LAW & MENTAL HEALTH PROFESSIONALS

NEW JERSEY

LAW & MENTAL HEALTH PROFESSIONALS SERIES

Bruce D. Sales and Michael O. Miller, Series Editors

ARIZONA: Miller and Sales
MASSACHUSETTS: Brant
NEW JERSEY: Wulach
TEXAS: Shuman

LAW & MENTAL HEALTH PROFESSIONALS

NEW JERSEY

James S. Wulach

AMERICAN PSYCHOLOGICAL ASSOCIATION
Washington, DC

First printing October 1991
Second printing March 1994

Published by
American Psychological Association
750 First Street, NE
Washington, DC 20002

Copies may be ordered from
APA Order Department
P.O. Box 2710
Hyattsville, MD 20784

In the UK and Europe, copies may be ordered from
American Psychological Association
3 Henrietta Street
Covent Garden, London
WC2E 8LU England

Text and cover design by Rubin Krassner, Silver Spring, MD
Composition by TAPSCO, Inc., Akron, PA
Printing by Edwards Brothers, Inc., Ann Arbor, MI
Technical editing by Patricia Loeber
Production coordination by Olin J. Nettles

Library of Congress Cataloging-in-Publication Data

Wulach, James S.
    Law & mental health professionals. New Jersey / James S.
      Wulach. p. cm.
    Includes bibliographical references and index.
    ISBN 1-55798-123-X
    1. Mental health personnel—Legal status, laws, etc.—
New Jersey. 2. Forensic psychiatry—New Jersey. 3. Psychology, Forensic. I. Title. II. Title: Law and mental health
professionals. New Jersey.
KFN2126.5.P73W8   1991
344.749′044—dc20
[347.4904444]

                                                     91-4263
                                                         CIP

Printed in the United States of America

Dedication

To my wife,
Sandra,
and daughters,
Laura and Suzanne

Contents

Section 5. Practice Related to the Law
5C. Civil/Criminal Matters   247

Section 5. Practice Related to the Law
5D. Criminal Matters   267

Acknowledgments

The research for this book was supported by Research Award 886-2995 from the Professional Staff Congress–City University of New York Research Foundation. The New Jersey Psychological Association provided support for an initial computerized legal search. The Graduate Studies Committee of John Jay College of Criminal Justice provided three credits of released time during the spring 1990 semester.

Special thanks go to Dorothy Cantor, who encouraged me to write this book. Lou Schlessinger and Stanley Moldawsky also provided encouragement. Bruce Sales and Michael Miller were generous with their editorial and personal support. Greg Reilly helped with an initial computer search. Those individuals who generously lent their time and expertise to reviewing drafts of this manuscript include psychologists Hirsch Silverman, Michael Kahn, Nina Thomas, Grace Smith, and Jeanne Scala and attorneys Eric Kleiner and James A. Louis.

Editors' Preface

The Need to Know the Law

For years, providers of mental health services (hereinafter mental health professionals, or MHPs) have been directly affected by the law. At one end of the continuum, their practice has been controlled by laws covering such matters as licensure and certification, third-party reimbursement, and professional incorporation. At the other end, they have been courted by the legal system to aid in its administration, providing such services as evaluating the mental status of litigants, providing expert testimony in court, and engaging in therapy with court-referred juveniles and adults. Even when not directly affected, MHPs find themselves indirectly affected by the law since their clients sometimes become involved in legal entanglements that involve mental status issues (e.g., divorce proceedings or termination of parental rights hearings).

Despite this pervasive influence, most professionals do not know about, much less understand, most of the laws that affect their practice, the services they render, and the clients they serve. This state of affairs is particularly troubling for several reasons. First, not knowing about the laws that affect one's practice typically results in the MHP's not gaining the benefits that the law may provide. Consider the law relating to the incorporation of professionals. It confers significant benefit, but only if it is known about and applied. The fact that it has been enacted by the state legislature does not help the MHP, any more than an MHP will be of help to a distressed person who refuses to contact the MHP.

Second, not knowing about the laws that affect the services they render can result in incompetent performance of, and liability for, the MHP either through the civil law (e.g., malpractice law) or through criminal sanctions. A brief example may help underscore this point. When an MHP is asked to evaluate a party to a lawsuit and testify in court, the court (the law's term for the judge) is asking the professional to assess and testify about whether that litigant meets some legal standard. The court is often not concerned with the defendant's mental health per se, although this may be relevant to the MHP's evaluation of the person. Rather, the court wants to know if the person meets the legal standard as it is set down by the law. Not knowing the legal standard means that the MHP is most likely evaluating the person for the wrong goal and providing the court with irrelevant information, at least from the court's point of view. Regretfully, there are too many cases in which this has occurred.

Third, not knowing the law that affects the clients that MHPs serve may significantly diminish their capability for handling their clients' distress. For example, a client who is undergoing a divorce and child custody dispute may have distorted beliefs about what may happen during the legal proceedings. A basic understanding of the controlling law in this area will allow the therapist to be more sensitive in rendering therapy.

The Problem in Accessing Legal Information

Given the need for this information, why have MHPs not systematically sought it out? Part of the reason lies in the concern over their ability to understand legal doctrines. Indeed, this is a legitimate worry, especially if they had to read original legal materials that were not collected, organized, and described with an MHP audience in mind. This is of particular concern since laws are written in terms and phrases of "art" that do not always share the common lay definition or usage, while some terms and phrases are left ambiguous and undefined or are used differently for different legal topics. Another part of the reason is that the law affecting MHPs and their clients is not readily available—even to lawyers. There are no compendiums that identify the topics that these laws cover, or present an analysis of each topic for easy reference.

To compound the difficulty, the law does not treat the different mental health professional disciplines uniformly or always specify the particular disciplines as being covered by it. Nor does the law emanate from a single legal forum. Each state enacts its own rules and regulations, often resulting in wide variations in the way a topic is handled across the United States. Multiply this confusion by the one hundred or so topics that relate to mental health practice. In addition, the law within a state does not come from one legal source. Rather, there are five primary ones: the state constitution; state legislative enactments (statutes); state agency administrative rules and regulations; rules of court promulgated by the state supreme court; and state and federal court cases that apply, interpret, and construe this existing state law. To know about one of these sources without knowing how its pronouncements on a given topic have been modified by these other sources can result in one's making erroneous conclusions about the operation of the law. Finally, mental health practice also comes under the purview of federal law (constitutional and statutory law, administrative rules and regulations, and case law). Federal law authorizes direct payments to MHPs for their services to some clients, sets standards for delivery of services in federal facilities (e.g., Veterans Administration Hospitals), and articulates the law that guides cases that are tried in federal courts under federal law.

Purposes of This Series

What is needed, therefore, is a book for each state, the District of Columbia, and the federal jurisdictions that comprehensively and accurately reviews and integrates all of the law that affects MHPs in that jurisdiction (hereinafter state). To ensure currency, regular supplements to these books will also need to be drafted. These materials should be written so that they are completely understandable to MHPs, as well as to lawyers. In order to accomplish these goals, the editors have tried to identify every legal topic that affects mental health practice, making each one the subject of a chapter. Each chapter, in turn, describes the legal standards that the MHP will be operating under and the relevant legal process that the MHP will be operating within. If a state does not have relevant law on an issue, then a brief explanation of how this law works in other states will be presented while noting the lack of regulation in this area within the state under consideration.

This type of coverage facilitates other purposes of the series. Although each chapter is written in order to state exactly what is the present state of the law and not argue for or against any particular approach, it is hoped that the comprehensiveness of the coverage will encourage MHPs to question the desirability of their states' approach to each topic. Such information and concern should provide the impetus for initiating legislation and litigation on the part of state mental health associations to ensure that the law reflects the scientific knowledge and professional values to the greatest extent possible.

In some measure, states will initially be hampered in this proactivity, since they will not know what legal alternatives are available and how desirable each alternative actually is. When a significant number of books in this series is available, however, it will allow for nationally oriented policy studies to identify the variety of legal approaches that are currently in use and to assess the validity of the behavioral assumptions underlying each variant, and ultimately lead to a conclusion as to the relative desirability of alternate approaches.[1] Thus, two other purposes of this book are to foster comprehensive analyses of the laws affecting MHPs across all states and the validity of the behavioral assumptions

---

1. Sales, B. D. (1983). The legal regulation of psychology: Professional and scientific interactions. In C. J. Scheirer & B. L. Hammonds (Eds.), *The master lecture series: Vol. 2: Psychology and law* (pp. 5–36). Washington, DC: American Psychological Association.

underlying these laws, and to promote political, legislative, and legal action to change laws that are inappropriate and impede the effective delivery of services. Legal change may be required because of gaps in legal regulation, overregulation, and regulation based on invalid behavioral and social assumptions. We hope this process will increase the rationality of future laws in this area and improve the effectiveness and quality of mental health service delivery nationally.

There are three remaining purposes for this series. First, although it will not replace the need for legal counsel, this series will make the MHP an intelligent consumer of legal services. This ability is gaining importance in an era of increasing professionalization and litigiousness. Second, it will ensure that MHPs are aware of the law's mandates when providing expert services (e.g., evaluation and testimony) within the legal system. Although chapters will not address how to clinically assess for the legal standard, provider competency will increase since providers now will be sure of the goals of their service (e.g., the legal standard that they are to assess for) as well as their roles and responsibilities within the legal system as to the particular topic at issue. Third and finally, each book will make clear that the legal standards that MHPs are asked to assess for by the law have typically not been translated into behavioral correlates. Nor are there discussions of tests, scales, and procedures for MHPs to use in assessing for the behavioral correlates of the legal standards in most cases. This series will provide the impetus for such research and writing.

Content and Organization of Volumes

Each book in this series is organized into six sections. Section 1 addresses the legal credentialing of MHPs. Section 2 deals with the different business forms for conducting one's practice. Section 3 then addresses insurance reimbursement and tax deductions that clients can receive for utilizing mental health services. With the business matters covered, the book then turns to the law directly affecting service delivery. Section 4 starts by covering the law that affects the maintenance and privacy of professional information. Section 5 then considers each area of law that may require the services of MHPs. It is subdivided into five parts: families and juveniles, other civil matters, topics that apply similarly in both civil and criminal cases, criminal matters, and voluntary and involuntary receipt of state services by the clients of mental health services. The last section of the book, Section 6, discusses the law that limits service delivery and sets liability for unethical and illegal behavior as a service provider.

Collectively, the chapters in these sections represent all topics pertaining to the law as it affects MHPs in their practices. Two caveats are in order, however. First, the law changes slowly over time. Thus, a supplement service will update all chapters on a regular basis. Second, as MHPs become more involved in the legal system, new opportunities for involvement are likely to arise. To be responsive to these developments, the supplements also will contain additional chapters reflecting these new roles and responsibilities.

Some final points about the content of this book are in order. The exact terms that the law chooses are used in the book even if they are a poor choice from an MHP's point of view. And where terms are defined by the law, that information is presented. The reader often will be frustrated, however, because as has already been noted, the law does not always define terms or provide detailed guidance. This does not mean that legal words and phrases can be taken lightly. The law sets the rules that MHPs and their clients must operate by; thus, the chapters must be read carefully. This should not be too arduous a task since chapters are relatively short. On the other hand, such brevity will leave some readers frustrated because chapters appear not to go far enough in answering their questions. Note that all the law is covered. If there is no law, however, there is no coverage. If a question is not answered in the text, it is because New Jersey law has not addressed the issue. Relatedly, if an obligation or benefit is created by a professional regulation (i.e., a rule of a professional organization) but is not directly recognized by the law, it is not covered. Thus, for example, professional credentials are not addressed in these volumes.

Finally, we want to point out that in some instances, the pronoun "he" is used generically to refer to both sexes. Most notably, the pronoun is used when quoting directly from the law. Legal language is generally consistent in its preference for using the masculine form of the pronoun; it is not always feasible to attempt a rewording.

Bruce D. Sales
Michael O. Miller
Series Editors

Author's Preface

This book is principally a treatment of state law applicable to MHPs. A comprehensive treatment of federal law, which is also relevant to the actions of MHPs, is beyond the scope of this work as it would expand it by volumes or require a more limited treatment of each subject. The sources of state law treated in this work include the state constitution, state statutes, state administrative rules, state judicial decisions, and state judicial rules.

The New Jersey Constitution establishes the framework for state government and describes various individual rights that occupy a high degree of importance in New Jersey. Citations to the New Jersey Constitution appear in the following form: art. 1, p. 10. This reference indicates that the citation is to the tenth paragraph of the first article in the New Jersey Constitution. The New Jersey Constitution is found in a separate volume of the *New Jersey Statutes Annotated*, published by the West Publishing Company.

Citations to state statutes, which result from legislation passed by the New Jersey Senate and Assembly, appear in the following form: N.J.S.A. 45:14B-1. This particular citation is a reference to the green bound volumes of statutes published by West entitled *New Jersey Statutes Annotated*. The number to the left of the colon is the title number; the number on the right of the colon is the particular section within the title.

This compilation of statutes and the New Jersey Constitution contain additional useful material. The compilers attempt to include a citation and a one-sentence summary of any reported cases that have discussed the statute or constitutional provision in question. A researcher may use these case annotations to begin research on how the statute or constitutional provision has been interpreted by the courts. The compilations also contain references to prior statutes that have been repealed. A review of these repealed statutes may be necessary to understand an earlier judicial opinion interpreting them or to resolve an ambiguity in the intent of the legislature in changing the statute.

State administrative rules are created by state agencies operating under the authority delegated to them by the legislature to carry out specific agency functions. For example, the legislation creating the State Board of Psychological Examiners does not list types of professional misconduct, but rather gives the Board the authority to make administrative rules delineating the various types of misconduct that can result in the suspension or revocation of a license. These rules do not appear in the green volumes of statutes but instead are kept in a three-ring notebook series entitled *New Jersey Administrative Code*. References to the administrative code appear in the following form: N.J.A.C. 13:42-3.1. The administrative rule referred to by this citation can be found in the volume of the three-ring series containing Section 42-3.1 of Title 13.

State judicial decisions are the product of judge-made law. Reported decisions typically are those of appellate courts. They consist of decisions of the New Jersey Supreme Court and of the appellate divisions of the superior courts. Citations to these decisions appear in the following form: State v. Maik, 114 N.J. Super. 470, 277 A.2d 235 (App. Div. 1971). This particular citation refers to a 1971 decision by the Appellate Division of the Superior Court. A reference to a New Jersey Supreme Court decision would appear in this manner: State v. Worlock, 117 N.J. 596, 569 A.2d 1314 (1990).

New Jersey Superior Court and Supreme Court decisions are reported separately in bound volumes published by the West Publishing Company. The decisions also appear in a reporter of cases in the geographic region including New Jersey, titled *Atlantic Reporter*. Both cases here (supra) are located in the second series of that compilation. The number 569 represents the volume in which the case appears, and 1314 is the page of the volume on which the report begins. The parties to the case are Worlock and the State of New Jersey.

State judicial rules, as contrasted with judicial decisions, are the product of judges acting in a legislative rather than a judicial capacity. In this role, judges make rules of general application in the courts, not usually in the context of deciding cases. The New Jersey Supreme Court promulgates court rules that relate to civil procedure, criminal procedure, civil appellate procedure, and practice in municipal and other courts.

Most rules, along with authoritative commentary, can be found in Pressler, *Current N.J. Court Rules*.[1] They appear in the following form: R. 1:8-1. This citation refers to Rule 1, Section 8-1. Rules of evidence may be proposed by the New Jersey Supreme Court, subject to legislative approval. They are compiled in Biunno, *Current N.J. Rules of Evidence*.[2] Rules of evidence are cited in the following manner: Evid. R. 63(1). They are also located in the *New Jersey Statutes Annotated*.

Although the focus of this work is on state rather than federal law applicable to MHPs in New Jersey, occasional reference is of

---

1. Pressler, S. B. (1990). *Current N.J. court rules*. Newark, NJ: Gann Law Books.
2. Biunno, R. J. (1990). *Current N.J. rules of evidence*. Newark, NJ: Gann Law Books.

necessity made to federal decisions interpreting or limiting state law. The citations to these decisions are from the United States District Court (F. Supp.), the United States Court of Appeals (F. or F.2d), and the United States Supreme Court (U.S., S.Ct., or L.Ed.). As is the case with the reports of state decisions, the number preceding the reporter is the volume number, and the number following is the page. References to federal legislation appear in the form 26 U.S.C. § 213(a) (1987). This particular citation to the United States Code, the repository of federal legislation, is from Title 26, Section 213(a), current as of 1987. In addition, there are citations to treatises and law review articles. These references may provide a fuller background of an issue of interest to MHPs.

Finally, although some chapters were updated until the manuscript went to press, the reader should consider the entire volume current as of May 1991.

James S. Wulach

Legal Credentialing

1.0

Licensure and Regulation of Mental Health Professionals

Each of the licensed mental health professions is governed by specific statutory and administrative laws that establish the licensing board, define terms, determine qualifications and procedures for licensure, provide exceptions to licensure, regulate conduct, and prescribe sanctions for violations. In addition to the specific laws governing the individual professions, there is a general law that governs all of the professions.[1] The general provisions are meant to augment and standardize the powers of the existing professional boards. Any specific laws that are inconsistent with the general provisions must be superceded by them.[2]

MHP Boards Covered by General Provisions

The act governing general provisions of professional boards includes, among others, the State Board of Medical Examiners (see Chapter 1.1), the New Jersey Board of Nursing (see Chapter 1.2), the State Board of Psychological Examiners (see Chapter 1.3), the State Board of Social Work Examiners (see Chapter 1.5), and the State Board of Marriage Counselor Examiners (see Chapter 1.8).[3] The boards are part of the Division of Consumer Affairs in the Department of Law and Public Safety.

---

1. N.J.S.A. 45:1-1 et seq.
2. N.J.S.A. 45:1-26.
3. N.J.S.A. 45:1-2.1.

Membership of Professional Boards

Although the individual boards may recommend the appointment of board members, the governor of New Jersey makes the final decision.[4] In addition to the regular board members, the governor must appoint two public members to each professional board. Public board members have all privileges except that they are not permitted to participate in the professional examination process. The public member must not have any relationship with any member of the profession that would prevent the member from representing the public. The governor must also appoint an additional board member from the governmental department most closely related to the profession.

Powers of the Attorney General

The attorney general is empowered to do the following:

1. recommend rules and regulations that govern the procedure for administrative hearings, complaints and answers, subpoenas, appointment of hearing examiners, and other procedural aspects of administrative hearings;

2. recommend rules and regulations governing disciplinary matters and arbitrary restrictions on initial licensures; and

3. recommend the initiation, modification, or setting aside of any enforcement action of a board.

If the licensing board does not take steps to conform with the recommendations of the attorney general within 30 days, he or she is empowered to promulgate such decisions unilaterally.

Grounds for Revocation, Suspension, or Refusal to Issue a License

Any board may refuse to admit a person to an examination or may suspend, revoke, or refuse to issue any license issued by the board upon proof that the applicant or licensee[5]

1. has obtained a license or authorization to sit for an examination through fraud, deception, or misrepresentation;

2. has engaged in the use of dishonesty, fraud, deception, misrepresentation, false promise, or false pretense;

---

4. N.J.S.A. 45:1-2.2.
5. N.J.S.A. 45:1-21.

3. has engaged in gross negligence, gross malpractice, or gross incompetence;

4. has engaged in repeated acts of negligence, malpractice, or incompetence;

5. has been convicted of any crime involving moral turpitude or any crime relating adversely to the activity regulated by the board (a plea of guilty, non vult, or nolo contendere shall be considered as a conviction);

6. has had the authority to engage in the profession revoked or suspended by any other state, agency, or authority;

7. has violated or failed to comply with the provisions of any act or regulation administered by the board; or

8. is incapable, for medical or any other good cause, of discharging the functions of a licensee in a manner consistent with the public's health, safety, and welfare.

In addition or as an alternative to revoking, suspending, or refusing to renew any license, a board may[6]

1. issue a letter of warning, reprimand, or censure;

2. assess civil penalties of not more than $2,500 for the first offense and not more than $5,000 for each additional offense;[7]

3. order a person to cease and desist from future violations or to correct any unlawful act or practice;

4. order a person to restore any money or property to an aggrieved party; or

5. order any licensee to secure medical or such other professional treatment as may be necessary to properly discharge licensee functions.

A board may also enter a temporary order suspending or limiting any license pending a full hearing, upon the request of the attorney general, if the request demonstrates a clear and imminent danger to the public health, safety, or welfare.

Investigative Powers of Boards

Any licensing board, as well as the attorney general and the director of the Department of Consumer Affairs, has the investigative power to[8]

---

6. N.J.S.A. 45:1-22.
7. N.J.S.A. 45:1-25.
8. N.J.S.A. 45:1-18.

1. require a written statement, under oath, from an applicant or licensee regarding any professional act;
2. examine any person under oath in connection with any professional act;
3. inspect any professional premises;
4. examine or impound any goods or item used in a professional service; or
5. examine or impound any record maintained by a licensee in the regular course of business.

Noncompliance With Investigation

If an applicant or licensee fails to comply with an order pursuant to an investigatory power of a board (supra), the attorney general may apply to the superior court and obtain an order adjudging such person in contempt of court, granting other relief, or suspending the license of a person unless and until compliance with the investigative demand is effected.[9]

If a person refuses to comply because such an act may tend to incriminate him or her, the person may still be ordered to comply by the attorney general.[10] Nevertheless, the individual cannot later be prosecuted in a criminal proceeding that arises out of and relates to the subject matter of the board investigation. However, perjury or forgery is still subject to separate legal sanctions.

---

9. N.J.S.A. 45:1-19.
10. N.J.S.A. 45:1-20.

1.1

Licensure and Regulation of Psychiatrists

The licensure and regulation of psychiatrists is governed by statutory law[1] that establishes a State Board of Medical Examiners, defines terms contained within the act, establishes qualifications and procedures for licensure of physicians, defines the practice of medicine, regulates the conduct of physicians, establishes exceptions to licensure, and prescribes sanctions for violations of the statute. Physicians are regulated also by the general licensing law that governs all boards and professions (see Chapter 1.0). There is no separate licensure provision pertaining to the practice of psychiatry; the law is a generic one that regulates the practice of medicine without regard to specialty.[2]

State Board of Medical Examiners

The State Board of Medical Examiners (Board) is the primary administrative body that licenses and regulates psychiatrists. It consists of 16 members appointed for 3-year terms by the governor. The Board is composed of two public members, one executive department designee, one designee of the Commissioner of Health, one osteopath, one podiatrist, one bioanalytical laboratory director, and nine physicians with M.D. degrees. The Board has the duty to[3]

1. regulate the granting, denial, revocation, renewal, and suspension of licenses;

---

1. N.J.S.A. 45:9-1 to 27.
2. The references to psychiatrists therefore apply generally to physicians.
3. N.J.S.A. 45:9-1.

2. sue and recover penalties from individuals practicing medicine illegally; and

3. employ personnel to assist the Board in carrying out its duties. In particular, the Board must employ a full-time medical director to assist it in carrying out its duties.[4] The medical director must have knowledge of the field of chemical dependency or addiction-oriented psychiatry, and among other duties, he or she must help develop procedures for the treatment and monitoring of impaired physicians. Such procedures must include notifying the Board when a practitioner fails to comply with the requirements of the treatment program or when a practitioner's impairment may jeopardize or improperly risk the health, safety, or life of a patient.

Licensure

Applicants will be licensed to practice medicine in New Jersey if they[5]

1. are at least 21 years of age, of good moral character, and a citizen of the United States;

2. graduated from high school and completed 2 years of premedical studies in college;

3. graduated from a school of medicine or osteopathy approved by the Board, after the completion of 4 years of course work;[6]

4. completed a 1-year internship in a hospital approved by the Board, or completed 1 year of acceptable postgraduate work in a school or hospital;[7]

5. committed no prior acts that would constitute grounds for disciplinary action (see subsequent text on disciplinary action); and

6. passed a written examination administered or recognized by the Board;[8] the Board recognizes the Federal Licensing Examination (FLEX) as its standard licensing examination.[9]

---

4. N.J.S.A. 45:9-19.6.
5. N.J.S.A. 45:9-6 to 14.
6. N.J.S.A. 45:9-8.
7. The Board may recognize 2 years of active military service as a commissioned officer and physician in a medical facility as the equivalent of the internship requirement. N.J.A.C. 13:35-1.4.
8. N.J.S.A. 45:9-15. Applicants may bypass this requirement if they meet one of the following criteria: (1) previously certified by the National Board of Medical Examiners or (2) currently licensed in another state of the United States. N.J.S.A. 45:9-13.
9. N.J.A.C. 13:35-3.1. Scores of 75 or over in both Component I and Component II shall be considered passing. The Board will grant a license by endorsement to applicants licensed in another state if such applicants meet statutory requirements and have passed the FLEX with scores of 75 or over in both components. N.J.A.C. 13:35-3.2. See also N.J.A.C. 13:35-3.3 and 4.

A temporary license may be granted to an applicant who is otherwise qualified except for being a citizen of another country. Fifth Pathway students in approved programs may enter graduate training without completing foreign social service or internship obligations and without obtaining Educational Commission on Foreign Medical Graduates certification.[10]

All licenses must be renewed biennially on or before July 1.[11] Failure to renew by July 1 results in suspension and a reinstatement fee if the licensee subsequently renews the license. The fee for a license is $225.00, and the fee for biennial registration is $160.00.[12] A licensee may register annually as a retired physician without paying a fee and may resume practice upon payment of the registration fee.

A physician must list on the biennial license renewal form the address of all practice locations, all health care facilities and health maintenance organizations with which he or she has an affiliation, and the name and address of the physician's malpractice insurer.[13] Such information must be updated within 21 days of any changes, additions, or deletions to the information.

Licensure of Physicians Graduated From Unaccredited Medical Schools

An applicant who is a graduate of a medical school not accredited by the Liaison Committee on Medical Education or the American Osteopathic Association must[14]

1. graduate from a medical school listed in the World Directory of Medical Schools published by the World Health Organization or from a medical school that was authorized by the country of domicile to confer a terminal degree for the plenary practice of medicine;

2. complete the full medical and educational curriculum, including clinical training, prescribed by the medical school and the country in which it is located;

3. obtain an unrestricted license to practice medicine in the country in which the medical training was received, if the applicant is a national of that country;

4. demonstrate, if the applicant completed the first 2 years of medical school in a foreign medical school and the last 2 years in clinical training programs in United States hospitals, that such a program would be approved by the Board;

---

10. N.J.A.C. 13:35-1.2.
11. N.J.S.A. 45:9-6.1.
12. N.J.A.C. 13:35-6.13.
13. N.J.S.A. 45:9-19.7.
14. N.J.A.C. 13:35-3.11.

5. pass an examination administered by the Educational Commission on Foreign Medical Graduates, FMGEMS or ECFMG, as applicable; and

6. complete all other statutory requirements, including the attainment of a score of at least 75 on the FLEX.

Exceptions to Licensing

The licensing law does not apply to[15] medical officers in the regular armed forces; medical residents;[16] state and county employees who are granted individual exemptions;[17] licensed physicians from other states who do not open an office; and licensed physicians from another state who, with the permission of the Board, temporarily manage the practice of a New Jersey licensed physician who is absent from the state. The Board is empowered to provide for the registration or issuance of permits to anybody engaging in the practice of medicine while in training, and to establish the scope of permissible practice by such individuals.[18]

Regulation

Disciplinary Actions Against a Licensed Physician

The Board may suspend, revoke, or refuse to grant a license if a person has[19]

1. been adjudicated insane;

2. demonstrated any physical, mental, or emotional condition or drug or alcohol use that impairs his or her ability to practice with reasonable skill or safety;

3. practiced criminal abortion;

4. been convicted of the crime of abortion or a crime of moral turpitude or has entered a plea that does not deny responsibility for such a crime;

5. been determined to be physically or mentally incapacitated;

---

15. N.J.S.A. 45:9-21.
16. Medical residents must be graduates of an approved medical school, who are in good standing. They must register with the Director of Graduate Medical Education at the training hospital, who shall certify them to the Board. The Board will then authorize them to practice medicine as residents at the training hospital. First-year residents shall be "Registered Residents" whereas advanced residents shall be "Permit Holders." N.J.A.C. 13:35-1.5.
17. Exempted physicians must satisfy all licensing criteria and take the FLEX examination at the earliest opportunity following appointment to their positions. To maintain employment, they must pass the FLEX and apply for licensure within 10 days thereafter. N.J.A.C. 13:35-3.7.
18. N.J.S.A. 45:9-19.12.
19. N.J.S.A. 45:9-16.

6. knowingly become employed by a physician who advertises illegally;

7. employed unlicensed persons to perform work only permitted to be performed by licensed physicians;

8. presented to the Board any illegally obtained license or certificate, or fraudulently obtained a license;

9. been found guilty of life-endangering gross malpractice or gross negligence while practicing medicine;

10. demonstrated professional incompetence to practice medicine;

11. advertised illegally (see Advertising Regulations infra);[20]

12. subverted or attempted to subvert the licensing examination process;[21]

13. charged excessive fees that are so high as to be manifestly unconscionable or overreaching under the circumstances;[22]

14. failed to maintain patient records for 7 years following the last entry;[23]

15. failed to provide copies of all pertinent objective data as well as a copy of the patient's record, or a summary of the record, within 30 days of a written request by the patient or an authorized representative, for a reasonable charge; a partial record may be supplied where the licensee reasonably believes that review by the patient of the full records would be harmful; however, the full record or a summary must be provided upon request to the patient's attorney, another licensed health care professional, or the patient's health insurance carrier, along with an explanation of the reasons for the refusal to provide the information to the patient;[24]

16. received directly or indirectly any fee, commission, rebate, gift, or other compensation for prescribing, ordering, or promoting the sale of any item;[25]

17. directly or indirectly billed a patient or third party for a device, appliance, or prescribed item without disclosing the actual cost of the item to the patient;[26]

18. sold "free samples";[27]

20. N.J.A.C. 13:35-6.10.
21. N.J.A.C. 13:35-3.10.
22. N.J.A.C. 13:35-6.11 and 12.
23. N.J.A.C. 13:35-6.5.
24. Id.
25. N.J.A.C. 13:35-6.4(a)1.
26. N.J.A.C. 13:35-6.4(a)2.
27. N.J.A.C. 13:35-6.4(a)4.

19. rendered any bill for the performance of services that were not actually performed (although charges for cancelled appointments are not prohibited);[28]

20. failed to follow requirements for the proper prescription of medication (infra);[29]

21. prescribed or dispensed a controlled dangerous substance in an indiscriminate manner or without good cause, or where the licensee reasonably knows or should have known that the substance is to be used for unauthorized consumption;[30] or

22. failed to notify the Board of information that reasonably indicates that another medical practitioner has demonstrated an impairment, gross incompetence, or unprofessional conduct that would present an imminent danger to a patient or to the public health, safety, or welfare.[31] The physician is immune from liability for notifying the Board except if false information is knowingly provided. Notification is not required if the physician learns of a practitioner's incompetence or impairment through rendering treatment to that person.

The accused must be given a hearing before the Board to contest any charges except where there has been a criminal conviction or a plea such as nolo contendere. The Board's findings must be based on a preponderance of the credible evidence.[32] Whenever there is an adverse finding, the Board must notify each licensed health-care facility and every board licensee with which the person is directly associated in his or her private medical practice.[33] If there is not an adverse finding, all information must remain confidential except that the Board may release it to a government agency for good cause after a hearing, with notice to the physician concerned.[34] Additional grounds for the refusal to grant or continue a license and additional regulatory powers are described in the general licensing law (see Chapter 1.0).

A person is guilty of a crime if he or she knowingly does not possess a license to practice medicine or knowingly had the license suspended, revoked, or limited by the Board, and if he or she[35]

1. engages in that practice;

2. exceeds the scope of practice permitted by the Board;

---

28. N.J.A.C. 13:35-6.4(a)5.
29. N.J.A.C. 13:35-6.3, 6.6, 6.7, 6.8.
30. N.J.S.A. 45:1-13.
31. N.J.S.A. 45:9-19.5.
32. N.J.S.A. 45:9-16.
33. N.J.S.A. 45:9-19.13.
34. N.J.S.A. 45:9-19.3.
35. N.J.S.A. 2C:21-20.

3. holds himself or herself out to the public as being eligible to engage in that practice;

4. engages in any activity for which such a license is a necessary prerequisite, including the ordering of controlled dangerous substances or prescription legend drugs from a distributor or manufacturer; or

5. practices medicine under a false or assumed name or falsely impersonates another licensed person.

A person is also guilty of a crime if he or she purposely destroys or alters any medical record in order to deceive any person concerning a patient.[36]

Medical Practitioner Review Panel

The Board is required to establish and maintain a Medical Practitioner Review Panel, consisting of nine members appointed by the governor for terms of 3 years.[37] Four of the members must be physicians, and one must be a board-certified psychiatrist or a physician experienced in the field of chemical dependency.

The review panel is required to receive notice from health-care facilities or health maintenance organizations of any disciplinary proceedings against physicians.[38] It must also receive notice from insurers regarding a medical malpractice claim settlement, judgment or arbitration award, or denial of, or surcharge on, the medical malpractice liability insurance coverage of a practitioner. The review panel also may receive referrals from the Board regarding complaints alleging professional misconduct from other health-care providers and consumers.

The review panel must promptly investigate any information received, and it is entitled to receive assistance, including that of the attorney general, in the conduct of its investigation. If the review panel has reasonable cause to believe that a practitioner represents an imminent danger to his or her patients, the panel must immediately notify the Board and the attorney general and recommend the immediate suspension or limitation of the practitioner's license pending further proceedings by the review panel or the Board. If such action is taken, the Board must notify each licensed health-care facility and health-maintenance organization, as well as each practitioner in the state with which the suspended practitioner is affiliated.

At the request of the panel or for good cause, an informal hearing may be scheduled before at least three review panel mem-

---

36. N.J.S.A. 2C:21-4.1.
37. N.J.S.A. 45:9-19.8.
38. N.J.S.A. 45:9-19.9.

bers. A practitioner who presents evidence to the panel is entitled to be represented by an attorney.

Upon completion of its review, the panel must prepare a report recommending one of the following dispositions:

1. recommend to the Board that the matter be referred to the attorney general for the initiation of disciplinary action;

2. defer making a recommendation pending the outcome of litigation or a disciplinary proceeding, if there is no evidence that the practitioner's professional conduct may jeopardize the health, safety, or life of a patient;

3. refer the practitioner to an appropriate licensed health-care practitioner program recognized by the Board and promptly notify the medical director of the Board of the referral; or

4. find that no further action is warranted.

The Board may affirm, reject, or modify any disposition of the review panel. After its consideration of the panel recommendation, the Board must notify the practitioner of the review panel's recommendation and the Board's determination. Any information concerning the professional conduct of a practitioner obtained by the review panel is confidential pending final disposition by the Board.[39]

Anybody acting as part of his or her official duties in the process of recommending or determining actions of the panel or Board is immune from liability if the action or recommendation was made without malice.[40] The attorney general will defend the individual in any civil suit, and the state will provide indemnification if any damages are awarded.

Advertising Regulations

The Board may suspend or revoke a license for unprofessional conduct in advertising, including[41]

1. any statement, claim, or format that is false, fraudulent, misleading, or deceptive;

2. any misrepresentation of a material fact;

3. the suppression, omission, or concealment of any material fact that the licensee should know is improper or that prohibits a prospective patient from making a full and informed judgment based on the advertisement;

---

39. N.J.S.A. 45:9-19.10.
40. N.J.S.A. 45:9-19.11.
41. N.J.A.C. 13:35-6.10.

4. any claim of professional superiority to the ordinary standards of the profession;

5. any promotion of a professional service that is beyond the licensee's ability to perform;

6. a technique or communication that appears to intimidate, exert undue pressure on, or unduly influence a prospective patient or consumer;

7. any personal testimonial attesting to the quality or competence of a service or treatment offered by a licensee;

8. the communication of any fact, data, or information that may personally identify a patient;

9. an offer to pay, give, or accept a fee or other consideration for the referral of a patient;

10. any print, language, or format that directly or indirectly obscures a material fact;

11. any guarantee of results from any procedure;

12. failure to provide factual substantiation to the Board to support the truthfulness of any questioned assertion or representation in the advertisement; or

13. in-person direct solicitation of prospective patients (although the offering of services to representatives of patients, such as employers, labor unions, and insurance carriers, is acceptable).

In addition, advertising relating to a fee shall be limited to the statement of a fixed fee or range of fees for routine services, in which all relevant considerations are discussed in an understandable manner. Unless it is otherwise specified, such fees shall be assumed to be effective for at least 90 days.

All offers of free services or discounts shall include a statement of the specific charges for all associated or reasonably anticipated services that are not included. There shall be no charge for any service whatsoever during a period of 72 hours from the time of the free service. The licensee is required to maintain a list of the patient names and dates of service for all patients who have received such services, as well as patient records, except for massive screening programs done off-site as a community service and that are sponsored by a governmental or nonprofit organization.

Any person offering free or discounted medical services shall file copies of such advertisements with the Board within 30 days of initial publication. Any such offer shall include the providing of results within 30 days of a written request by the patient.

The responsibility for the form and content of any advertisement shall be jointly and severally that of each licensee who is a principal, partner, or officer of the firm or entity identified in the advertisement.

The licensee is required to keep printed, audiotaped, or videotaped copies of the advertisement for at least 3 years and to make such copies available to the Board upon request.

All advertisements circulated away from the office premises shall disclose the nature of the practice and the name and address or telephone number of at least one of the principal practitioners. The public service corporation or trade name may also be included.

All testimonials shall truthfully reflect the actual experience of the patient and shall include the following statements:

1. "This procedure may not be suitable for every patient. All patients must be evaluated by a physician as to the appropriateness of performing the procedure" (or words to that effect); and

2. "The above testimonial represents the individual's response and reaction to the procedure; however, no medical procedure is risk-free. Associated potential risks and complications should be discussed with the physician rendering this procedure" (or words to that effect).

If the person giving a testimonial received any compensation, that fact shall be disclosed in the advertisement.

All testimonial advertisements should be backed by documentation including the name, address, and telephone number of the person in the advertisement; the amount of compensation; and a notarized statement and release verifying the truthfulness of the information.

Medication Regulations

All doctor's orders and prescriptions written by unlicensed physicians must be properly countersigned.[42] Licensed physicians must advise all patients by adequate notice, such as a pamphlet in the waiting room, that a patient may request to substitute a generic drug for any prescribed medication.[43] Every prescription must include the prescriber's full name, address, telephone number, and academic degree or identification of the type of professional practice.

Each prescription must include the full name, age, and address of the patient; the date; the name, strength, and quantity of the drug; and adequate instructions for usage beyond "as directed."[44] The prescription should include the number of refills permitted

---

42. N.J.A.C. 13:35-6.3.
43. N.J.A.C. 13:35-6.6(a).
44. N.J.A.C. 13:35-6.6(b).

and the prescriber's Drug Enforcement Agency number when it is required. In addition, the prescription must be signed by hand. Every prescription blank must be imprinted with the words "substitution permissible" and "do not substitute."

With regard to the prescription of Schedule II controlled dangerous substances, the quantity of each drug must be stated by word in addition to number.[45] The practitioner must not prescribe more than a 30-day supply.

With regard to narcotic drugs, a prescription should not be used for detoxification or maintenance. (However, narcotic drugs may be dispensed for these circumstances by those practitioners separately registered and authorized to do so in a narcotics treatment program.) A physician who is not authorized to dispense narcotics may do so on a daily emergency basis for not more than 3 days, while arrangements are being made for patient referral to a program.

Narcotics regulations do not extend to the administering or dispensing of narcotic drugs in a hospital as an adjunct to surgical treatment.[46] Nor do they apply to prescribing or dispensing narcotic drugs to people with intractable pain from which no relief is possible or for which no cure has been found. However, the practitioner must attempt to taper the dosage periodically or try other treatment modalities to reduce addiction propensity.

No physician may prescribe or administer any amphetamine or sympathomimetic amine drug or compound designated as a Schedule II controlled dangerous substance except for the treatment of narcolepsy, hyperkinesis, drug-induced brain dysfunction, epilepsy, depression refractory to other treatments, or senile apathetic behavior.[47] Also, the use of these drugs for immediate use in a hospital for acute conditions is permitted, or for the differential diagnosis of depression, or in approved research. The prescribing or dispensing of such drugs for use in weight management, dieting, or fatigue is specifically prohibited. The violation of these regulations may result not only in professional misconduct (supra), but also in criminal penalties for distribution of a controlled dangerous substance and for gross malpractice in the practice of medicine.

Although it is less relevant to psychiatrists, the prescription of laetrile is also closely monitored and requires special quadruplicate forms.[48]

---

45. *Id.*
46. N.J.A.C. 13:35-6.6(f).
47. N.J.A.C. 13:35-6.7.
48. N.J.A.C. 13:35-6.8.

Investigations by the Board

The Board has broad powers to investigate violations of the statute.[49] It is empowered to issue subpoenas and to compel attendance and testimony of witnesses. Investigatory regulations of the general licensing law also apply (see Chapter 1.0).

Penalties for Violations

In addition to the penalties listed previously under "Disciplinary Actions," the Board may sue to impose financial penalties against those who do not comply with its investigatory procedures.[50] Also, the Board may sue to impose financial penalties against those who engage in the illegal practice of medicine.[51] Finally, apart from the Board, both civil and criminal actions may be instituted in other courts for behavior that violates such law.

---

49. N.J.S.A. 45:9-2.
50. *Id.*
51. N.J.S.A. 45:9-22. The general licensing law allows boards to impose significant financial penalties without suit in another court (see Chapter 1.0).

1.2

Licensure and Regulation of Psychiatric Nurses

The licensure and regulation of psychiatric nurses is governed by statutory law[1] that establishes a New Jersey Board of Nursing, defines the practice of nursing, accredits schools of professional nursing, establishes qualifications and procedures for the licensure of nurses, establishes exceptions to licensure, regulates the conduct of licensed nurses, provides for administrative hearings, and prescribes criminal sanctions for violations of the statute. In addition, the Board promulgates rules and regulations to carry out the provisions of the chapter. Nurses are regulated also by the general licensing law, which governs all boards and professions (see Chapter 1.0). There is no separate licensure pertaining to the practice of psychiatric nursing; the law is a generic one that regulates the practice of nursing without regard to specialty.[2]

Board of Nursing

The New Jersey Board of Nursing (Board) is the primary administrative body that licenses and regulates nurses. It consists of 10 members appointed for 5-year terms by the governor. Seven members of the Board must be registered professional nurses, two must be licensed practical nurses, and one must be a public member appointed by the governor. The Board has the duty to[3]

---

1. N.J.S.A. 45:11-1 to 45:11-44.
2. This law also pertains to practical nursing, but this discussion is limited to professional nursing because psychiatric nurses will have the additional education required by the latter category.
3. N.J.S.A. 45:11-24.

1. regulate the granting, denial, revocation, renewal, and suspension of licenses;
2. hold hearings and issue subpoenas to compel documents and testimony on any matters pertaining to the regulation of nursing; and
3. prescribe standards and curricula for schools of nursing and approve schools of nursing that meet those criteria.

Licensure

The statutes and rules pertaining to licensure set out the qualifications applicants must meet, the fees and examination procedure, and exemptions to the rules.[4] The Board must issue a license to anyone who

1. is at least 18 years of age;
2. is of good moral character;
3. is not a habitual user of drugs, nor has violated narcotics laws;
4. holds a diploma from an accredited 4-year high school;
5. has completed a 3-year course of study and graduated from an accredited school of professional nursing or its equivalent;[5] and
6. has passed a written examination administered by the Board.

The Board may grant a license by endorsement to those applicants who have been licensed in another state. The written examination may be waived if the applicant has the educational requirements and passing scores in his or her state board examinations equal to those required in New Jersey.[6]

Nurses trained in foreign countries may qualify for the written examination and licensure if they provide proof of 4 years of high school or the equivalent, proof of graduation from an approved school of professional nursing or a valid certificate issued by the Commission on Graduates of Foreign Nursing Schools, and verification of licensure in a foreign country if such verification is available. Educational deficiencies must be remedied by course work in an accredited course in an approved school of nursing.[7] All foreign nursing candidates must submit to the Board a certificate from the Commission on Graduates of Foreign Nursing Schools.[8]

---

4. N.J.S.A. 45:11-26.
5. *Id.* and N.J.A.C. 13:37-2.1.
6. N.J.A.C. 13:37-5.1 and 2.
7. N.J.A.C. 13:37-4.1 to 4.3.
8. N.J.A.C. 13:37-4.6.

Applicants may be issued temporary work permits for employment in approved institutions pending the administration and successful passing of the examination for licensure.[9]

All licenses expire at the end of the biennial calendar year. Applicants for renewal must complete a renewal form and mail in a license fee ($24.00) on or before that date. An additional reregistration fee ($34.00) is required if the license has expired.[10]

Regulation

Disciplinary Actions Against a Licensed Nurse

The Board may refuse to grant or renew or may revoke or suspend a license on any of the following grounds:[11]

1. dishonesty,

2. unfitness or incapacity,

3. conduct derogatory to nursing,

4. fraud or willful misrepresentation in an application for license or renewal,

5. willful or repeated violations of the nursing law,

6. conviction of a crime involving moral turpitude, or

7. fraud or willful misrepresentation in connection with a license application or renewal.

The general licensing law provides additional grounds for action and additional disciplinary powers to the Board (see Chapter 1.0).

Investigations and Hearings by the Board

The Board is required to hold a hearing whenever it exercises disciplinary regulation, and its decisions are subject to review by appeal to the Superior Court of New Jersey.[12] The accused is required to receive notice at least 10 days prior to the hearing. The licensee is entitled to representation by an attorney and has the right to cross-examine witnesses and to offer evidence. Either the Board or the licensee may issue subpoenas to compel the appearance and testimony of witnesses and the production of records. The court may order a rehearing on any action within 2 years and may permit

---

9. N.J.A.C. 13:37-3.5 and 4.4.
10. N.J.S.A. 45:11-28 and N.J.A.C. 13:37-12.1.
11. N.J.S.A. 45:11-32.
12. N.J.S.A. 45:11-32.

an individual who has been disciplined to reapply for a new license. The hearings and procedures are also subject to the provisions of the general licensing law (see Chapter 1.0).

The Board is entitled to sue (for financial penalties in the New Jersey Superior Court) any unlicensed person for practicing professional nursing or for using the abbreviation "R.N."[13] Determinations by the Board may also form the basis for a civil suit against the nurse (see Chapters 6.5 and 6.6).

---

13. N.J.S.A. 45:11 27-38. This provision is probably superceded by the general licensing law, which allows the Board to confer significant financial penalties on those who violate the licensing laws.

1.3

Licensure and Regulation of Psychologists

The licensure and regulation of psychologists is governed by statutory law[1] that establishes a State Board of Psychological Examiners, defines the practice of psychology, bars the practice of medicine by psychologists, establishes qualifications and procedures for the licensure of psychologists, establishes exceptions to licensure, regulates the conduct of licensed psychologists, provides for administrative hearings, establishes a psychologist–client privilege, prescribes criminal sanctions for violations of the statute, and regulates the disclosure of patient information to third-party payors.[2] In addition, the Board promulgates rules and regulations to carry out the provisions of the statute. Psychologists are regulated also by the general licensing law that governs all boards and professions (see Chapter 1.0).

State Board of Psychological Examiners

The State Board of Psychological Examiners (Board) is the primary administrative body that licenses and regulates psychologists. It consists of seven members appointed for 3-year terms by the governor. A majority of the Board must be licensed practicing psychologists who represent equitably the diverse fields of psychology.[3] The Board has the duty to[4]

---

1. N.J.S.A. 45:14B-1 to 46.
2. Disclosure to third-party payors is discussed in Chapter 3.1.
3. N.J.S.A. 45:14B-9.
4. N.J.S.A. 45:14B-13.

1. regulate the granting, denial, revocation, renewal, and suspension of licenses; and
2. hold hearings and issue subpoenas to compel documents and testimony on any matters pertaining to the regulation of psychology.

Licensure

The statutes and rules pertaining to licensure set out the qualifications applicants must meet, the fees and examination procedure, and exemptions to the rules. The Board shall issue a license to anyone who[5]

1. is at least 21 years of age;
2. is of good moral character;
3. is not engaged in any practice or conduct that would be a ground for suspending, revoking, or refusing to issue a psychology license;
4. has received a doctoral degree in psychology, or a closely allied field, from a recognized institution;[6]
5. has practiced psychology under the supervision of a licensed psychologist for the equivalent of 2 years, full time, with at least 1 year subsequent to receiving the doctoral degree;[7] and
6. has passed a written and oral examination in theoretical and applied psychology.

The written examination must be sponsored by the American Association of State Psychology Boards (AASPB). A satisfactory score is defined minimally as one standard deviation below the national mean. Passing candidates are then entitled to take a taped oral examination, which will be based on a 20-page work sample in clinical, counseling, industrial, organizational, or school psychology.[8]

---

5. N.J.S.A. 45:14B-14-23.
6. The applicant in a closely allied field must have completed 40 doctoral credits specifically in psychology and 20 additional graduate credits in other psychology courses. In addition, the doctoral dissertation must be psychological in nature. N.J.A.C. 13:42-2.1. Alternatively, an applicant who has at least 5 years of acceptable experience in the field of applied psychology after completing a doctorate with a clearly psychological dissertation may also be admitted to the licensing examination. N.J.A.C. 13:42-2.2.
7. The supervisor must be licensed for 3 years as a psychologist, or the equivalent, or be a Board-certified psychiatrist (who can provide only one third of the total supervision).
8. N.J.A.C. 13:42-3.1.

Failure in either the written or the oral segments of the examination shall entitle the Board to limit reexamination to the segment failed.[9] A candidate may appeal a failure within 45 days of notification of the results.[10]

The examination may be waived for persons who are licensed in another state or who hold a diploma from a nationally recognized psychological board or agency (such as a diplomate of the American Board of Examiners in Professional Psychology).[11] However, such waivers shall only be extended to those who have passed the AASPB examination at the same level as the passing level in New Jersey for that examination.[12]

All licenses expire biennially on June 30. Applicants for renewal must complete a renewal form and mail in a biennial license fee ($140.00) on or before that date. An additional reregistration fee ($25.00) is required if the license has expired.[13]

Exceptions to the Regulations

The law does not restrict the activities and services of all persons who call themselves psychologists. Eight classes of persons are allowed exemptions. Without complying with the above-mentioned licensing procedures, they may use the title of psychologist in their official duties as[14]

1. an employee of an accredited academic institution, a governmental institution or agency, or a research facility;

2. an employee of a business organization, provided that the purposes of the organization do not include the practice of psychology;

3. an employee of a nonprofit bona fide community agency, supported substantially by public funds, provided that the individual is under the direct supervision of a licensed practicing psychologist;

4. an employee of a private elementary or secondary school that requires its psychologists to be certified as school psychologists by the New Jersey State Department of Education;

5. a student of psychology or a psychology intern preparing for the practice of psychology under qualified supervision in an

---

9. N.J.A.C. 13:42-3.4.
10. N.J.A.C. 13:42-1.1.
11. N.J.S.A. 45:14B-20 and N.J.A.C. 13:42-3.3.
12. N.J.A.C. 13:42-3.2.
13. N.J.S.A. 45:14B-21 to 23 and N.J.A.C. 13:42-1.2.
14. N.J.S.A. 45:14B-6.

approved training facility, provided that the individual is designated by such titles as "psychological intern" or "psychological trainee";

6. a practicing psychologist for 10 consecutive days, if he or she is licensed in another state and gives the Board a summary of qualifications and 10 days' written notice;

7. a practicing psychologist for 2 years, if he or she has a temporary permit; or

8. a practicing psychologist for not more than 3 years under the supervision of a licensed psychologist, if he or she has completed all the requirements for licensing except the supervision requirement.[15]

Regulation

Disciplinary Actions Against a Licensed Psychologist

The Board may refuse to grant or renew or may revoke or suspend a license on any of the following grounds of misconduct:[16] use of fraud or deception in the application process; practice of psychology under a false or assumed name; conviction of a crime of moral turpitude; drug or alcohol abuse that interferes with professional duties; violation of the psychology statute or any regulations or code of ethics issued by the Board; professional negligence or misconduct; and illegal advertising.

More specifically, misconduct can include:[17]

1. failing in a willful or grossly negligent manner to comply with federal, state, or local laws, rules, or regulations governing the practice of psychology;

2. exercising undue influence on a patient or client, including the promotion of the sales of services, goods, appliances, or drugs in an exploitative manner for financial gain;

3. fee splitting;

4. permitting any person to share in the fees for professional services, other than a partner, employee, permit holder under supervision, associate in a professional firm or corporation, or psychologist subcontractor or consultant;

5. making claims of professional superiority that cannot be substantiated;

---

15. N.J.A.C. 13:42-2.5.
16. N.J.S.A. 45:14B-24.
17. N.J.A.C. 13:42-4.1.

6. failing to respond within 30 days to a written communication from the Board and to make available any relevant records with respect to an inquiry;

7. abandoning or neglecting a client under and in need of immediate professional care without making reasonable arrangements for the continuation of such care, or abandoning a professional employment without reasonable notice and under circumstances that seriously impair the delivery of professional care to clients;

8. willfully harassing, abusing, or intimidating a patient or colleague relative to delivery of patient services;

9. failing to maintain a record for each patient that accurately reflects the patient contact with the practitioner; all patient records must be retained for at least 6 years;

10. using the word "doctor" without also indicating the specific degree;

11. failing to exercise appropriate supervision over persons who are authorized to practice only under the supervision of a licensed or license-eligible professional;

12. failing to make available to a patient or, upon a patient's request, to another licensed health practitioner copies of reports relating to the patient, or failing to complete forms or reports required for the reimbursement of a patient by a third party; reasonable fees may be charged for such services, but prior payment for the professional services to which such reports relate shall not be required as a condition for making such reports available; a practitioner may, however, withhold information from a patient if he or she believes release of such information would adversely affect the patient's health; there is no requirement to release to the parent of a minor information relating to venereal disease or abortion except with the minor's consent;

13. guaranteeing that satisfaction or a cure will result from the performance of professional services;

14. ordering of excessive tests, treatment, or treatment facilities;

15. claiming or using any secret method of treatment or diagnostic technique that the licensee refuses to divulge to the Board;

16. having physical contact of a sexual nature in the treatment of sexual dysfunction as well as in other psychological practice, or in therapy groups, devising activities that promote or allow explicit physical sexual contact between group members;

17. participating in a conflict of interest, including (a) participation in dual relationships including research or treatment with em-

ployees, tenants, students, supervisees, close friends, or relatives; (b) within an institution, failure to attempt to prevent distortion, misuse, or suppression of psychological findings; (c) failure to attempt to prevent misuse of one's influence or work; (d) exploitation of the trust and dependency of clients; and (e) failure to inform all parties involved of a conflict of interest that has arisen and to take appropriate action;

18. in the undertaking of research, failing to (a) minimize the possibility that the findings will be misleading, (b) provide thorough discussion of the limitations of the data and alternative hypotheses, (c) reveal contrary or disconfirming data, (d) disclose the actual authors of work in proportion to their professional contributions, or (e) treat research participants ethically;

19. in supervisory positions, failing to (a) provide adequate and timely evaluations; (b) provide informed choice, confidentiality, and due process to subordinates; or (c) provide appropriate working conditions, constructive consultation, and opportunities;

20. failing to accurately and objectively represent one's competence, education, training, and experience; for example, psychologists should not claim as evidence of professional qualifications any degree that was not obtained from an accredited academic institution;

21. in financial arrangements with clients, failing to (a) safeguard the best interests of the client; (b) assist clients to understand financial arrangements in advance of incurring a financial obligation to the psychologist, including the specific fee, the extent to which it will be covered by insurance, and whether installment payments are acceptable; (c) assist clients in finding needed services in the instances where payment of the usual fee would be a hardship; or (d) refuse the giving or receiving of a commission, rebate, or other form of remuneration for referral of clients;

22. failing to ensure competence consistent with one's professional responsibilities, including (a) not seeking continuing education; (b) as a teacher, not carefully preparing instruction so that it is accurate, current, and scholarly; (c) undertaking any activity in which one's personal problems are likely to lead to inadequate performance or harm, or failing to seek competent professional assistance in order to determine whether to suspend, terminate, or limit the scope of one's professional and/or scientific activities when personal problems arise; (d) failing to remain abreast of and follow relevant statutes, regulations, and standards; (e) engaging in or condoning inhumane practices or those that result in discrimination in hiring, promotion,

or training; and (f) failing to have an understanding of psychological or educational statistics while making decisions based on test results;

23. improper advertising;

24. failing to maintain professional confidentiality and to safeguard information about an individual that has been obtained by a psychologist in the course of professional duties, unless (a) there is a clear and imminent danger to the individual or the public or when there is probable cause to believe that there is a likelihood of danger to a potential victim of a patient, as judged by the psychologist in accordance with the standards of the profession; in such cases, information should be revealed only to appropriate professional workers, public authorities, and the threatened individuals or their representatives; (b) the information contained in clinical or consulting relationships is discussed only for professional purposes and only with persons clearly connected with the case; (c) personal information obtained is revealed with prior consent of the clients or where the identity of the clients or persons involved is adequately disguised; (d) the originator and other persons involved have given their express permission to share confidential communications with the individual concerned; or (e) research subjects grant explicit permission for their identity to be revealed; the psychologist assumes responsibility for adequately disguising the source; when confidential records are to be maintained, the psychologist makes provision for the protection of confidential information;

25. having improper professional relationships, including (a) failure to make full use of all of the professional technical and administrative resources that best serve the interests of consumers; psychologists are responsible for understanding the areas of competence in the profession and related professions; (b) following discovery of violations of ethical standards by other psychologists, failure to attempt to rectify the situation informally; if the violation does not seem amenable to an informal solution or is of a more serious nature, failure to bring such unethical activities to the attention of the appropriate authorities (if an informal solution is not reached); (c) failure to terminate a clinical or consulting relationship when it is reasonably clear that the consumer is not benefitting from it, and failure to offer help to the consumer to find alternative sources of assistance; (d) as employees, failure to notify responsible persons and to propose modification or termination when services are being used in a way that is not beneficial to participants; (e) exploitation of one's professional relation-

ships with clients, supervisors, students, employees, or research participants sexually or otherwise, or sexual harassment (defined as deliberate or repeated comments, gestures, or physical contacts of a sexual nature that are unwanted by the recipient) condoned or engaged in; and

26. participating improperly in assessment and/or testing in which there is (a) failure to provide the client an explanation of the nature and the purposes of the test and the test results in language that the client can understand unless there is an explicit exception to this right agreed on in advance; (b) failure to utilize established scientific procedures and observe relevant professional standards when one is responsible for the development and standardization of psychological tests and other assessment techniques; (c) failure in reporting test results to indicate reservations regarding validity or reliability resulting from testing circumstances or inappropriateness of the test norms; (d) failure to make every effort to avoid and prevent the misuse of obsolete measures; (e) inability to demonstrate that the validity of the programs and procedures used in arriving at interpretations are based on appropriate evidence in offering test scoring and interpretation services; the public offering of an automated test interpretation is considered as a professional-to-professional consultation; (f) the encouragement or promotion of the use of psychological assessment techniques by inappropriately trained or otherwise unqualified persons through teaching, sponsorship, or supervision.

In addition, the Board is governed by regulations in the general licensing law that provide for the revocation and refusal to grant a license and also specify alternative penalties and dispositions (see Chapter 1.0).

Improper Advertising

Licensed psychologists may engage in advertising.[18] However, the following proscriptions are considered improper advertising, a form of professional misconduct punishable by the Board with denial, suspension, or revocation of a license:[19]

1. any statement, claim, or format that is false, fraudulent, misleading, or deceptive;

2. any misrepresentation of a material fact;

3. the suppression, omission, or concealment of any material fact that the licensee should know is improper or that prohibits a

---

18. N.J.A.C. 13:42-4.1(a).
19. *Id.* and N.J.S.A. 45:14B-24(g).

prospective patient from making a full and informed judgment based upon the advertisement;

4. any claim of professional superiority to the ordinary standards of the profession;

5. any promotion of a professional service that is beyond the licensee's ability to perform;

6. a technique or communication that appears to intimidate, exert undue pressure on, or unduly influence a prospective patient or consumer;

7. any personal testimonial attesting to the quality or competence of a service or treatment offered by a licensee;

8. the communication of any fact, data, or information that may personally identify a patient;

9. an offer to pay, give, or accept a fee or other consideration for the referral of a patient;

10. any format or partial format that is unprofessional;

11. any print, language, or format that directly or indirectly obscures a material fact;

12. offers of gratuitous services or discounts in connection with professional services (although fee negotiation and the rendering of free professional services is not prohibited);

13. failure to provide factual substantiation to the Board to support and substantiate the truthfulness of any questioned assertion or representation in an advertisement; and

14. in-person direct solicitation of prospective patients or consumers (although the offering of services to representatives of patients such as employers, labor unions, and insurance carriers is acceptable).

In addition, advertising relating to a fee shall be limited to the statement of a fixed fee or range of fees for routine services, in which all relevant considerations are discussed in an understandable manner. Unless it is otherwise specified, such fees shall be assumed effective for at least 90 days. All advertising shall include the name and address or telephone number of the licensee and also any other principals, partners, or officers in a firm or organization, each of whom shall be responsible for the advertisement. Psychologists are required to keep printed, audiotaped, or videotaped copies of their advertisements for at least 3 years and to make such copies available to the Board upon request.

Investigations and Hearings by the Board

The Board is required to hold a hearing whenever it exercises disciplinary regulation, and its decisions are subject to review by appeal to the Superior Court of New Jersey.[20] The hearing must be public unless the accused requests a private hearing, and there must be at least 20 days' written notice of the hearing. The Board has the power to issue subpoenas, review any documents, and compel testimony.[21] The proceedings are also governed by the general licensing law (see Chapter 1.0).

The Board is entitled to sue, in the New Jersey Superior Court, any unlicensed person for practicing psychology.[22] The suit may be for both financial penalties and an order of prevention or restraint against continuing to practice illegally.

Determinations by the Board may also form the basis for a civil suit against the psychologist (see Chapters 6.5 and 6.6).

---

20. N.J.S.A. 45:14B-24. The hearing regulations are governed by the Administrative Procedure Act, N.J.S.A. 52:14B-1 et seq., and the Uniform Administrative Procedure Rules, N.J.A.C. 1:1. *See also* N.J.A.C. 13:42-4.1(b).
21. N.J.S.A. 45:14B-13.
22. N.J.S.A. 45:14B-26. The general licensing law allows the Board to institute its own significant penalties for practicing without a license (see Chapter 1.0).

1.4

Subdoctoral and Unlicensed Psychologists

The status of subdoctoral-level psychologists is an important issue, as it pertains both to the law and to the practice of psychology. For example, in some states master's-level psychologists have the right to practice independently, while in other states the laws recognize that these professionals can be a valuable aid to doctoral-level mental health professionals. New Jersey law does not squarely fit either position.

Psychologists Exempted From Licensure

As was already noted in Chapter 1.3, the law provides that a person must be licensed by the State Board of Psychological Examiners in order to use the title psychologist, although it does provide an exception for the following eight classes of persons who may use the title in the performance of their official duties as[1]

1. an employee of an accredited academic institution, a governmental institution or agency, or a research facility;

2. an employee of a business organization, provided that the purposes of the organization do not include the practice of psychology;

3. an employee of a nonprofit bona fide community agency, supported substantially by public funds, provided that the individual is under the direct supervision of a licensed practicing psychologist;

---

1. N.J.S.A. 45:14B-6.

4. an employee of a private elementary or secondary school that requires its psychologists to be certified as school psychologists by the New Jersey State Department of Education;

5. a student of psychology or as a psychology intern preparing for the practice of psychology under qualified supervision in an approved training facility, provided that the individual is designated by such titles as "psychological intern" or "psychological trainee";

6. a practicing psychologist for 10 consecutive days, if he or she is licensed in another state and gives the Board a summary of his or her qualifications and 10-days' written notice;

7. a practicing psychologist for 2 years, if he or she has a temporary permit; or

8. a practicing psychologist for not more than 3 years under the supervision of a licensed psychologist, if he or she has completed all the requirements for licensing except the supervision requirement.[2]

Individuals not licensed nor falling under one of these exemptions may not call themselves psychologists or use psychological or psychology in their title. They may not independently practice psychology or psychotherapy. They may, however, practice as a consultant if they neither advertise nor perform psychological services.

Rights and Responsibilities of Subdoctoral and Licensed Psychologists

Even if a person can use the title psychologist by being exempted from licensure under one of the above categories, it is not clear whether that individual will have all of the same rights and responsibilities as a licensed person. In areas such as confidentiality and privileged communications laws (see Chapters 4.2 and 4.3), the law is ambiguous. Clients of lawyers, whose privileged communications are the basis for the psychologist privilege,[3] are protected if the attorney is a person authorized or reasonably believed by the client to be authorized to practice law.[4] However, the psychologist privilege refers only to "licensed practicing psychologists." Consequently, "It is unclear whether all of the exceptions and lim-

---

2. N.J.A.C. 13:42-2.5.
3. N.J.S.A. 45:14B-28.
4. N.J.S.A. 2A:84A-20.

itations contained in the lawyer–client privilege, Rule 26, are applicable to the psychologist's privilege."[5]

In the only case related to this issue, an unlicensed marriage counselor, under supervision of a licensed marriage counselor, was held to be covered under the marriage counselor's privilege. However, the court stated in dicta (i.e., nonbinding opinion) that if the marriage counselor had been a psychologist, he could not have claimed any privilege because the "psychologist privilege . . . applies to *licensed* practicing psychologists alone."[6]

There are certain other issues, such as malpractice (see Chapter 6.5), where it is also not clear whether an exempted psychologist would be held to the same standard of care as a licensed psychologist. The determination will be made on a case-by-case basis, and there is no present New Jersey case law. In other areas, however, such as insurance reimbursement (see Chapter 3.1), unlicensed psychologists are excluded.

---

5. Biunno, R. J. (1990). Comment to Evid. R. 26A-1. *Current N.J. rules of evidence*, Newark, NJ: Gann Law Books.
6. Touma v. Touma, 140 N.J. Super. 544, 549, 357 A.2d 25, 27 (1976).

Licensure, Certification, and Regulation of Social Workers

The licensure, certification, and regulation of social workers is governed by statutory law[1] that establishes a State Board of Social Work Examiners (Board), defines terms contained in the act, establishes qualifications and procedures for the licensure and certification of three classes of social workers, and provides for confidentiality between social workers and their clients. In addition, this Board is authorized to promulgate rules and regulations to carry out the provisions of the statute. Social workers are also regulated by the general licensing law that governs all boards and professions (see Chapter 1.0).

State Board of Social Work Examiners

The State Board of Social Work Examiners is the primary administrative body that licenses and regulates social workers.[2] It consists of three members who have been actively practicing social work for the preceding 5 years, two social-work educators, and one doctoral-level social worker. There must also be two public members and a representative of the Department of Human Services on the Board. Members are appointed by the governor for 3-year terms.

The Board has the duty to[3]

---

1. N.J.S.A. 15 BB-1 to 13.
2. N.J.S.A. 15 BB-10.
3. N.J.S.A. 15 BB-11.

1. administer the provisions of the Social Worker Licensing Act;
2. examine and pass on the qualifications of all social-work applicants for licensure or certification;
3. evaluate and supervise all licensure and certification exams and procedures;
4. adopt rules and regulations that are necessary to perform its duties and to enforce provisions of the licensing law;
5. establish standards for the continuing education of social workers;
6. prescribe or change the charges for examinations, certifications, licensures, renewals, and other services; and
7. establish social-work specialty advisory committees that must advise and assist the Board in establishing educational criteria for licensure and certification, in developing administrative rules and regulations, and in developing appropriate examinations.

Licensure and Certification

The law defines two types of social work and establishes three classes of social workers.

Social work is defined as[4]

the activity directed at enhancing, protecting or restoring a person's capacity for social functioning, whether impaired by physical, environmental, or emotional factors. The practice of social work includes policy and administration, clinical social work, planning and community organization, social work education, and research.

Clinical social work is defined as[5]

the professional application or social work methods and values in the assessment and psychotherapeutic counseling of individuals, families, or groups. Clinical social work services shall include, but shall not be limited to: assessment; psychotherapy; client-centered advocacy; and consultation.

Certified social workers must have a baccalaureate degree in social work from an educational program accredited by the Council on Social Work Education.

Licensed social workers must have a master's degree in social work from a program accredited by the Council on Social Work Education. They must also pass an examination provided by the Board.

---

4. N.J.S.A. 15 BB-3.
5. *Id.*

Licensed clinical social workers must have a master's degree in social work from a program accredited by the Council on Social Work Education, or a doctorate in social work from an accredited institution. They must have at least 2 years of full-time experience under the supervision of an eligible or licensed clinical social worker (or other acceptable supervisor). They must have satisfactorily completed course requirements established by the Board to ensure adequate training in clinical social work. Finally, they must pass an examination administered by the Board.

Applicants may be exempted from the examination requirements if they demonstrate to the Board that they are licensed or registered in another jurisdiction of the United States that requires substantially the same educational and experiential requirements for licensure as does New Jersey.[6] In addition, within 180 days after the Board establishes procedures for licensure, applicants who meet specified criteria may be "grandfathered" as certified social workers, licensed social workers, or licensed clinical social workers, depending on their education and experience.[7]

Regulations

The law does not yet describe specific conduct that would be grounds for revocation, suspension, or refusal to issue a license. However, social workers are subject to the general licensing law, which provides a detailed list of such behaviors (see Chapter 1.0). The law governing confidentiality (see Chapter 4.2) and privileged communications (see Chapter 4.3) is discussed elsewhere.

Only licensed clinical social workers are permitted to engage in the independent practice of clinical social work for a fee.[8] Certified social workers are forbidden to practice clinical social work, and a licensed social worker is permitted to practice clinical social work only under the supervision of a licensed clinical social worker.

The Social Worker's Licensing Act prohibits people from representing themselves as social workers, certified social workers, licensed clinical social workers, or any other title that includes the words "social worker" or "social work" without the appropriate certification or licensure.[9] Likewise, only those who are certified or licensed may use related abbreviations such as "LSW," "CSW," or "LCSW."

---

6. N.J.S.A. 15 BB-7.
7. N.J.S.A. 15 BB-8.
8. N.J.S.A. 15 BB-4(c).
9. N.J.S.A. 15 BB-4(a).

At the time of license renewal, all applicants must submit a sworn statement that a social-work certificate or license has not been revoked or suspended in any other jurisdiction.[10] In addition, renewal applicants must demonstrate the completion of any continuing education requirements specified by the Board.

Exceptions to the Regulations

The law does not restrict the activities and services of all persons who call themselves social workers or who offer services similar to social work. Specifically, the law does not apply to the following persons:[11]

1. licensed professionals acting within the scope of their profession and training, as long as they do not claim to have a certificate or license in social work;

2. social-work students enrolled in an approved program, so long as the students are practicing as part of a supervised course and are designated by the title "social work intern";

3. school social workers who are certified by the Department of Education,[12] so long as they limit their practice to their official duties;

4. members of the clergy who perform services within the scope of their duties without separate charge, or others whose services are performed under the auspices and control of a legally established church (with or without charge);

5. persons engaged in the intervention, prevention, or treatment of drug or alcohol abuse, so long as they do not use regulated social-work titles; and

6. state employees, who are subject to civil service regulations, in the regular course of their employment.

---

10. N.J.S.A. 15 BB-10.
11. N.J.S.A. 15 BB-5.
12. N.J.A.C. 6:11-12.10.

1.6

Endorsement and Regulation of School Psychologists

The New Jersey State Department of Education, Bureau of Teacher Preparation and Certification, regulates and endorses persons as school psychologists who are employed in primary and secondary school settings.[1] The endorsement is entirely independent of the State Board of Psychological Examiners, with school psychologists being exempted from the regular licensure procedures for services provided as school employees (see Chapter 1.3).[2]

Endorsement

The requirements for endorsement as a school psychologist include[3]

1. a bachelor's degree from an accredited college with a minimum of 30 semester hour credits distributed in at least three of the following fields: English, social studies, science, fine arts, mathematics, and foreign languages;

2. an advanced program of at least 60 semester hour credits in graduate courses in an accredited and approved college or university program or its equivalent, with 12 credits in educational foundations, 6 credits in education of the handicapped, 18 credits in testing and clinical techniques, and 12 credits in personality and behavioral development;

---

1. N.J.S.A. 18A:4-15 and 18A:6-38. N.J.A.C. 6:11-12.14.
2. N.J.S.A. 45:14B-6.
3. N.J.A.C. 6:11-12.14.

3. an externship of 450 supervised hours in a school clinic, child guidance clinic, or other approved clinic;[4] the supervision must be by a qualified school psychologist or by personnel approved by the Commissioner of Education; and

4. as part of the 450-hour externship, at least 100 hours in testing mentally retarded children; at least 50% of the externship must be in the psychological services division of a public school system or the equivalent.

Duties

School psychologists are trained both in course work and during their externships to perform such duties as conducting diagnostic studies; writing reports; counseling pupils, parents, and faculty; participating in staff planning and evaluation conferences; conducting conferences with special personnel; developing cooperative relationships with the community; providing in-service programs for faculty members; and utilizing available community resources.

---

4. Although 450 hours of supervised externship are required for the standard certificate, a provisional certificate can be obtained after 350 hours.

Endorsement and Regulation of School Counselors, Social Workers, and Substance Awareness Coordinators

The New Jersey State Department of Education, Bureau of Teacher Preparation and Certification, regulates and endorses persons as school counselors, school social workers, and substance awareness coordinators who are employed in primary and secondary school settings.[1] The endorsement is entirely independent of the State Board of Psychological Examiners, with school mental health professionals being exempted from the regular licensure procedures for services provided as school employees (see Chapter 1.3).[2]

School Guidance Counselors

Duties

The duties of school guidance counselors include studying and assessing individual pupils with respect to their status, abilities, interests, and needs; counseling with teachers, students, and parents regarding personal, social, educational, and vocational plans and programs; and developing cooperative relationships with community agencies in assisting children and families.[3]

Requirements for Endorsement

The requirements for an endorsement as a school guidance counselor are[4]

---

1. N.J.S.A. 18A:4-15 and 18A:6-38. N.J.A.C. 6:11-12.13.
2. N.J.S.A. 45:14B-6.
3. N.J.A.C. 6:11-12.13.
4. *Id.*

1. a bachelor's or higher degree;
2. a standard New Jersey teacher's certificate, or the completion of the professional course work required for such a certificate;
3. one year of successful teaching experience; and
4. a program of college studies including 30 credits of postbaccalaureate work in five areas including specified course work in guidance and counseling, testing and evaluation, psychology, sociological foundations, and electives.

School Social Workers

The requirements for endorsement of school social workers are[5]

1. a bachelor's degree based on a 4-year curriculum in an accredited college; and
2. three years of successful teaching experience or 3 years of approved social work experience or a combination of both, or a master's degree from an accredited school of social work; or
3. for an applicant without a master's degree from an accredited school of social work, 24 undergraduate credits within five areas including psychology, education, sociology, social case work, mental hygiene, medical information, and community organization and public welfare services.

Substance Awareness Coordinator

Duties

The duties of the substance awareness coordinator are to[6]

1. assist with the in-service training of school district staff concerning substance abuse issues;
2. serve as an information resource for substance abuse curriculum development and instruction;
3. assist the district in revising and implementing substance abuse policies and procedures;
4. develop and administer intervention services in the district;
5. provide counseling services to pupils regarding substance abuse problems; and

---

5. N.J.A.C. 6:11-12.10.
6. N.J.S.A. 18A:40A-18C.

6. cooperate with juvenile justice officials in the rendering of substance abuse treatment services, where necessary and appropriate.

Requirements for Endorsement

The following requirements are necessary to be endorsed as a substance awareness coordinator:[7]

1. a bachelor's degree from an accredited institution in health, human services, psychology, or social work or in a field leading to teacher certification;

2. a program of studies beyond the bachelor's degree that meets the approval of the New Jersey State Department of Education and that includes the following seven topics: fundamentals of drug and alcohol abuse and dependency; child and adolescent development; curriculum planning, implementation, and staff development in chemical health education; coordination and delivery of intervention and referral services in a school setting; evaluation and counseling of drug- and alcohol-affected students and their families; development and coordination of substance abuse intervention and referral services; development and coordination of prevention program services; and the development of school drug and alcohol policies and procedures; and

3. satisfactory completion of a state-approved 300-hour school district residency lasting between 6 months and 1 year (candidates who meet the educational requirements may be employed provisionally while they complete the residency requirement).

---

7. N.J.A.C. 6:11-12.5.

1.8

Licensure and Regulation of Marriage Counselors

The licensure and regulation of marriage counselors is governed by statutory law[1] that establishes a State Board of Marriage Counselor Examiners, defines the practice of marriage counseling, bars the practice of medicine by marriage counselors, establishes qualifications and procedures for the licensure of marriage counselors, establishes exceptions to licensure, regulates the conduct of licensed marriage counselors, provides for administrative hearings, establishes a marriage counselor–client privilege, and prescribes sanctions for violations of the statute. In addition, the Board promulgates rules and regulations to carry out the provisions of the chapter. Marriage counselors are regulated also by the general licensing law that governs all boards and professions (see Chapter 1.0).

State Board of Marriage Counselor Examiners

The State Board of Marriage Counselor Examiners (Board) is the primary administrative body that licenses and regulates marriage counselors. It consists of seven members appointed for 3-year terms by the governor. Five members of the Board must be licensed practicing marriage counselors.[2] The Board has the duty to[3]

1. regulate the granting, denial, revocation, renewal, and suspension of licenses; and

---

1. N.J.S.A. 45:8B-1 to 33.
2. N.J.S.A. 45:8B-9.
3. N.J.S.A. 45:8B-13.

2. hold hearings and issue subpoenas to compel documents and testimony on any matters pertaining to the regulation of marriage counseling.

Licensure

The statutes and rules pertaining to licensure set out the qualifications applicants must meet, the fees and examination procedure, and exemptions to the rules.[4] The Board must issue a license to anyone who

1. is at least 21 years of age;

2. is of good moral character;

3. is not engaged in any practice or conduct that would be a ground for suspending, revoking, or refusing to issue a license;

4. has received at least a master's degree in social work; or a post-master's degree in marriage and family counseling; or a doctorate in marriage or pastoral counseling, psychology, sociology of the family, family life education, or a closely allied field of study; or an M.D. with equivalent course work;[5]

5. has passed a written and oral examination in theoretical and applied marriage counseling; the examination may be waived for persons who are licensed in another state;[6] and

6. has practiced counseling for the equivalent of 5 years under supervision, full time, 2 years of which have included marriage counseling under the supervision of a qualified marriage counselor.

All licensed supervisors must have prior approval by the Board for each supervisee they plan to supervise.[7] Unsupervised independent practice by the candidate is prohibited. The supervisor must meet with the supervisee for at least 1 hour per week. The final professional responsibility for the welfare of the client rests with the supervisor. The supervisor, not the candidate, must bill and accept fees.[8]

---

4. N.J.S.A. 45:8B-15 to 24.
5. All applicants must complete a course of study containing 12 credit hours of human development, 6 credit hours of marital studies and therapy, 9 credit hours of family studies and therapy, 3 credit hours of professional studies, 9 credit hours of supervised clinical work, and 6 credit hours of research methodology. N.J.A.C. 13:34-4.2.
6. N.J.S.A. 45:8B-21.
7. N.J.A.C. 13:34-3.3.
8. N.J.A.C. 13:34-3.4.

Two years of "supervised experience" in marriage counseling requires a minimum of 17 hours per week of actual marriage and family counseling client contact, with a minimum of 1 hour of individual supervision for every 5 hours of client contact. A minimum of 850 hours of counseling with couples and families and a minimum of 170 hours of individual supervision is required. Individuals may prorate the experience requirements over 3 years instead of 2.[9]

All licenses expire annually on June 30. Applicants for renewal must complete a renewal form and mail in a license fee ($65.00) on or before that date. An additional reregistration fee ($50.00) is required if the license has expired.[10]

Exceptions to the Regulations

The law does not restrict the activities and services of all persons who call themselves marriage counselors. Seven classes of persons are allowed exemptions; without complying with the above-mentioned licensing procedures, one may use the title of marriage counselor in his or her official duties[11]

1. as an employee of an accredited academic institution, a governmental institution or agency, or a research facility;

2. as an employee of a private organization, provided the marriage counseling duties are under the direct supervision of a licensed marriage counselor who has received prior Board approval for the supervision arrangements;

3. as a student of counseling or as a marriage counseling intern preparing for the practice of marriage counseling under qualified supervision in an approved training facility, provided that the individual is designated by such title as "marriage counseling intern" or other titles clearly indicating training status;

4. as an employee of a nonprofit bona fide community agency, supported wholly or in major part by public funds;[12]

5. as a practicing marriage counselor for 10 consecutive days, if he or she is licensed in another state and gives the Board a summary of qualifications and 10-days' written notice;

---

9. N.J.A.C. 13:34-4.1.
10. N.J.S.A. 45:8B-22 and N.J.A.C. 13:34-1.1.
11. N.J.S.A. 45:8B-6.
12. N.J.A.C. 13:34-3.1.

6. as a practicing marriage counselor for 1 year, if he or she has a temporary permit;[13] or

7. as a practicing marriage counselor for not more than 3 years under the supervision of a licensed marriage counselor, if he or she has completed all the requirements for licensing except the supervision requirement.

Employees of organizations who are exempted from the licensing law may only perform marriage counseling functions at the employer's place of business and under the eligible organization's control. This right to practice does not confer the privilege of unsupervised, independent practice.[14]

Regulation

Disciplinary Actions Against a Licensed Marriage Counselor[15]

The Board may refuse to grant or renew or may revoke or suspend a license on any of the following grounds: use of fraud or deception in the application process, practice of marriage counseling under a false or assumed name, conviction of a crime of moral turpitude, drug or alcohol abuse that interferes with professional duties, violation of the marriage counseling statute or any regulations or code of ethics issued by the Board, or professional negligence or misconduct.

Professional or occupational misconduct in the practice of marriage counseling by licensed individuals includes the following:[16]

1. failing in a willful or grossly negligent manner to comply with federal, state, or local laws, rules, or regulations governing the practice of the profession;

2. exercising undue influence on a patient or client, including the promotion of the sales of services, goods, appliances, or drugs in an exploitative manner for financial gain;

3. fee splitting;

---

13. If a candidate for licensure has not completed the supervision requirement prior to the filing of the application, he or she may request a temporary permit. Holders of temporary permits must arrange for a supervisor to provide the Board with a written statement detailing the proposed supervision, which must be approved by the Board. The supervisor must document the supervisory experience with the Board every 6 months. N.J.A.C. 13:34-3.4.
14. N.J.A.C. 13:34-3.1.
15. N.J.S.A. 45:8B-25.
16. N.J.A.C. 13:34-2.1.

4. failing to respond within 30 days to a written communication from the Board and to make available any relevant records with respect to an inquiry;

5. abandoning or neglecting a client under and in need of immediate professional care without making reasonable arrangements for the continuation of such care, or abandoning a professional employment without reasonable notice and under circumstances that seriously impair the delivery of professional care to clients;

6. willfully harassing, abusing, or intimidating a client or colleague relative to delivery of patient services;

7. failing to maintain a record for each client that accurately reflects the client's contact with the practitioner; all client records must be retained for at least 6 years;

8. using the word "doctor" without also indicating the specific degree;

9. failing to make available to a client or, upon a client's request, to another licensed health practitioner copies of reports relating to the client, or failing to complete forms or reports required for the reimbursement of a client by a third party; reasonable fees may be charged for such services, but prior payment for the professional services to which such reports relate shall not be required as a condition for making such reports available; a practitioner may, however, withhold information from a client if he or she believes release of such information would adversely affect the client's health; there is no requirement to release to the parent of a minor information relating to venereal disease or abortion except with the minor's consent;

10. guaranteeing that satisfaction or a cure will result from the performance of professional services;

11. ordering of excessive tests, treatment, or treatment facilities;

12. claiming or using any secret method of treatment or diagnostic technique that the licensee refuses to divulge to the Board;

13. having physical contact of a sexual nature between marriage counselor and client, or in therapy groups, promoting or allowing physical contact of a sexual nature between group members;

14. charging of excessive fees for services; a fee is excessive when a licensee of ordinary prudence would be left with a definite and firm conviction that the fee is so high as to be manifestly unconscionable under the circumstances; or

15. unprofessional advertising (infra).

In addition, the Board is governed by regulations in the general licensing law that provide for the revocation and refusal to grant a license and also specify alternative penalties and dispositions (see Chapter 1.0).

Professional Standards in Advertisements

Licensed marriage counselors may engage in advertising. However, the following proscriptions are considered improper advertising, a form of professional misconduct punishable by the Board with denial, suspension, or revocation of a license:[17]

1. any statement, claim, or format that is false, fraudulent, misleading, or deceptive;

2. any guarantee of services;

3. the suppression, omission, or concealment of any material fact that the licensee should know is improper or that prohibits a prospective client from making a full and informed judgment based upon the advertisement;

4. any claim of professional superiority to the ordinary standards of the profession;

5. any promotion of a professional service that is beyond the licensee's ability to perform;

6. a technique or communication that appears to intimidate, exert undue pressure on, or unduly influence a prospective client or consumer;

7. any personal testimonial attesting to the quality or competence of a service or treatment offered by a licensee;

8. the communication of any fact, data, or information that may personally identify a client;

9. an offer to pay, give, or accept a fee or other consideration for the referral of a client;

10. any format or partial format that is unprofessional;

11. any print, language, or format that directly or indirectly obscures a material fact;

12. offers of gratuitous services or discounts in connection with professional services (although fee negotiation and the rendering of free professional services is not prohibited);

13. failure to provide factual substantiation to the Board to support and substantiate the truthfulness of any questioned assertion or representation in an advertisement; or

---

17. N.J.A.C. 13:34-2.1.

14. an offer of marriage and family counseling services by a proprietary organization that fails to designate the licensed marriage counselor.

Unlicensed individuals who are authorized to practice marriage and family counseling as exceptions to the licensing statute (supra) are obligated to disclose the name of the unlicensed individual and the fact of nonlicensure in any advertising.[18]

Investigations and Hearings by the Board

The Board is required to hold a hearing whenever it exercises disciplinary regulation, and its decisions are subject to review by appeal to the Superior Court of New Jersey.[19] The hearing shall be public unless the accused requests a private hearing, and there shall be at least 20-days' written notice of a hearing. The Board has the power to issue subpoenas, review any documents, and compel testimony.[20] The conduct of all hearings must conform to the requirements of the Administrative Procedure Act, as amended and supplemented.[21]

The Board is entitled to sue, in the New Jersey Superior Court, any unlicensed person for practicing marriage counseling. The suit may be for both financial penalties and an order of prevention or restraint against continuing to practice illegally.[22]

Investigations, hearings, and suits by the Board are also governed by the general licensing law (see Chapter 1.0), which provides additional powers to the Board. Determinations by the Board may also form the basis for a civil suit against the marriage counselor (see Chapters 6.5 and 6.6).

18. N.J.A.C. 13:34-3.7.
19. N.J.S.A. 45:8B-25.
20. N.J.S.A. 45:8B-13.
21. N.J.S.A. 54:14B-1 et seq. and N.J.A.C. 13:34-1.7.
22. N.J.S.A. 45:8B-27 and 28.

1.9

Licensure and Regulation of Hypnotists

In some states, the law regulates hypnosis and the professional title "hypnotist" by prescribing education, experience, and skills. In these states, MHPs would have to obtain certification in order to use the title of hypnotist. Because New Jersey does not have such a law, MHPs may use the title hypnotist at their own discretion. The use of hypnotically induced testimony in the courtroom, however, is regulated (see Chapter 5D.12).

1.10

Licensure and Regulation of Polygraph Examiners

In some states, the law regulates polygraph examinations and the professional title "polygraph examiner" by prescribing education, experience, and skills. In these states, MHPs would have to obtain certification in order to use the title of polygraph examiner. Because New Jersey does not have such a law, MHPs may use the title polygraph examiner at their own discretion. The use of polygraph evidence in court, however, is strictly limited by case law (see Chapter 5C.3).

1.11

Sunset of Credentialing Agencies

A sunset law is a means by which the legislature or other branch of government reviews and revises the facets of state government from entire departments to small commissions. Such laws work by automatically terminating the authority of an agency to continue, or of a regulation to remain in force, until after a mandatory review extends the termination date. In New Jersey, there are no statutory sunset provisions. However, administrative rules of various agencies, including professional licensing boards, are subject to automatic sunset provisions as the result of a standing executive order of the governor.

Operation of the Executive Order

Every administrative rule that is adopted pursuant to the Administrative Procedure Act,[1] including all of the state professional licensing boards, must contain a provision that the rule will expire on a date no more than 5 years after the date of its adoption.[2] Any amendment to a rule must also automatically expire no more than 5 years after its adoption. At the time of expiration, the agency may choose to reenact the rule, amend it, or let it lapse indefinitely.

The sunset provision does not apply to any administrative rule that is adopted in compliance with federal law or that would violate state or federal law if applied.[3]

---

1. N.J.S.A. 52:14B-1 et seq.
2. Executive Order 66 (1978).
3. *Id.*

Forms of Business Practice

2.1

Sole Proprietorships

Mental health professionals who practice alone and without any formal organization are termed sole proprietors. Unlike partnerships and professional corporations (see Chapters 2.2 and 2.3), there is no law directly regulating this type of business entity. Rather, sole proprietors must abide only by the laws regulating businesses in general.

2.2

Professional Corporations

Mental health professionals who do not work for an employer typically organize their business in one of three forms: sole proprietorship (see Chapter 2.1), partnership (see Chapter 2.3), or professional corporation (PC or PA).[1] The value of the professional corporation is that it offers many of the tax and practice benefits of regular incorporation. Note that if MHPs wish to incorporate, they must do so under the PC law, since professionals are not permitted to incorporate their practice under the regular incorporation laws.[2]

Benefits of Incorporation

There are three main benefits to incorporation of an MHP practice. First, certain tax deductions are available only to a PC (e.g., deductions for the purchase of health insurance, death benefits, and retirement plans). Second, where there is more than one shareholder (MHP) in the corporation, the professional liability of each MHP (e.g., liability for malpractice) is jointly shared by all, thereby reducing the financial burden on any one person. Third, meeting the requisites of corporation law, such as holding shareholder

---

1. Because the law discussed in this chapter applies to many types of professionals, this section can serve only as an introduction rather than a comprehensive analysis.
2. N.J.S.A. 14A:17-1 to 18.

meetings and issuing regular reports, forces professionals to become more sensitive to the business aspects of their practice.[3]

Incorporation and Operation Procedures

A PC must be organized for the purpose of engaging in one category of professional service (e.g., provision of psychological services); it cannot change that practice after incorporation.[4] Thus it may be formed only by professionals licensed or certified to perform services for which the corporation is organized. Furthermore, all of the shareholders, directors, officers, agents, and professional employees of the PC must also be licensed or certified members of that profession.[5]

The PC must be organized pursuant to the law that governs all aspects of regular incorporation, such as the requirements of adopting the articles of incorporation, the bylaws, the methods of dividing the shares, and so forth. The general incorporation law controls where there is no contrary provision in the PC law.[6]

A PC may employ ancillary personnel to work within the organization. These employees must work under the supervision of licensed or certified personnel and must not hold themselves out as being authorized to engage in the independent practice of the profession for which the PC is licensed. This provision does not expand the requirements of the licensing laws nor the criteria of the state boards regarding the practice of the professions.[7]

Liability and Accountability

Professional corporations differ from regular corporations in one critical way: Each shareholder is jointly and severally liable for all the services provided by the corporation.[8] This means that individual shareholders are liable for their own acts to the same degree as if engaged in an individual practice. Additionally, if more than one person is a part of the practice, each shareholder is potentially

---

3. For more information on whether to incorporate and the particular benefits and liabilities involved, MHPs should seek the advice of a tax consultant and a business planning attorney.
4. N.J.S.A. 14A:17-5.
5. N.J.S.A. 14A:17-10.
6. N.J.S.A. 14A:17-15.
7. N.J.S.A. 14A:17-7.
8. N.J.S.A. 14A:17-8.

responsible for the professional acts of the other members of the PC.

The PC is accountable to the board that grants professional licenses or certificates to its shareholders (e.g., the State Board of Psychological Examiners). It cannot engage in any acts that are prohibited to like professionals who are not incorporated, and if any member of the PC becomes legally disqualified to render professional services, the PC must terminate the person's employment immediately and transfer all shares held by that person within 90 days, at book value, either to the corporation or another qualified person. Other methods of transfer and computation of the value of the shares in such an eventuality may be provided for within the articles of incorporation or the bylaws.[9]

Termination of the Professional Corporation

The PC continues "perpetually" until voluntary or involuntary dissolution occurs pursuant to the laws governing dissolution of regular corporations.[10]

---

9. N.J.S.A. 14A:17-13.
10. *Id.*

Partnerships

A partnership[1] is a form of doing business whereby two or more persons, each of whom is a co-owner, enter into a "for-profit" agreement. It allows the partners to pool their resources to undertake projects that would be financially difficult for one person. But the law may find that any joint endeavor is a partnership whether or not the persons labeled it as such. Such a finding could result in a forced sharing of profits and debts. Thus MHPs should be aware of this form of business whether they form a partnership or merely work in a close business relationship with other persons that could be construed as a partnership.

Formation of a Partnership

A partnership is formed when two or more persons agree to carry on as co-owners of a business for profit.[2] The intent to share profits is the most important factor in determining whether a partnership exists. For instance, two psychiatrists who work out of a co-owned building under a common name will not have partnership status forced upon them unless there also is an intent to share the profits of their services. Partners, however, do not have to share equally in profits and losses. Generally, they are assigned to the partners according to their respective shares in the partnership. For example,

---

1. Because the law discussed in this chapter applies to many types of businesses, an attempt is made only to introduce the reader to it rather than present a comprehensive analysis.
2. N.J.S.A. 42:1-6.

where a partnership consists of two persons, one of whom initially contributed $50,000 and the other $100,000, the latter may legitimately take 66% of the profits. Partners may agree, however, to allocate partnership income and losses in different proportions, although the Internal Revenue Service will not recognize losses in excess of a partner's investment in a partnership.

A mere sharing of rental income does not invoke partnership status.[3] Similarly, the presence of a profit-sharing plan will not be determinative of whether there is a partnership. Nor does the partnership require a formal declaration or filing of business purpose. Rather, any agreement between the parties that meets the above definition, even an oral one, suffices to initiate a partnership.

Rights and Duties Between Partners

A partnership is more than a business relationship: The law imposes duties on the partners governing their interactions. For instance, the partners have equal rights in the management and conduct of business.[4] Each partner has the right to inspect the partnership books,[5] receive all information that may affect the partnership,[6] demand a formal accounting,[7] and rely on the other partners to report all benefits to the partnership.[8]

In fact, the law views each partner as an agent of the partnership. Thus each person's acts bind each of the other partners[9] as long as these acts are within the partner's authority. In no event can a partner individually assign the partnership property in trust for creditors, dispose of the goodwill of the business,[10] do any other act that makes it impossible to carry on the ordinary business of the partnership, acknowledge responsibility in any suit against the partnership, or submit a partnership claim or liability to arbitration or reference.

Perhaps most important, any wrongful act or omission of any partner acting in the ordinary course of the business of the partnership that results in a loss, injury, or penalty accrues to all of the partners.[11] Therefore, if any partner misapplies money or

---

3. N.J.S.A. 42:1-7.
4. N.J.S.A. 42:1-18(5).
5. N.J.S.A. 42:1-19.
6. N.J.S.A. 42:1-20.
7. N.J.S.A. 42:1-22.
8. N.J.S.A. 42:1-21.
9. N.J.S.A. 42:1-9.
10. The reputation of the business. As it pertains to the sale of a business, it is equal to the difference between the purchase price and the value of the net assets.
11. N.J.S.A. 42:1-13.

property of a third party, the partnership is bound to make good the loss.[12] The partners are jointly and severally liable for the above, which means that a wronged person may sue one, several, or all of the partners. In fact, an injured person could sue only the non-injuring partners if desired.[13]

Dissolution of a Partnership

A partnership is dissolved by[14]

1. the terms of the partnership agreement;
2. the express will of any partner to dissolve when no definite term or particular undertaking is specified; that is, where the partners have not agreed to carry out a particular business activity for a specified length of time and one of the partners wishes to dissolve the partnership, that person may do so;
3. the expulsion of any partner from the business in accordance with such a power conferred by the agreement between the partners;
4. a violation of the agreement between the partners, where one of the partners expressly intends for the partnership to dissolve;
5. any event that makes it unlawful for the business of the partnership to be carried on or for the members to carry it on;
6. the death of any partner;
7. the bankruptcy of any partner or the partnership; or
8. the decree of the court when

   a. a partner has been declared a lunatic[15] in any judicial proceeding or is shown to be of unsound mind;
   b. a partner becomes in any other way incapable of performing his or her part of the partnership contract;
   c. a partner has been guilty of such conduct as tends to affect prejudicially the carrying on of the business;
   d. a partner willfully or persistently commits a breach of the partnership agreement, or otherwise so conducts himself or herself in matters relating to the partnership that it is not reasonably practicable to carry on the business in partnership with that partner;

---

12. N.J.S.A. 42:1-14.
13. N.J.S.A. 42:1-15.
14. N.J.S.A. 42:1-31.
15. This term is contained in the law and would now apply to a guardianship and/or conservatorship proceeding (see Chapters 5A.2 and 5A.3).

e. the business of the partnership can only be carried on at a loss; or

f. other circumstances render a dissolution equitable.

Generally, the dissolution of a partnership terminates the authority of the partners except to wind up the partnership affairs.[16] This does not absolve the partners of whatever liability may have accrued to the partnership prior to dissolution, however.

---

16. N.J.S.A. 42:1-33.

2.4

Health Maintenance Organizations

A health maintenance organization (HMO) is a health care program whereby an individual or a group pays a single fee, usually annually, to receive health care services at little or no additional cost. The services are provided by HMO employees or by professionals who contract with the organization on a fee-for-service basis. The overall costs are kept lower by limiting the organization expenses to the prepaid amount and by centralized administration.

Benefits for Mental Health Services

The law[1] provides that an HMO must offer basic health care services, including periodic examinations and office visits, obstetrical care, pediatric care, surgical care, anesthesia, inpatient medical care, radiology, consultations, emergency services, diagnostic laboratory services, inpatient hospital care, skilled nursing services, home health services, ambulance services, health and nutritional education, and preventive health services. Two forms of mental health services are also required:

1. short-term (not to exceed 20 visits) outpatient evaluative and crisis intervention mental health services; and

2. medical social services, which must include assistance in dealing with the physical, emotional, and economic impact of illness and disability through services such as prehospitalization and

---

1. N.J.A.C. 8:38-1.2. *See also* N.J.S.A. 26:2J-1 et seq.

posthospitalization planning, referral to agencies, and related family counseling.

While social workers provide medical social services (see Chapter 1.5), psychiatrists and psychologists must presumably provide short-term mental health services. Although patients must be reimbursed by third-party payors for services performed by a psychologist (see Chapter 3.1), an HMO is not obligated to employ psychologists on its staff.

In addition, every individual and group health insurance policy providing hospital-medical expense benefits issued or renewed in New Jersey must provide coverage for alcoholism treatment ordered by a physician including inpatient or outpatient care in a licensed health care facility, treatment at a licensed detoxification facility, and treatment at a state-approved residential treatment facility (see Chapter 3.1).[2]

Any mental health services beyond those described are considered supplemental and are not required by law.

---

2. N.J.A.C. 11:4-15.1.

2.5

Preferred Provider Organizations

A preferred provider organization (PPO) is a group of health care providers and/or hospitals that contracts with employers, unions, or third-party payors (such as Blue Cross/Blue Shield) to provide services to the employees, members, or insured for a discounted fee in return for an exclusive service arrangement. The service providers see the patients in their own offices. There is no law regulating the formation, organization, or operation of PPOs in New Jersey. The law neither expressly permits nor forbids such organizations.

2.6

Individual Practice Associations

An individual practice association (IPA) is a group of health care providers that contracts to provide services for an organization that provides a prepaid health plan, frequently an HMO.[1] The members of the IPA practice in their own offices but are compensated by the organization on a fee-for-service or fee-per-patient basis.

There is no New Jersey law regulating the formation or operation of IPAs. They would be governed by contract law principles, however.

---

1. An IPA is a new form of health care organization, and an exact definition has yet to be widely adopted.

Hospital, Administrative, and Staff Privileges

The law in many states governs which classes of MHPs are eligible for agency and hospital staff and administrative privileges. With few exceptions, New Jersey law does not directly differentiate between classes of MHPs either in agency privileges or in hospital administrative positions. However, the law does require physicians to be in certain agency and administrative positions (infra). Staff privileges at hospitals are largely governed by the rules and regulations of the Department of Health.

Agency and Administrative Positions

The law requires that the New Jersey State Commissioner of Health be a physician.[1] The person with overall professional responsibility for a mental hospital is the medical director, who must be a physician.[2] The medical director may appoint physician chiefs of service, whose responsibilities are to administer individual units in a mental hospital. Although these laws do not differentiate between classes of MHPs directly, the effect is to permit psychiatrists to qualify for the positions, while excluding other MHPs.

One statute that does differentiate between psychiatrists and other MHPs requires that the clinical director of a screening service, short-term care facility, or psychiatric facility "shall be a psychiatrist, however, those persons currently serving in the capacity will not be affected by this provision. This provision shall not alter any

---

1. N.J.S.A. 26:1A-3.
2. N.J.S.A. 30:1 et seq.

current civil service laws designating the qualifications of such position."[3]

Hospital Staff Privileges

The Commissioner of Health, with the approval of the board of health, is authorized to create regulations, standards, and procedures relating to the licensing of health care facilities and other health services.[4] Such regulations require an organized medical staff in each hospital. Each member of the medical staff must be qualified for membership and for performance of the clinical privileges granted to him or her.[5]

Qualifications and procedures for admission to staff membership must be established that conform to the rules of the hospital.[6] Medical staff bylaws must conform generally to the bylaws of the medical staff approved by the New Jersey Medical Society, the Joint Commission on Accreditation of Hospitals, or the American Osteopathic Association. All applications for membership, privileges, or initial appointment to the medical staff must include the verification of credentials, periodic review of privileges, and the obtaining of information about any disciplinary action from the New Jersey Board of Medical Examiners or other relevant professional licensing board or the Federal Clearinghouse.[7]

Any hospital that has a separate, designated psychiatric service must have a physician director who is board certified in psychiatry or eligible and planning to take the boards within 2 years.[8] The social worker assigned to the inpatient psychiatric unit must have at least a Master of Social Work (M.S.W.) degree from a graduate school accredited by the Council on Social Work Education, or a bachelor's degree from an accredited social work program and 1 year of experience in social work or mental health.[9] Nurses on the psychiatric care unit must be directed by a registered nurse with at least a baccalaureate degree in a health-related field from an accredited college and 2 years of clinical psychiatric experience, or with 4 years of clinical psychiatric experience. In addition, the psychiatric care unit must have psychological services, including testing, provided by a licensed psychologist.[10]

---

3. N.J.S.A. 30:4-27.2.
4. N.J.S.A. 26:2H-5(b).
5. N.J.A.C. 8:43B-6.2.
6. *Id.*
7. N.J.A.C. 8:43G-16.1.
8. N.J.A.C. 8:43G-26.3.
9. *Id.*
10. N.J.A.C. 8:43G-26.7.

Beyond these provisions, the law neither requires nor denies hospital or staff privileges to different classes of MHPs; instead, the law delegates such decisions to the individual hospital medical staffs.

2.8

Zoning for Community Homes

Zoning regulations are the laws by which state and local governments guide the rate and type of growth of communities, including
their residential and commercial buildings. These laws can be, and
have been, used to exclude certain classes of people thought to be
undesirable from particular communities or from areas within
communities in some states. For example, some zoning boards have
prohibited community homes for the mentally disordered from
locating in single-family residential neighborhoods even though
such a placement would be in the best interests of the community
home residents.

New Jersey law partially prohibits such discrimination by designating certain community homes as family residences. This law
provides that[1]

> Community residences for the developmentally disabled and
> community shelters for victims of domestic violence shall be a
> permitted use in all residential districts of a municipality, and the
> requirements therefore shall be the same as for single family
> dwelling units located within such districts.

It is important to note that a "community residence for the
developmentally disabled" is defined by statute to mean a group
home, half-way house, intermediate care facility, supervised
apartment, or other such facility providing food, shelter, and personal guidance that houses not more than 15 mentally ill or developmentally disabled people.[2] Community residences for the
mentally ill are required to be preapproved by the Division of

---

1. N.J.S.A. 40:55D-66.1 et seq.
2. N.J.S.A. 40:55D-66.2.

Mental Health and Hospitals of the Department of Human Services,[3] and community shelters for domestic violence also must be preapproved by the Department of Human Services.[4]

Community residences and shelters housing more than six residents (other than staff) may be required by a municipality to apply for a conditional use permit from its planning board. The planning board's standards and specifications for such a conditional use must be reasonably related to the health, safety, and welfare of the residents of the district.[5]

A municipality may prohibit any community residence or shelter from being established within 1,500 feet of an existing one. Likewise, prohibition is permitted if the municipality houses more than 50 such persons or their number exceeds more than 0.5% of its population.[6]

Family day care homes, which contract with the Division of Youth and Family Services to provide day care for 3–5 children for 15 hours or more per week, are also exempted from municipal zoning laws and must be considered a home occupation rather than a special use.[7] Likewise, municipalities are prohibited from zoning ordinances that discriminate between children of a family, foster children placed with the family by the Division of Youth and Family Services, and children placed in group homes.[8]

3. *Id.* and N.J.S.A. 26:2H-1 et seq.
4. *Id.* and N.J.S.A. 30:14-1 et seq.
5. N.J.S.A. 40:55D-66.1 and 7.
6. N.J.S.A. 40:55D-66.1.
7. N.J.S.A. 40:55D-66.4.
8. N.J.S.A. 30:4C-26.

Insurance Reimbursement and Deductions for Services

3.1

Insurance
Reimbursement
for Services

Health insurance carriers (insurers) typically have provisions providing reimbursement for mental health services. The policies frequently limit reimbursement to certain classes of health care providers, usually physicians, and to particular types of services. New Jersey law provides that insurers must reimburse psychiatrists and psychologists in certain situations. The law strictly limits the amount of patient information that psychologists must make available to insurance companies for reimbursement purposes. There are no laws pertaining to services by other MHPs, which means that insurers may deny claims by them or their clients if they are not specifically included in the policy.

Types of Insurance Affected

Although some states prohibit the denial of reimbursement for psychiatric or psychological services in certain types of insurance policies, New Jersey only prohibits the denial of reimbursement for alcoholism benefits in health insurance policies.

Required Coverage of Psychiatric Services

The law requires insurance policy benefits for both inpatient and outpatient treatment of alcoholism, including detoxification, to the same extent that any other sickness is covered in the policy.[1] If a policy only defines benefits in terms of inpatient days, outpatient treatments must be considered equivalent to inpatient days and afforded the same kind of coverage.[2] Outpatient treatment may be given at a hospital or residential treatment facility or as aftercare at a detoxification facility, provided by certified alcoholism counselors and MHPs.

While the statute requires that treatment be prescribed by a physician, presumably psychologists would also be reimbursed for services within their expertise, as required by the Psychology Licensing Act (see Chapter 1.3).

Prohibiting Denial of Reimbursements for Psychological Services

The law[3] prohibits the denial of reimbursement for services that are within the lawful scope of licensed psychologists, whether they are performed by a physician or a psychologist. The statement in an insurance policy that such reimbursable services must be performed by a physician or psychiatrist is interpreted by state law to include psychologists. The law extends to health maintenance organizations (HMOs) that recognize psychologists as licensed health care providers.[4]

Psychologists are entitled to reimbursement to the same extent that benefits are provided to psychiatrists for equivalent mental health services. According to the Psychology Licensing Act (see Chapter 1.3), although psychologists are not entitled to practice medicine, they are authorized to provide diagnosis, assessment, and psychotherapy.[5]

Although the courts in New Jersey have not ruled on the question, it is probable that the federal ERISA statute, regulating those companies that design their own self-insured employee benefit plans, preempts all state "mandated provider" laws, including the New Jersey statute prohibiting the denial of reimbursement to psychologists.[6] Consequently, a company that self-insures probably is free to design a plan either reimbursing or denying any claims for psychological services.

---

1. N.J.S.A. 17B:27-46.1 and N.J.A.C. 11:4-15.1 et seq.
2. N.J.A.C. 11:4-15.2.
3. N.J.S.A. 17B:27-50 and 17B:26-2(e).
4. N.J.S.A. 26:2J-2.
5. N.J.S.A. 45:14B-2.
6. 29 U.S.C. §§ 1001-1461 (1982). See Note, ERISA Preemption of State Mandated Provider Laws, 1985 DUKE L. J. 1194. See also Rapp v. Travelers Insurance Co., 869 F.2d 1498 (Table) (1989).

Disclosures by Psychologists to Insurance Companies

Third-party payors (insurance companies) are regulated in obtaining treatment information about psychologists' patients even if a waiver of confidentiality has been signed.[7] The disclosures are limited to administrative information, diagnostic information (DSM–III–R code), status of the patient (voluntary or involuntary, inpatient or outpatient), and the reason for continuing psychological services. Such reason is limited to an assessment of the patient's current level of functioning and level of distress (both described by the terms *mild, moderate, severe,* or *extreme*).[8] Third-party payors are prohibited from further disclosure of this treatment information except where required by law or in legal disputes to settle payment claims.[9]

If the third-party payor believes that the psychological treatment is neither usual, customary, nor reasonable, the payor may request and pay for an independent review by a professional review committee.[10] The request shall be in writing to the treating psychologist, who must then notify the State Board of Psychological Examiners.[11] The Board will then assign two "reviewers" who shall conduct a confidential review of the case, according to statutory guidelines, and then certify to the insurance company whether the treatment was usual, customary, or reasonable. Such certification will determine whether reimbursement will be paid. Patients must sign a detailed revocable authorization to disclose information to the reviewers before the review may begin.[12] The Board is required to appoint psychologists in each of the major theoretical orientations to the independent professional review committee and to establish rules and regulations for reviewing procedures.[13]

The law is limited to disclosures by psychologists to third-party payors and does not apply to other MHPs.

7. N.J.S.A. 45:14B-31 et seq.
8. N.J.S.A. 45:14B-32.
9. N.J.S.A. 45:14B-39.
10. N.J.S.A. 45:14B-33.
11. N.J.S.A. 45:14B-34.
12. N.J.S.A. 45:14B-36.
13. N.J.S.A. 45:14B-45 and 46.

3.2

Mental Health Benefits in State Insurance Plans

In some states, including New Jersey, the law mandates that any health insurance plan provided for state government employees must include certain mental health benefits.[1] The law states,[2]

> Maximums of $10,000 per calendar year and $20,000 for the entire period of the person's coverage under the plan shall apply to eligible expenses incurred because of mental illness or functional nervous disorders, and such may be reapplied to a covered person.

Under New Jersey's current insurance plan, mental health benefits may be reapplied to an individual up to a $100,000 lifetime maximum. These amounts are payable yearly after a $100 deductible, at the rate of 80% of the first $2,000 of major medical expenses and 100% thereafter.

As in any state-authorized insurance reimbursement plan (see Chapter 3.1), both inpatient and outpatient treatment for alcoholism that is prescribed by a physician must also be reimbursed as any other disease, not subject to the maximums for mental disorders.[3]

Any eligible service that is performed lawfully by a licensed psychologist must be reimbursed under the same conditions as those applicable to physicians (see Chapter 3.1).[4]

---

1. N.J.S.A. 52:14-17.28 et seq. and N.J.A.C. 17:9-1.1 et seq.
2. N.J.S.A. 52:14-17.29.
3. *Id.*
4. *Id.*

3.3

Tax Deductions for Services

Payments for mental health services may be deductible as either an individual medical deduction or as a business expense, depending on the nature of the service and the use by the recipient taxpayer.

Mental Health Services as a Medical Deduction

Professional services relating to the diagnosis or treatment of mental or emotional disorders are allowable as medical deductions under both federal and state law. The expenses must be actually paid for the medical care of the taxpayer, spouse, or dependent, minus compensation for insurance or otherwise. The deduction is limited to that amount of net expenses greater than 7.5% of the taxpayer's federal adjusted gross income and 2% of the taxpayer's New Jersey gross income.[1]

Federal law obviously allows for a deduction for services performed by a psychiatrist physician. It also provides that[2]

> Amounts paid psychologists who are qualified and authorized under State law to practice psychology for services rendered by them in connection with the diagnosis, cure, mitigation, treatment or prevention of disease, or for the purpose of affecting any structure or function of the body, constitute expenses paid for medical care within the meaning of section 23(x) of the Internal

---

1. I.R.C. Reg. 1.213-2 and N.J.S.A. 54A:3-3.
2. Rev. Rul. 143, 1953-2 C.B. 129.

Revenue Code and may be deducted in computing net income for Federal income tax purposes, to the extent provided therein.

The Internal Revenue Service (IRS) further allows deductions for payments made to other types of mental health providers:[3]

> Accordingly it is held that amounts paid for medical services rendered by practitioners, such as chiropractors, psychotherapists, and others rendering similar type services, constitute expenses for "medical care" within the provisions of section 213 of the Code, even though the practitioners who perform the services are not required by law to be, or are not (even though required by law) licensed, certified, or otherwise qualified to perform such services.

Similarly, state tax deductions are allowed for mental health services:[4]

> Each taxpayer shall be allowed to deduct from his gross income medical expenses for himself, his spouse, and his dependents with respect to such expenses that were paid during the taxable year and to the extent that such medical expenses exceed two percent of the taxpayer's gross income. In the case of a nonresident, gross income shall mean gross income which such nonresident would have reported if he had been subject to tax during the entire taxable year as a resident.

"Medical care" refers to amounts paid

1. for the diagnosis, cure, mitigation, treatment, or prevention of disease or for the purpose of affecting any structure or function of the body; and

2. for transportation primarily for and essential to medical care referred to in Item 1 above.

Because New Jersey follows federal law, this provision will be interpreted by reference to the federal law noted above. And because the IRS interprets "medical care" to include services provided by nonpsychiatric providers, taxpayers can deduct those services like other medical expenses when they file their New Jersey income tax returns.

Mental Health Services as a Business Deduction

The use of mental health services by a business is deductible as a trade or business expense. Federal law provides that "there shall

---

3. Rev. Rul. 91, 1963-1 C.B. 54.
4. N.J.S.A. 54A:3-3.

be allowed as a deduction all the ordinary and necessary expenses paid or incurred during the taxable year in carrying on any trade or business."[5] The key words are "ordinary and necessary." Ordinary has been defined as "common and accepted."[6] Necessary means "appropriate and helpful."[7]

Mental Health Services Received by MHPs

Mental health professionals may not deduct the cost of their basic professional education as a business expense. However, MHPs may deduct education courses if (1) they are employed or self-employed; (2) they meet the minimum requirements of the job or profession; and (3) the course maintains or improves job skills, or the person is required by the employer or by law to take the course to keep the present salary or position.[8]

The educational expenses will not be deductible if they are part of a program of study that will lead to a new trade or business.[9] Licensed psychiatrists are permitted to deduct expenses associated with training at a psychoanalytic institute, including personal psychoanalysis, under this rule.[10] In a tax court decision, a clinical social worker was also permitted a deduction for her own psychoanalysis.[11] In a similar vein, a psychiatrist has been permitted a deduction for his own psychotherapy.[12] Although the law is unsettled in this area, the trend is to permit educational business deductions for the expense of personal psychotherapy if the experience improves the MHP's job skills.

---

5. 26 U.S.C. 162(a).
6. Welch v. Helvening, 290 U.S. 111, 114, 54 S.Ct. 8, 9, 78 L.Ed. 212, 214 (1933).
7. *Id.* at 290 U.S. 113, 54 S.Ct. 9, 78 L.Ed. 214.
8. I.R.C. Reg. 1.162-5(a).
9. I.R.C. Reg. 1.162-5(b)(3).
10. *Id.* example (4).
11. Voigt v. Comm'r, 74 T.C. 82 (1980), *nonacq.*, 1981-33.
12. Porter v. Comm'r, T.C. Memo. 1986-70.

Privacy of Professional Information

4.1

Extensiveness, Ownership, Maintenance, and Access to Records

An MHP's records are an important, required part of a practice. Because the law does not speak to the issue, it is assumed that MHPs own these records. New Jersey law, however, does regulate other issues relating to a psychologist's, psychiatrist's, and marriage counselor's records; the law does not speak to other MHPs.

Psychologists and Marriage Counselors

Extensiveness of Records

Maintaining such records is not only necessary for the conduct of a good mental health practice, but is also required by the State Board of Psychological Examiners[1] and the State Board of Marriage Counselors.[2] The administrative codes for both professions state that professional misconduct that is grounds for revocation, suspension, or refusal to renew a license exists if there is failure to maintain a record for each patient that accurately reflects the patient contact with the practitioner.

Maintenance of Records

This rule for psychologists goes on to provide that such records must be maintained for a minimum of 6 years in most cases: "Unless otherwise provided by law, all patient records shall be retained

---

1. N.J.A.C. 13:42-4.1(a)(1)(ix).
2. N.J.A.C. 13:34-2.1(a)(6).

for at least six years."[3] The rule for marriage counselors is identical in substance.[4]

Client Access

The law provides that licensed psychologists[5] and licensed marriage counselors[6] engage in unprofessional conduct if they fail to make available to the client or, upon his or her request, to another licensed health practitioner copies of reports relating to the patient. This includes the failure to complete forms or reports necessary for third-party reimbursement. Reasonable fees may be charged for such services, but payment cannot be required as a condition for releasing the information.

A psychologist or marriage counselor may, however, withhold information from a patient if he or she reasonably believes it would adversely affect the patient's health. In addition, these professionals are not required to release to the parent or guardian of a minor records or information relating to venereal disease or abortion, except with the minor's consent.

Access by the State Boards of Examiners

Both psychologists[7] and marriage counselors[8] must divulge any client information, answer any questions under oath, and produce relevant books, records, and papers when they are subpoenaed by their respective state boards. The board in question has broad investigative powers to compel witnesses and records in "any matter pertaining to its duties" under the Practicing Psychology Licensing Act. This is also true under the Marriage Counseling Act.

Hospital Medical Review Boards

Certified hospitals and extended care facilities are required to establish utilization review committees for the purposes of reducing morbidity and mortality and for the improvement of the care of patients provided in the institution. Such committees are entitled to full access to all hospital records concerning the care and treatment of patients.[9] Thus, records documenting psychological or other mental health services delivered in a hospital would be available to the review committee. Requests for nonhospital records of a hospital patient would be covered by confidentiality and privileged communications law (see Chapters 4.2 and 4.3).

---

3. N.J.A.C. 13:42-4.1(a)(1)(ix).
4. N.J.A.C. 13:34-2.1(a)(6)(i).
5. N.J.A.C. 13:42-4.1(a)(1)(xi).
6. N.J.A.C. 13:34-2.1(a)(8).
7. N.J.S.A. 45:14B-13.
8. N.J.S.A. 45:8B-13.
9. N.J.S.A. 2A:84A-22.8.

These records must remain confidential except to the patient's attending physician, the chief administrative officer of the hospital, the medical executive committee of the hospital, representatives of government agencies under the provisions of state and federal law, and insurance companies that authorize the carrier to request and be given such information and data (see Chapter 6.4).

Liability for Violation

Violation of the above laws may result in suspension, revocation, or failure to renew a psychologist's or marriage counselor's license. Furthermore, since these laws set the standard for psychologists and marriage counselors in New Jersey, failure to abide by it may result in civil liability (see Chapters 1.3, 1.8, and 6.5). Note that since these laws only pertain to licensed psychologists and marriage counselors, the standard for unlicensed professionals (see Chapter 1.4) may not be the same.

Psychiatrists

Extensiveness of Records

Physicians are required to prepare and maintain patient records. Although there are no requirements regarding the adequacy of such records, presumably if the records were insufficient to perform reasonable medical services, the physician would be demonstrating "professional incompetence to practice medicine," which is grounds for the State Board of Medical Examiners to suspend or revoke a license.[10]

Maintenance of Records

The physician is required to maintain medical records for 7 years from the date of the last entry.[11]

Client Access

Copies of all records and reports are required to be furnished to the patient or an authorized representative within 30 days of a request. A reasonable charge may be made for such services.[12] However, no physician is permitted to charge a patient an extra fee for services rendered in completing a medical claim form in connection with a health insurance policy.[13]

---

10. N.J.S.A. 45:9-16(a).
11. *Id.*
12. N.J.S.A. 45:9-16(b) and (c).
13. N.J.S.A. 45:9-22.1.

Where the physician reasonably believes that review by the patient of requested records would be deleterious to the patient's best interests, a partial record may be supplied.[14]

Access by the State Board of Medical Examiners

The Board has broad powers to investigate violations of the licensing law "in any matter pertaining to its duties," including the subpoena of witnesses and presumably of documents and records.[15]

Hospital Medical Review Boards

Certified hospitals and extended care facilities are required to establish utilization review committees for the purposes of reducing morbidity and mortality and for the improvement of the care of patients provided in the institution. Such committees are entitled to full access to all hospital records concerning the care and treatment of patients.[16] Thus, a psychiatrist's records documenting services delivered in a hospital would be available to the review committee. Requests for nonhospital records of a hospital patient would be covered by confidentiality and privileged communications law (see Chapters 4.2 and 4.3).

These records must remain confidential except to the patient's attending physician, the chief administrative officer of the hospital, the medical executive committee of the hospital, representatives of government agencies under the provisions of state and federal law, and insurance companies that authorize the carrier to request and be given such information and data (see Chapter 6.4).

Liability for Violation

Violation of the above laws may result in suspension or revocation of the psychiatrist's license. Furthermore, since the law sets the standard of behavior for psychiatrists in New Jersey, failure to abide by it may result in civil liability (see Chapters 1.1 and 6.5).

---

14. N.J.S.A. 45:9-16(b) and (c).
15. N.J.S.A. 45:9-2.
16. N.J.S.A. 2A:84A-22.8.

Confidential Relations and Communications

Generally, a confidential communication is written or verbal information conveyed by the client to an MHP in the course of a professional relationship. Confidentiality originated in professional ethics codes[1] arising from a belief that effective psychotherapy required a guarantee from the therapist that no information obtained in the course of evaluation or treatment would be given to others. Although the law in some states has adopted this concern by mandating criminal penalties for violations of confidentiality for some professionals, all MHPs may be liable in civil suits initiated by clients who have been harmed by breaches of confidentiality (see Chapter 6.5). The remainder of this chapter only pertains to psychologists, psychiatrists, marriage counselors, and social workers.

Psychologists

Psychologists Covered Under These Statutes

The statutes concern the confidential communications of licensed psychologists. It is unclear whether the courts would apply the statute to a client who reasonably, but erroneously, believes that he or she is in a professional relationship with a licensed psychologist.[2]

---

1. E.g., see APA (1990). Ethical principles of psychologists. *American Psychologists, 45,* 390–395.
2. N.J.S.A. 2A:84A-20 and 45:14B-28.

Scope of the Duty

Confidential communications are covered under both regulatory and statutory law. The Board of Psychological Examiners has defined the "failure to maintain professional confidentiality," including the "failure to safeguard information about an individual that has been obtained by a psychologist in the course of his or her teaching, practice, or investigation," as a type of professional misconduct. Such misconduct is grounds for the Board to revoke, suspend, or refuse to renew or grant a license.[3]

The primary authority for the protection of confidential communications is derived from the Psychology Licensing Act, which provides that[4]

> The confidential relations and communications between a licensed practicing psychologist and individuals, couples, families or groups in the course of the practice of psychology are placed on the same basis as those provided between attorney and client, and nothing in this act shall be construed to require any such privileged communications to be disclosed by any such person.

This statute does more than establish a duty of confidentiality: It also creates a psychologist–client privilege (see Chapter 4.3).[5] The duty of confidentiality, rather than being based on the ethical standards of psychologists, is derived from the law pertaining to confidential relations and communications between attorney and client.[6]

The attorney–client privilege states that[7]

> communications between lawyer and his client in the course of that relationship and in professional confidence, are privileged, and a client has a privilege (a) to refuse to disclose any such communication, and (b) to prevent his lawyer from disclosing it, and (c) to prevent any other witness from disclosing such communication if it came to the knowledge of such witness (i) in the course of its transmittal between the client and the lawyer, or (ii) in a manner not reasonably to be anticipated, or (iii) as a breach of the lawyer–client relationship, or (iv) in the course of a rec-

---

3. N.J.A.C. 13:42-4.1(a)(1)(xxiv).
4. N.J.S.A. 45:14B-28.
5. In many states, the law clearly distinguishes between confidentiality and privileged communications. Confidentiality law refers to maintenance of confidences outside of legal proceedings. Privileged communications law refers to the maintenance of confidences within legal proceedings. New Jersey, however, does not apparently draw this distinction as clearly. For example, in the statute just cited, the confidential communications law refers to privileged communications between psychologist and client. In addition, it places the relationship on the same basis as that between attorney and client, which applies a uniform standard both inside and outside legal proceedings.
6. N.J.S.A. 2A:84A-20.
7. N.J.S.A. 2A:84A-20(1).

ognized confidential or privileged communication between the client and such witness. The privilege shall be claimed by the lawyer unless otherwise instructed by the client or his representative.

Although this section places confidential psychologist–client relations under the attorney–client privilege, as will be noted later (see Chapter 6.5), the standard of due care for malpractice is the one ordinarily practiced by average members of the profession. Under this rule, it is not clear whether New Jersey psychologists would be held to the standard customarily exercised by psychologists as defined by practice standards or that exercised by attorneys. If the courts chose the former, an inconsistency in the law would be created, although it is clearly the more rational approach.

Another ambiguity created by drafting the attorney–client privilege into the psychologist confidentiality statute arises if the psychologist is unlicensed or unauthorized to practice psychology (see Chapter 1.4). Clients of lawyers are assured of confidentiality if the attorney is a person authorized or reasonably believed by the client to be authorized to practice law.[8] However, the psychologist privilege refers only to "licensed practicing psychologists." Consequently,[9]

> It is unclear whether all of the exceptions and limitations contained in the lawyer–client privilege, Rule 26, are applicable to the psychologist's privilege.

Limitations on the Duty

The duty regarding confidentiality has several limitations. First, the Board of Psychological Examiners may subpoena attendance of witnesses and production of documents or other information pertaining to investigations of violations of the rules, regulations, or orders of the Board.[10]

Second, the psychologist must break confidentiality if there is a clear and imminent danger to the individual or the public or when there is probable cause to believe that there is a likelihood of danger to a potential victim of a patient, as judged by the psychologist in accordance with the standards of the profession. In such cases, information should be revealed only to appropriate professional workers, public authorities, and the threatened individuals or their representatives.[11]

---

8. N.J.S.A. 2A:84A-20.
9. Evid. R. 26A-1.
10. N.J.S.A. 45:14B-13.
11. N.J.A.C. 13:42-4.1(a)(1)(xxiv). *See also* McIntosh v. Milano, 168 N.J. Super. 466, 403 A.2d 500 (1979), a malpractice case that litigated this issue.

Third, the psychologist may break confidentiality in professional work where the identity of the clients, research subjects, or other persons involved is adequately disguised or where the originator and other persons involved have given their express permission to share confidential communications with the individual concerned. When confidential records are to be maintained, the psychologist must make provision for the protection of confidential information.[12]

Fourth, confidential communications to psychologists protected by the "attorney–client" privilege do not extend to (psychological) services sought or obtained to further the commission of a crime or a fraud.[13] Nor does privileged communication apply to communications relevant to a breach of duty between the psychologist and patient (which might later be raised in a legal proceeding, such as a failure to pay a bill).[14] Also, a patient waives his or her privileged communication rights if he or she contracts not to exercise the privilege, or if he or she knowingly makes a voluntary disclosure regarding the privileged matter.[15]

A fifth exception to confidential communications is the statutory requirement (see Chapter 5A.8) that "any person having a reasonable cause to believe that a child has been subjected to child abuse or acts of child abuse shall report the same immediately to the Division of Youth and Family Services by telephone or otherwise."[16]

Another statutory requirement enables physicians, hospitals, and clinics to treat minors, without parental consent, for venereal disease or drug abuse.[17] The physician has the discretionary authority to decide whether to notify the parents about such treatment.[18] It is possible that this law would be interpreted to include psychological treatment as well, a prospect based upon the broad treatment rights conferred on psychologists under the Psychology Licensing Act.

A final exception to confidential communications occurs in criminal proceedings to determine competency to stand trial or in

---

12. *Id.*
13. However, the superior court ruled that a Department of Corrections regulation excepting inmate–patient communications from the psychotherapist-patient privilege when it is believed that disclosure is more important to interests of substantial justice or safety was invalid as being broader than a situation that presents clear and imminent danger to the inmate or others. Matter of Rules Adoption Regarding Inmate–Therapist Confidentiality (N.J.A.C. 10A:16-4.4), 224 N.J. Super. 252, 540 A.2d 212 (App. Div. 1988).
14. N.J.S.A. 2A:84A-20.
15. N.J.S.A. 2A:84A-29.
16. N.J.S.A. 9:6-8.10.
17. N.J.S.A. 9:17A-4.
18. N.J.S.A. 9:17A-5.

release following an insanity verdict. Such information would be admissible in court only for the purpose of clarifying an individual's mental condition and not to prove other issues such as innocence or guilt.[19]

Liability for Violation

Several types of penalties may be imposed for violations of confidentiality. First, as was noted earlier, the law[20] provides that the State Board of Psychological Examiners may suspend, revoke, or refuse to renew the license of any psychologist who fails to "maintain professional confidentiality." Clients harmed by a breach of confidentiality may also bring a civil suit for recovery of damages based on several legal theories. Although there is no law in New Jersey directly addressing civil remedies for breach of confidentiality, Chapters 6.5 and 6.6 describe actions that have been used in other states with varying degrees of success. There is no reason to believe that such suits would be barred in New Jersey.

Marriage Counselors

The primary authority for the protection of confidential communications is derived from the Practicing Marriage Counseling Act, which states,[21]

> Any communication between a marriage counselor and the person or persons counseled shall be confidential and its memory preserved. This privilege shall not be subject to waiver, except where the marriage counselor is a party defendant to a civil, criminal, or disciplinary action arising from such counseling, in which case, the waiver shall be limited to that action.

This statute does more than establish a duty of confidentiality: It also creates a marriage counselor–client privilege (see Chapter 4.3).[22]

The duty regarding confidentiality has several limitations. First, the State Board of Marriage Counseling Examiners may by subpoena compel the attendance of witnesses and the production of

---

19. N.J.S.A. 2C:4-10.
20. N.J.A.C. 13:42-4.1.
21. N.J.S.A. 45:8B-29.
22. In many states, the law clearly distinguishes between confidentiality and privileged communications. Confidentiality law refers to maintenance of confidences outside of legal proceedings. Privileged communications law refers to the maintenance of confidences within legal proceedings. New Jersey, however, does not apparently draw this distinction as clearly. For example, in the statute just cited, the confidential communications law refers to privileged communications between marriage counselor and client.

documents or other information pertaining to investigations of violations of the rules, regulations, or orders of the Board.[23]

Second, the duty of confidential communications does not apply where the marriage counselor is required by law to report patient information. This includes the child abuse reporting law (see Chapter 5A.8).[24]

Third, confidentiality must be broken when there is a probability that clients may become dangerous to others.[25] In such situations, the marriage counselor must take whatever steps are reasonably necessary to protect a potential victim of the client, such as warning the victim or calling the police. As the court in the case of *McIntosh v. Milano* emphasized, the principle of confidentiality does not apply to many situations where it becomes necessary to protect the welfare of the individual or of the community, as in reporting patients with infectious diseases or gunshot wounds or those who are about to commit a fraud or crime.[26] Although the defendant in this case was a psychiatrist, the court opinion frequently refers to the legal duties of "therapists," which strongly implies that marriage counselors would be governed by the same principles as psychiatrists.

Liability for Violation

Several types of penalties may be imposed for violations of confidentiality. First, the State Board of Marriage Counselors may revoke, suspend, or refuse to renew a license for violation of the marriage counseling statute.[27] Furthermore, because this law prescribes a standard of conduct, failure to abide by it may result in civil liability (see Chapter 6.5). Clients may also bring suit on the basis of other legal theories. Although there is no law in New Jersey directly addressing civil remedies for breach of confidentiality, Chapter 6.6 describes actions that have been used in other states with varying degrees of success. There is no reason to believe that such suits would be barred in New Jersey.

Psychiatrists

Scope and Limitations of the Duty

While there is no specific obligation of physician–patient confidentiality in the physician licensing statute, the regulations of the

---

23. N.J.S.A. 45:8B-13.
24. N.J.S.A. 9:6-8.10.
25. McIntosh v. Milano, *supra.*
26. *Id.,* p. 485.
27. N.J.S.A. 45:8B-25.

Board of Medical Examiners require confidentiality of treatment records except in the following circumstances:[28]

1. when subpoenas are issued by the Board of Medical Examiners or the Office of the Attorney General;
2. where laws or regulations require the waiving of confidentiality, such as the reporting of communicable diseases, gunshot wounds, suspected child abuse (see Chapter 5A.8), evaluations of competency to stand trial (see Chapter 4.3), or when the patient's treatment is the subject of peer review (see Chapter 6.4);
3. to assist another licensed health care professional who is providing or has been asked to provide treatment to the patient, even absent the patient's request, if it is in the best interests of the patient; or
4. when there is a good faith belief that the patient because of a mental or physical condition may pose an imminent danger to himself or herself or to others; pertinent information may be released to law enforcement agencies or other health care professionals to minimize the threat of danger.

Liability for Violation

Violations of this law may result in suspension, revocation, or refusal to renew the physician's license (see Chapter 1.1). Furthermore, because this law prescribes a minimum standard of conduct, failure to abide by it may result in civil liability (see Chapter 6.5). Clients may also bring suit on the basis of other legal theories. Although there is no law in New Jersey directly addressing civil remedies for breach of confidentiality, Chapter 6.6 describes actions that have been used in other states with varying degrees of success. There is no reason to believe that such suits would be barred in New Jersey.

Social Workers

Social Workers Covered Under These Statutes

The statutes concern the confidential communications of licensed and certified social workers. Presumably, the courts would not apply the statute to a client who reasonably, but erroneously, believes that he or she is in a professional relationship with a licensed social worker.

---

28. N.J.A.C. 13:35-6.5.

Scope of the Duty

The law states that certified or licensed social workers[29]

> shall not be required to disclose any confidential information that the social worker may have acquired from a client or patient while performing social work services for that patient or client.

Limitations on the Duty

The law specifically describes several limitations on the duty of confidentiality, and there are other implied limitations. Disclosure is required if[30]

1. disclosure is required by other state law, such as the law requiring the reporting of child abuse (see Chapter 5A.8);
2. failure to disclose the information presents a clear and present danger to the health or safety of an individual;
3. the social worker is a defendant to a civil, criminal, or disciplinary action, in which case a waiver of the "privilege" shall be limited to that case;
4. the client is a defendant in a criminal proceeding and the use of the privilege would violate the defendant's right to a compulsory process or the right to present testimony and witnesses on that person's behalf; or
5. a client agrees to waive confidentiality or privilege, but if the person received services as part of a family, every member of the family who received services must agree to a waiver.

Although not specified, it is likely that disclosure will be required of social workers upon the request of the Social Work Licensing Board in the performance of its duties. In addition, disclosure of limited information will probably apply in certain civil proceedings where the social worker is a defendant, such as in a contract dispute over nonpayment of fees. Finally, the courts will probably rule that any breach of confidentiality on the part of the social worker will be considered an implied waiver.

Liability for Violation

Although there are no specific penalties described in the Social Worker Licensing Act for the breach of confidentiality, the general licensing law provides for the revocation, suspension, or nonrenewal of a professional license, by the appropriate board, if any statutory provision is violated (see Chapter 1.0). Furthermore, since this law prescribes a minimum standard of conduct, failure to abide

---

29. N.J.S.A. 15 BB-13.
30. N.J.S.A. 15 BB-13(a) through (e).

by it may result in civil liability from a malpractice suit (see Chapter 6.5). Clients may also bring suit on other legal theories. Although there is no law in New Jersey directly addressing civil remedies for breach of confidentiality, Chapter 6.6 describes actions that have been used in other states with varying degrees of success. There is no reason to believe that such suits would be barred in New Jersey.

New Legislation

As this book went to press, the New Jersey Legislature passed a significant confidentiality bill (S-3063).[31] The new law provides immunity to licensed psychologists, physicians, marriage counselors, and clinical social workers in any malpractice suit where a patient has committed a violent act, unless the MHP has incurred a duty to protect the potential victim and has failed to discharge that duty. The immunity also protects MHPs against liability for disclosure of confidential communications required to comply with this law.

The duty to warn and protect a potential victim arises if the patient has communicated a threat of imminent, serious physical violence against a readily identifiable individual (including him- or herself) and if the circumstances are such that a reasonable practitioner would believe that the patient intended to carry out the threat; or if the circumstances are such that a reasonable practitioner would believe that the patient intended to commit such an act of imminent serious violence, even without a specific verbal threat.

The MHP could discharge the duty to warn and protect by doing any of the following: arranging for voluntary or involuntary hospitalization of the patient, advising the local police department of the threat and the identity of the intended victim, warning the intended victim, or warning the parent if the intended victim (including oneself) is a minor.

When the duty to warn and protect arises from the receipt of a confidential and privileged communication from a patient in a drug or alcohol program governed by federal law, the MHP may be required initially to obtain a court order authorizing disclosure, in accordance with 42 U.S.C. 290dd-3 and 42 U.S.C. 290ee-3.

This law supersedes existing statutes and administrative regulations governing the conduct of MHPs (see Chapters 1.1, 1.3, 1.5, 1.8, and 4.3).

---

[31] N.J.S.A. 2A:53A.

4.3

Privileged Communications

Two primary areas of law exist that attempt to protect the client's communications from disclosure. The most well-known is confidentiality law whose principles originated in professional ethics codes and have now been incorporated in legislation and court rulings (see Chapter 4.2). It is designed to encourage frank discussion and the exchange of reliable information and to protect the client from improper disclosure of information by the MHP in most situations. It does not, however, protect the client from court orders requiring the MHP to disclose information.

For protection in the courtroom, the communications must be covered under a privileged communication statute. Psychologists, psychiatrists, and marriage counselors must be knowledgeable of this law so that they can advise their clients of the limits of confidential information. Except for victim counselors working in a victim counseling center,[1] there are no privileged communications laws for MHPs other than those mentioned; therefore, their clients' disclosures can be revealed in a court hearing if the MHP is required to testify.

The privileges, assertion and waiver of privileges, and limitations on the scope of the privileges will be discussed separately for psychologists, marriage counselors, psychiatrists, and social workers. The chapter will conclude with a section on the general liability of mental health professionals for violation of privileged communication statutes.

---

1. N.J.S.A. 2A:84A-22.13 et seq.

Psychologists

Privilege for Psychologists

As was noted in Chapter 4.2, the law provides that[2]

> The confidential relations and communications between a licensed practicing psychologist and individuals, couples, families, or groups in the course of the practice of psychology are placed on the same basis as those provided between attorney and client, and nothing in this act shall be construed to require any such privileged communications to be disclosed by any such person.

The statute protects communications between a client and a licensed psychologist and places these communications between psychologists and their clients on the same basis as the attorney–client privilege. Thus, in order to understand the scope of the privilege for psychologists, we need to understand how it works for attorneys. The following statute addresses the latter privilege:[3]

> Communications between lawyer and his client in the course of that relationship and in professional confidence, are privileged, and a client has a privilege (a) to refuse to disclose any such communication, and (b) to prevent his lawyer from disclosing it, and (c) to prevent any other witness from disclosing such communication if it came to the knowledge of such witness (i) in the course of its transmittal between the client and the lawyer, or (ii) in a manner not reasonably to be anticipated, or (iii) as a breach of the lawyer–client relationship, or (iv) in the course of a recognized confidential or privileged communication between the client and such witness.

From this statute it is apparent that the attorney–client privilege allows clients to prevent the interrogation of their attorneys as to information exchanged in the course of their professional relationship. The privilege also includes employees working under the attorney who come into contact with confidential information obtained in the scope of their employment. These same rules will apply to psychologists. However, the attorney–client privilege is not completely identical to the psychologist privilege and may differ

---

2. N.J.S.A. 45:14B-28. In many states, the law clearly distinguishes between confidentiality and privileged communications. Confidentiality law refers to maintenance of confidences outside of legal proceedings. Privileged communications law refers to the maintenance of confidences within legal proceedings. New Jersey, however, does not apparently draw this distinction as clearly. For example, in the statute just cited, the privileged communications law refers to the confidential communications between psychologist and client. In addition, it places the relationship on the same basis as that between attorney and client, which applies a uniform standard both inside and outside legal proceedings.
3. N.J.S.A. 2A:84A-20(1).

in limited areas, such as the extent to which clients are privileged with unlicensed or unauthorized practitioners (see Chapters 1.4 and 4.2).

Assertion and Waiver of the Privilege

The court will not assume that a privilege exists merely on the assertion that the psychologist has seen the client in a professional capacity. Rather, it will decide whether the privilege exists, typically after an in camera examination (i.e., in a private setting rather than in the courtroom) of the psychologist and the material asserted to be privileged. The court will seek to determine whether the person is a licensed psychologist, whether the material is of a confidential nature, whether the client has waived the privilege, and whether the communication constitutes an exception to confidentiality and privilege.

Limitations on the Scope of the Privilege

The privilege extends only to communications in which the client seeks psychological services and reasonably expects the exchange of information to be kept confidential. The scope of the privilege is limited by a number of statutory limitations. For example, the Board of Psychological Examiners may by subpoena compel the attendance of witnesses and the production of documents or other information pertaining to investigations of violations of the rules, regulations, or orders of the Board.[4]

Confidential communications to psychologists protected by the attorney–client privilege do not extend to (psychological) services sought or obtained to further the commission of a crime or a fraud.[5] Nor does privileged communication apply to communications relevant to a breach of duty between the psychologist and patient (which might later be raised in a legal proceeding).[6] In addition, a patient waives his or her privileged communication rights if he or she contracts not to exercise the privilege, or if he or she knowingly makes a voluntary disclosure regarding the privileged matter.[7] Also, the privilege may not always be upheld in child custody proceedings (see Chapter 5A.6).

---

4. N.J.S.A. 45:14B-13.
5. However, the superior court ruled that a Department of Corrections regulation excepting inmate–patient communications from the psychotherapist–patient privilege when it is believed that disclosure is more important to interests of substantial justice or safety was invalid as being broader than a situation that presents clear and imminent danger to the inmate or others. Matter of Rules Adoption Regarding Inmate–Therapist Confidentiality (N.J.A.C. 10A: 16-4.4), 540 A.2d 212, 224 N.J. Super. 252 (App. Div. 1988).
6. N.J.S.A. 2A:84A-20.
7. N.J.S.A. 2A:84A-29.

A final exception to privileged communications occurs in criminal proceedings, in evaluations of competency to stand trial and in the release of individuals found not guilty by reason of insanity. The information would be admissible in court only for the purpose of clarifying the mental condition and not to prove other issues such as innocence or guilt.[8]

Marriage Counselors

Privilege for Marriage Counselors

The marriage counselor–client privilege states,[9]

> Any communication between a marriage counselor and the person or persons counseled shall be confidential and its memory preserved. This privilege shall not be subject to waiver, except where the marriage counselor is a party defendant to a civil, criminal, or disciplinary action arising from such counseling, in which case, the waiver shall be limited to that action.

Assertion and Waiver of the Privilege

Courts have held that the marriage counselor privilege extends not only to licensed marriage counselors, but also to qualified members of other professions such as psychologists, physicians, and social workers, who may also claim the privilege.[10] The court will not assume that a privilege exists merely on the assertion that the marriage counselor has seen the client in a professional capacity. Rather, it will decide whether the privilege exists, usually after an in camera examination (i.e., in a private setting rather than in the courtroom) of the MHP and the material asserted to be privileged. The court will seek to determine whether the person is a marriage counselor within the meaning of the statute, whether the client has waived the privilege, and whether the communication constitutes an exception to confidentiality and privilege.

Limitations on the Scope of the Privilege

While the statutory language of the marriage counseling privileged communication law creates the strongest privilege of any of the mental health professions, it is not absolute. First, there is the statutory waiver of privilege in court proceedings in which the marriage counselor is a party. This would include situations in which the marriage counselor is being sued for malpractice or is suing the client.

---

8. N.J.S.A. 2C:4-10.
9. N.J.S.A. 45:8B-29.
10. Wichansky v. Wichansky, 126 N.J. Super. 156, 313 A.2d 222 (1973).

Second, there are other statutes that require a breach of confidentiality regardless of the privileged communication statute. Thus, the State Board of Marriage Counseling Examiners may by subpoena compel the attendance of witnesses and the production of documents or other information pertaining to investigations of violations of the rules, regulations, or orders of the Board.[11] Also, the privilege may not always be upheld in child custody proceedings (see Chapter 5A.6).

Third, confidentiality must be broken and testimony may later be required in situations when there is a probability that clients may be dangerous to others, including their children.[12]

Finally, there are several customary waivers that courts apply to privileged communication statutes that may also be applied to this statute, despite the absolute language, on the grounds that the legislation did not intend to exclude such a waiver. An example of this might occur in a situation where the services of the marriage counselor were sought to aid the client in planning a crime or tort, or to escape detection following the commission of a crime or tort. A court has held that a marriage counselor was not entitled to assert the privilege independently, after both a husband and a wife, whom he had counseled, entered into a consent order waiving the privilege.[13] In another case a defendant who had been counseled subsequently murdered his wife. The court held that the marriage counselor's privilege was outweighed by the court's constitutional duty to ensure a fair criminal trial with all relevant evidence.[14]

Psychiatrists

Privilege for Psychiatrists

The physician–patient privilege states,[15]

> Except as otherwise provided in this act, a person, whether or not a party, has a privilege in a civil action or in a prosecution for a crime or violation of the disorderly persons law or for an act of juvenile delinquency to refuse to disclose, and to prevent a witness from disclosing, a communication, if he claims the privilege.

---

11. N.J.S.A. 45:8B-13.
12. McIntosh v. Milano, 168 N.J. Super. 466, 403 A.2d 500 (1979).
13. Touma v. Touma, 140 N.J. Super. 544, 357 A.2d 25 (1976).
14. State v. Roma, 140 N.J. Super. 582, 357 A.2d 45 (1976).
15. N.J.S.A. 2A:84A-22.2.

Assertion and Waiver of the Privilege

The court will not assume that a privilege exists merely on the assertion that the psychiatrist has seen the client in a professional capacity. Rather, it will decide whether the privilege exists, usually after an in camera examination (i.e., in a private setting rather than in the courtroom) of the MHP and the material asserted to be privileged.[16] The court will seek to determine whether[17]

> (a) the communication was a confidential communication between patient and physician, and (b) the patient or the physician reasonably believed the communication to be necessary or helpful to enable the physician to make a diagnosis of the condition of the patient or to prescribe or render treatment therefor, and (c) the witness (i) is the holder of the privilege or (ii) at the time of the communication was the physician or a person to whom disclosure was made because reasonably necessary for the transmission of the communication or for the accomplishment of the purpose for which it was transmitted or (iii) is any other person who obtained knowledge or possession of the communication as the result of an intentional breach of the physician's duty of nondisclosure by the physician or his agent or servant and (d) the claimant is the holder of the privilege or a person authorized to claim the privilege for him.

Limitations on the Scope of the Privilege

The scope of the privilege will not extend to the following situations:

1. extraneous communications between physician and patient that were not made for the purpose of diagnosis or treatment;[18]

2. any relevant communication when the issue is the commitment or mental competence of a patient;[19]

3. any suit for monetary damages against the patient for conduct that constitutes a felony offense;[20]

4. any proceeding where the issue is the validity of a document such as a will of a patient, or where the issue involves the inheritance of a deceased patient;[21]

5. any legal action or suit in which the condition of a patient (or of any party claiming through the patient) is an element or factor of the claim or defense;[22]

---

16. D. v. D., 108 N.J. Super. 149, 260 A.2d 255 (1969). *See also* Fitzgibbon v. Fitzgibbon, 197 N.J. Super. 63, 484 A.2d 46 (1984).
17. *Id.*
18. *Id.*
19. N.J.S.A. 2A:84A-22.3.
20. *Id.*
21. *Id.*
22. N.J.S.A. 2A:84A-22.4. However, psychiatrists acting as marriage counselors may be protected by claiming the marriage counselor privilege (supra).

6. information that the physician or the patient reported to a public official or office as a legal requirement;[23]

7. a finding, supported by sufficient independent evidence, that the services of the physician were sought to aid anyone in planning a crime or a tort, or to escape detection following the commission of a crime or tort;[24]

8. a request by a patient, while holder of the privilege, that caused the physician to testify in any action on any matter regarding the privileged communication;[25]

9. a subpoena of the Board of Medical Examiners compelling attendance of witnesses and production of documents or other information pertaining to investigations of violations of the rules, regulations, or orders of the Board;[26] or

10. in criminal proceedings, evaluations of competency to stand trial and the release of individuals found not guilty by reason of insanity; the information would be admissible in court only for the purpose of clarifying the mental condition and not to prove other issues such as innocence or guilt.[27]

Social Workers

Privilege for Social Workers

The law governing confidential communications between certified and licensed social workers and their clients does not specifically authorize a privileged communication protection.[28] However, the use of the term *privilege* several times in the itemized exceptions to confidentiality implies that a privileged communication protection was intended. Privilege is likely to be upheld unless[29]

1. disclosure is required by other state law;

2. failure to disclose the information presents a clear and present danger to the health or safety of an individual;

3. the social worker is a defendant to a civil, criminal, or disciplinary action, in which case a waiver of the "privilege" shall be limited to that case;

---

23. N.J.S.A. 2A:84A-22.5.
24. N.J.S.A. 2A:84A-22.6.
25. N.J.S.A. 2A:84A-22.7.
26. N.J.S.A. 45:9-2.
27. N.J.S.A. 2C:4-10.
28. N.J.S.A. 15 BB-13.
29. N.J.S.A. 15 BB-13(a) through (e).

4. the client is a defendant in a criminal proceeding and the use of the privilege would violate the defendant's right to a compulsory process or the right to present testimony and witnesses on that person's behalf; or

5. a client agrees to waive confidentiality or privilege, but if the person received services as part of a family, every member of the family who received services must agree to a waiver.

Although not specified, it is likely that privilege will not apply if the Social Work Licensing Board requests information or testimony in the performance of its duties. In addition, disclosure of limited information will probably apply in certain civil proceedings where the social worker is a defendant, such as in a contract dispute over nonpayment of fees. Finally, the courts will probably rule that any breach of confidentiality on the part of the social worker will be considered an implied waiver.

Liability for Violation

Mental health professionals who improperly testify despite the privileged communications law may face civil liability for violation of confidential communications (see Chapters 1.1, 1.3, 1.8, and 6.5). In addition, the board of examiners for each licensed profession may suspend, revoke, or refuse to renew the license of a mental health professional who has broken confidentiality by violating the privileged communication statute.

The law has not addressed the issue of whether an MHP must advise a client of the limits of confidentiality, for instance, that criminal responsibility evaluations are not privileged. However, it is good practice, and some courts in the future may consider it an ethical duty to inform clients about such potential "side effects" of treatment.

Search, Seizure, and Subpoena of Records

Search of an MHP's office and seizure of any records may occur within the context of a criminal investigation of the MHP or the client. Our discussion in this chapter is limited to the latter situation. If a court, during a civil or criminal action, demands information from an MHP that was obtained during the course of a professional relationship with a client, it will usually come via a subpoena. Both types of request, search or subpoena, are important to MHPs because they provide major exceptions to confidentiality (see Chapter 4.2) and privileged communication law (see Chapter 4.3). Note, however, that the seizure of records does not necessarily mean that they will ultimately be admissible in court. That determination will be made at trial.

Search and Seizure

The law in this area concerns a government official's[1] search or seizure of things or places in which an individual has a reasonable expectation of privacy. Although warrantless searches are sometimes permissible, they are generally restricted to exigent circumstances such as the reasonable possibility of dangerous persons or weapons in an arrested person's apartment.[2] However, search and seizure are typically authorized by a written order from a municipal court judge,[3] directing any law enforcement officer (without naming

---

1. Thus, this area of law does not govern private individuals acquiring evidence on their own.
2. State v. Miller, 126 N.J. Super. 572, 316 A.2d 16 (App. Div. 1974).
3. R. 3:5-1 et seq.

him or her) to search for specific items.[4] It provides that a search warrant may be issued[5]

> to search for and seize any property, including documents, books, papers and any other tangible objects, obtained in violation of the penal laws of this State or any other state; or possessed, controlled, designed or intended for use or which has been used in connection with any such violation; or constituting evidence of or tending to show any such violation.

The judge must be satisfied that there is "probable cause" that the objects of the search exist. The warrant must identify the property to be seized, describe the person or place to be searched, and specify the hours when it may be executed. The basis for the warrant's issuance and the names of the persons whose affidavits or testimony have been taken in support must also be stated on the warrant.[6] The warrant must be executed within 10 days after its issuance.[7]

The officer taking property must give a copy of the warrant and a receipt for the property to the person from whom the property is taken, or leave the warrant on the premises if no person is present.[8] A warrant may be executed after an unannounced entry onto the premises, if the officer has reason to believe that an announcement would result in destruction of the property.[9] Furthermore, contraband other than that described in the warrant may be seized if it is in plain view when the warrant is being executed.[10]

The return of property must be made promptly, and an inventory of any property held must be made. Persons objecting to any aspect of a search should contact an attorney because police officers may respond with appropriate force to execute the search warrant. If there is a dispute regarding the seized property, a person may apply promptly to the New Jersey Superior Court for a hearing to determine whether the search or seizure was illegal. If there was an illegal search, the property will be returned promptly after the hearing, and it will not be permitted as evidence in court.[11]

Subpoena

A subpoena is a written order of the court compelling a witness to appear and give testimony. It must contain the name of the

---

4. R. 3:5-3.
5. R. 3:5-2.
6. R. 3:5-3.
7. R. 3:5-5.
8. *Id.*
9. State v. Kuznitz, 105 N.J. Super. 33, 250 A.2d 802 (1969).
10. State v. Scott, 156 N.J. Super. 421, 383 A.2d 1210 (1978).
11. R. 3:5-7.

court, title of the legal action, and the time and place where the testimony is to be given.[12] The subpoena may also extend to documentary evidence such as books, papers, documents, or other designated objects (this is typically referred to as a subpoena duces tecum).[13] Service of a subpoena is made by delivering a copy directly to the witness and tendering the small fee for one day's attendance allowed by law.[14] No payment of fees is required in a criminal trial or for an indigent defendant.[15]

A witness may be compelled to testify at a court hearing[16] or a deposition[17] or by a public officer authorized to take evidence[18] (e.g., State Board of Psychological Examiners). If the subpoena commands production of documentary evidence that would be unreasonable or oppressive, the witness may make a timely motion to quash or modify the subpoena or, in a civil suit, to condition compliance upon payment of the reasonable cost of producing the evidence.[19]

Furthermore, it should be noted that mere issuance of a subpoena, which is done by the court clerk, does not indicate that a privileged communication with a psychologist, marriage counselor, or psychiatrist is overcome (see Chapter 4.3). Rather, the MHP must assert the privilege until the client expressly waives it or the court orders the privilege waived as a matter of law (e.g., where the person holding the privilege, the client, disclosed the information in such a way as to extinguish its confidential nature; see Chapter 4.3). Failure by an MHP to initially assert a statutory privilege may result in both revocation or suspension of licensure and civil liability (see Chapters 1.1, 1.3, 1.8, and 6.5).

Failure to appear at the time and place specified in the subpoena may result in contempt of court proceedings and commitment to jail until there is consent to testify or until the matter is discharged by law.[20]

---

12. R. 1:9-1 et seq.
13. R. 1:9-2.
14. R. 1:9-3.
15. R. 1:9-1.
16. *Id.*
17. R. 4:14-7.
18. R. 1:9-6.
19. R. 1:9-2.
20. R. 1:9-5 and 1:10. *See also* N.J.S.A. 2A:10-1 and 2C:29-9.

4.5

State Freedom of Information Act

Some states have laws regulating the extent to which government agencies may withhold information, including reports and other data collected by MHPs. New Jersey, however, does not have an overarching statute regulating the dissemination of government information.

New Jersey has enacted an Open Public Meetings Act, known as the Sunshine Law, which does require open meetings of most state and local governmental boards and agencies.[1] The act also requires written disclosure of most information discussed in such meetings. However, the public may be excluded whenever such a board discusses any material that constitutes[2]

> an unwarranted invasion of individual privacy such as any records [of] social service, medical, health . . . or similar program or institution operated by a public body pertaining to any specific individual admitted to or served by such institution or program, including but not limited to information relative to the individual's personal and family circumstances, and any material pertaining to admission, discharge, treatment, progress or condition of any individual, unless the individual concerned . . . shall request in writing that the same be disclosed publicly.

Consequently, it is unlikely that professional reports and other data collected by MHPs will be disclosed through the operation of this law.

---

1. N.J.S.A. 10:4-6 *et seq.*
2. N.J.S.A. 10:4-12.

Practice Related to the Law

Families and Juveniles

5A.1

Competency to Marry

In order to marry, many states require a minimum mental status. New Jersey does not have such a requirement. The law[1] does provide, however, that persons under 18 years of age cannot marry without their parent's or guardian's consent. If the person is under 16, the approval of a county or superior court judge is also required. Although the law has not imposed guidelines on the judge's decision, it presumably might involve consultation with an MHP regarding the person's competency to understand and appreciate the consequences of his or her decision.

1. N.J.S.A. 37:1-6.

5A.2

Guardianship for Adults

Individuals who are unable to conduct their day-to-day affairs because of an emotional or cognitive disability may be appointed a guardian who will control their lives much as parents oversee the lives of their children. There are two classes of persons for whom guardianship may be obtained: minors and incapacitated persons. This chapter is limited to a discussion of guardianships for incapacitated persons. Guardianship for minors is discussed in Chapter 5A.11. An MHP may become involved in this process by being asked to evaluate the person and testify as to whether the person meets the test for a guardianship, and/or by providing therapeutic services to the person after a guardianship has been imposed.

Application for Guardianship

An incapacitated person or anyone interested in the person's welfare[1] may file a complaint in the superior court for a determination of mental incompetency. The complaint shall include the names and addresses of all potentially interested parties such as the next of kin and the person or institution having the care of the alleged incompetent.

---

1. R. 4:83-1. Although a "mere stranger" cannot initiate a complaint, a court ruling has permitted a social service agency to petition when it has been requested to render protective services to the alleged incompetent person. *In re* Bennett, 180 N.J. Super. 406, 434 A.2d 1155 (Law Div. 1981).

The incompetency complaint must be accompanied by an affidavit stating the value of the property of the alleged incompetent. In addition, there must be[2]

> the affidavits of two [licensed] physicians which state that the alleged incompetent is unfit and unable to govern himself and to manage his affairs and which shall set forth with particularity the circumstances and conduct of the alleged incompetent upon which this opinion is based, including a history of his condition.[3]

These affidavits must be based upon a personal examination not more than 20 days prior to the filing of the complaint. In the event that the alleged incompetent refuses the examination, an affidavit of one such physician is required.

Guardianship Hearing

If the court is satisfied with the sufficiency of the incompetency complaint, it shall require at least 20 days' notice to all interested parties before a hearing. The alleged incompetent must be served personally with the notice that states that he or she may appear at the hearing in person or by an attorney and that there is the right to a jury trial.[4] The notice must include the appointment of an attorney for the alleged incompetent, with the right to change counsel. If the alleged incompetent has refused to submit to two physical examinations, the court shall order such evaluations and enclose names, addresses, and appointment times.[5]

Unless a trial by jury is demanded, the court shall take testimony in open court. However, if the alleged incompetent has been continuously confined in a public institution for more than 2 years because of chronic mental retardation, the court may determine the issue of competency on the basis of the affidavits if the parties agree. Likewise, no hearing is necessary for veterans who have been rated incompetent by a federal agency and who require a guardian to receive federal funds.[6] In nonjury cases the court may take physician testimony by telephone with the consent of the alleged incompetent.[7]

---

2. R. 4:83-2.
3. If the person is confined to a public institution, one of the physicians must be an administrator of patient care in such institution. Any physician must not have a financial interest in the outcome of the hearing.
4. N.J.S.A. 3B:12-24 and R. 4:83-4.
5. R. 4:83-4.
6. R. 4:83-9. This rule follows the Uniform Veterans Guardianship Law.
7. R. 4:83-6.

Appointment and Authority of Guardian

The superior court determines mental incompetency after a guardianship hearing. The court may appoint a guardian for the person, a guardian for the estate, or a guardian for the person and the estate. The spouse must be granted the guardianship if husband and wife are living together at the time the incompetency arose. If there is no spouse who meets these requirements, the guardianship shall be offered to the next of kin.[8] However, if none of them will accept the guardianship, or if it is proven that it will not be in the best interest of the incompetent or the estate to appoint one of them, then the court may appoint any proper guardian.[9]

Guardians have the same powers, rights, and duties respecting their ward that parents have toward their minor children, except that the guardian is not legally obligated to provide for the ward from his or her own funds.[10] In particular, the guardian has the following powers and duties except as modified by a court order:[11]

1. to have custody of the ward and establish the ward's residence in or out of the state;
2. to provide for the care, comfort, and maintenance of the ward and to arrange for the ward's training and education wherever appropriate;
3. to take reasonable care of the ward's clothing, furniture, vehicles, and personal property;
4. to institute an action to compel the performance of any person with a duty to support the ward or to pay money for the welfare of the ward; and
5. to receive money for the support of the ward's care and education.

Special Medical Guardian

In emergency situations, if the prompt rendering of medical treatment is necessary in order to deal with a substantial threat to the

---

8. N.J.S.A. 3B:12-25.
9. *Id.* and R. 4:83-6(c). The next of kin, determined in accordance with the traditional table of consanguinity, is absolutely entitled to the guardianship unless such appointment is clearly contrary to the best interests of the incompetent or his estate. *In re* Roll, 117 N.J. Super. 122, 283 A.2d 764 (App. Div. 1971).
10. N.J.S.A. 3B:12-56.
11. N.J.S.A. 3B:12-57.

patient's life or health, the court may appoint a special guardian of a patient to make decisions solely respecting medical treatment.[12] The court must find the patient to be incompetent, unconscious, underage, or otherwise unable to consent to medical treatment, and there must be no general or natural guardian immediately available. An application to a superior court judge may be made by a hospital, nursing home, treating physician, relative, or other appropriate person. Testimony may be taken by telephone to expedite the proceeding.

Guardians for Persons Receiving Services From the Division of Developmental Disabilities

The Commissioner of Human Services or any parent, spouse, relative, or interested party, on behalf of an alleged mental incompetent who is receiving services from the Division of Developmental Disabilities, may bring an action in the superior court to designate a guardian.[13] The verified complaint must include two affidavits, one from an officer of the Division and the other from a licensed psychologist or physician. The affidavits must include facts explaining why the alleged incompetent[14]

> suffers from a significant chronic functional impairment to such a degree that the person either lacks the cognitive capacity to make decisions for himself or to communicate, in any way, decisions to others. . . . "[S]ignificant chronic functional impairment" includes, but is not limited to, a lack of comprehension of concepts related to personal care, health care or medical treatment.

If a family member initiates a guardianship proceeding but the administrative head of the functional services unit disagrees either with the need for a guardian or the choice of guardian, the chief of the Bureau of Guardianship Services must determine whether to take legal action in the proceeding.[15]

The alleged incompetent must be represented by the Public Advocate or a court-appointed attorney, who may retain an independent expert to render an incompetency opinion, at the expense of the state. If there is no objection, a guardian may be appointed in a summary hearing.

---

12. R. 4:83-12.
13. N.J.S.A. 30:4-165.7 and R. 4:83-10.
14. N.J.S.A. 30:4-165.8.
15. N.J.A.C. 10:43-7.1.

Termination of the Guardianship

The authority and responsibility of a guardian of a person or an estate terminates if the ward or guardian dies, if the guardian resigns or is removed by the court, or if there is a court judgment adjudicating the restoration of competency.[16] If the incompetent person or an interested party files a complaint alleging the restoration of competency, verified by affidavit that describes supporting facts, the court is required to take oral testimony in open court, with or without a jury, and may render a judgment that he or she has returned to competency and that the estate be returned to that person's control.[17]

---

16. N.J.S.A. 3B:12-64.
17. R. 4:83-7.

5A.3

Conservatorship for Adults

As an alternative to appointing guardians of the person and/or the estate of an incompetent ward (see Chapters 5A.2 and 5A.11), New Jersey conservatorship law allows the court to appoint someone to manage the finances of a consenting adult who is no longer able to take care of his or her property and/or financial affairs. This chapter focuses on the adults in this group. Conservatorship for minors is discussed in Chapter 5A.12. An MHP may become involved in this process by being asked to evaluate the person and to testify as to the person's ability to manage his or her finances, and/or by providing therapeutic services to the person after a conservatorship has been imposed.

Application for Conservatorship

A *conservatee* is defined as a person who has *not* been declared judicially incompetent (as in the case of guardian and ward), but who by reason of advanced age, illness, or physical infirmity is unable to care for or manage his or her property or has become unable to provide for himself or herself or others dependent upon him or her for support.[1] An action for the appointment of a conservator for such an individual's estate and financial affairs may be brought by the conservatee or in his or her behalf by the spouse, the adult children or next of kin, any person having concern for the well-being of the conservatee, a public agency, or the chief

---

1. N.J.S.A. 3B:13A-1.

administrator of a licensed institution where the conservatee is a patient or receives services.[2]

The complaint must be filed in the superior court and should state[3]

1. the conservatee's age and residence;
2. the names and addresses of the conservatee's heirs;
3. the spouse and adult children of the conservatee, or if there are none, the next of kin;
4. the person with whom the conservatee resides, or the administrator of an institution where he or she lives; and
5. the nature, location, and value of all the conservatee's property.

The Conservatorship Hearing

The court may appoint a conservator only if the conservatee does not object.[4] The court, without a jury, is required to take testimony in open court to determine whether the conservatee, by reason of advanced age, illness, or physical infirmity, is unable to care for or manage his or her property or has become unable to provide for himself or herself or others dependent upon the conservatee for support. The court may appoint a lawyer for the conservatee if it concludes that one is necessary to adequately protect his or her interests. If the conservatee is unable to attend the hearing by reason of disability and he or she does not have an attorney, the court must appoint a guardian ad litem to conduct an investigation to determine whether the conservatee objects to the conservatorship.

Authority and Responsibilities of the Conservator

The court may appoint a person or a qualified financial institution as the conservator, in the following order of priority, unless there is "good cause" to prioritize otherwise:[5]

1. a nominee of the conservatee,
2. the conservatee's spouse,

---

2. N.J.S.A. 3B:13A-5.
3. R. 4:83-11(a).
4. R. 4:83-11(b).
5. N.J.S.A. 3B:13A-8.

3. an adult child of the conservatee or persons closest in kinship, or

4. any other proper person or financial institution.

The authority of the conservator entitles him or her to spend, with reasonable discretion, as much of the income or principal of the conservatee as he or she chooses for the support, maintenance, education, and general use and benefit of the conservatee and his or her dependents.[6] The conservator must take into account the size of the estate, the probable duration of the conservatorship, and the accustomed standard of living of the conservatee and members of the household.[7] A conservator's powers are limited in that power over the property extends only to the investment of income, or the expenditure and distribution of income and principal, unless other powers are specifically conferred by the court.[8]

Termination of the Conservatorship

Upon the application of the conservatee, the court is required to terminate the conservatorship. The conservator must then return all funds and property under his or her control to the conservatee.[9] If the conservator resigns, dies, or is removed for good cause by the court, the court may appoint another conservator in the same manner as the original appointment.[10] A conservatorship may also be terminated by the death of the conservatee or upon a finding of mental incompetency (see Chapter 5A.2).[11]

---

6. N.J.S.A. 3B:13A-18.
7. N.J.S.A. 3B:13A-20.
8. N.J.S.A. 3B:13A-34.
9. N.J.S.A. 3B:13A-33.
10. N.J.S.A. 3B:13A-35.
11. N.J.S.A. 3B:13A-34.

Annulment

Whereas a divorce dissolves what was once a valid, functioning marriage, annulment is the process whereby a marriage is declared void and is legally held never to have existed. This result can have legal significance. For instance, a widowed spouse of a worker receives compensation benefits until the widow remarries, and if the second marriage ceases by virtue of annulment rather than divorce, the person regains the benefits. MHPs may be involved in an annulment proceeding directly through evaluation and testimony, or indirectly when they are working with persons who are contemplating the dissolution of their marriage.

Grounds for Annulment

A marriage may be judicially annulled if[1]

1. either of the spouses has another husband or wife living at the time of an additional marriage;
2. the spouses are relatives prohibited by law from marrying;
3. either spouse was physically and incurably impotent (incapable of sexual intercourse) at the time of the marriage, without knowledge by the other person;
4. either spouse lacked capacity to marry, owing to a lack of understanding because of a mental condition or the influence of drugs or alcohol;

---

1. N.J.S.A. 2A:34-1.

5. there was a lack of meaningful mutual assent to the marital relationship because of significant duress or fraud that has not subsequently been ratified or accepted in the marriage;

6. either spouse requesting annulment was under 18 years old at the time of the marriage; or

7. the court believes annulment would be equitable.

Courts have annulled marriages on the grounds of fraud in cases of concealed pregnancy from another man[2] and concealed heroin addiction.[3] However, several courts have held that fraudulent concealment of mental illness or prior institutionalization is not grounds for annulment.[4]

---

2. B.v.S., 99 N.J. Super. 429, 240 A.2d 189 (1968).
3. Costello v. Porzelt, 116 N.J. Super. 380, 282 A.2d 432 (1971).
4. Houlahan v. Horzepa, 46 N.J. Super. 583, 135 A.2d 232 (1957).

5A.5

Divorce

Prior to 1971, divorce law in New Jersey (and in many states today) required the petitioning party to allege fault by the other spouse. This changed when New Jersey included a "no-fault" divorce provision in the divorce law. Now, litigation typically centers around property division, child support, spousal maintenance, or child custody (see Chapter 5A.6). Aside from custody assessments, MHPs become involved in divorce issues by providing counseling and psychotherapy to individuals, couples, or families who are contemplating, participating in, or recovering from a divorce.

Divorce Procedure

The dissolution of marriage is initiated by a summons and complaint in the New Jersey Superior Court (Chancery Division, Family Part). The complaint is required to state a summary of the alleged facts constituting the legal action, the statutes relied upon by the plaintiff, the names and addresses of the parties, the names and addresses of any children, and a statement of any previous family actions between the parties.[1] The spouse is then required to file an acknowledgment of service of process or answer the complaint prior to a judicial hearing.[2]

Upon a judicial finding that the marriage should be dissolved, the court will make provisions for division of property, support payments, and child custody. These matters are incorporated into

---

1. R. 5:4-2.
2. N.J.S.A. 2A:34-11.

a decree of dissolution that is final when entered. Unless one of the parties challenges the initial dissolution decision by the trial court that the marriage is irretrievably broken, either spouse may remarry even though other issues are appealed, such as child custody or support payments.

Causes for Divorce

Divorce from the bond of matrimony may be adjudicated for the following causes:[3]

1. adultery;
2. willful and continued desertion for 12 months or more, demonstrated by the fact that the parties no longer cohabit as husband and wife;
3. extreme mental or physical cruelty that endangers the safety or health of the plaintiff;
4. separation for 18 months, provided that the spouses have resided in separate habitations during that time and that there is no reasonable prospect of reconciliation;[4]
5. voluntary induced addiction or habitual drunkenness for a period of 12 months or more;
6. institutionalization for mental illness for a period of 2 years subsequent to the marriage;
7. imprisonment for 18 or more consecutive months after marriage, provided that the spouses have not resumed cohabitation following release; or
8. deviant sexual conduct without the consent of the plaintiff.

---

3. N.J.S.A. 2A:34-2.
4. The fact of the 18-month separation creates a statutory presumption that there is no reasonable prospect of reconciliation.

5A.6

Child Custody After Marital Dissolution

Child custody determinations can result from four types of changes in the legal status of the marriage: annulment, legal separation, divorce, and modification of a divorce decree. MHPs may become involved in this determination in one of two ways. First, the judge or a party may request an evaluation of the mental status of a parent, proposed parent, or child, possibly culminating in a court appearance as an expert witness. Second, an MHP who has provided services to the family unit, whether diagnostic or therapeutic, may be subpoenaed by either party to present evidence as a witness.

Criteria to Establish Court Jurisdiction

The New Jersey Superior Court, Chancery Division, Family Part, has jurisdiction to make orders determining the custody and visitation of minor children.[1] The authority of the court to assume jurisdiction over the child is generally a factual determination based on the domicile of the child and parents.

If the child is living in New Jersey at the commencement of the dissolution proceeding, the court automatically assumes jurisdiction. Also, if the parents were divorced in another state or country, the superior court assumes jurisdiction if the minor children of the marriage are inhabitants of New Jersey.[2] Even if a child is in New Jersey temporarily, the courts will assume jurisdiction of the case if it is necessary to protect the child from an unfit custodian,

---

1. N.J.S.A. 9:2-1 et seq. A "minor" or "child" refers to a person under 18 years of age.
2. N.J.S.A. 9:2-1.

or for some other limited purpose that would be necessary for the best interests of the child.[3]

In any custody proceeding, for good cause and upon its own motion, the court may appoint a guardian ad litem, an attorney, or both to represent the minor child's interests.[4] The court has the authority to award a fee to such individuals and to assess the cost between the litigating parties.

Legal Standards in Custody Determinations

It is the public policy of the state to assure minor children of frequent and continuing contact with both parents after separation or divorce and to encourage parents to share the rights and responsibilities of child rearing.[5] In any custody proceeding, the rights of both parents are considered equal.

Prior to a final disposition of a case, the judge must make a temporary order of custody unless the parties agree otherwise. The legal standard is that of the best interests of the child:[6]

> The court shall determine temporary custody based upon the best interests of the child with due regard to the caretaking arrangement that previously existed. No child shall be taken forcibly or against the will of the parent having custody by the other parent without a court order.

In a final custody decision, the court has three options:[7]

1. joint custody to both parents (see infra),
2. sole custody to one parent with appropriate visitation for the noncustodial parent, or
3. any other custody arrangement as the court may determine to be in the best interests of the child.

In making a custody award, the court must consider, but will not be limited to, the following factors:[8]

1. the parents' ability to agree, communicate, and cooperate in the best interests of the child;

---

3. Vannucchi v. Vannucchi, 113 N.J. Super. 40, 272 A.2d 560 (App. Div. 1971).
4. N.J.S.A. 9:2-4.
5. Id.
6. N.J.S.A. 9:2-3.
7. N.J.S.A. 9:2-4.
8. Id.

2. the parents' willingness to accept custody and any history of unwillingness to allow visitation not based on substantiated abuse;

3. the interaction and relationship of the child with his or her parents and siblings;

4. the history of domestic violence, if any;

5. the safety of the child and the safety of either parent from physical abuse by the other parent;

6. the preference of the child when he or she is of sufficient age and capacity to reason so as to form an intelligent decision;

7. the needs of the child;

8. the stability of the home environment offered;

9. the quality and continuity of the child's education;

10. the fitness of the parents (but the parent shall not be deemed unfit unless the parent's conduct has a substantial adverse effect on the child);

11. the geographical proximity of the parents' homes;

12. the extent and quality of the time spent with the child prior to or subsequent to the separation;

13. the parents' employment responsibilities; and

14. the age and number of the children.

The court must order any custody arrangement that is agreed to by both parents unless it is contrary to the best interests of the child.[9] In any case in which the parents cannot agree to a custody arrangement, the courts may require each parent to submit a custody plan that the court must consider in awarding custody. In its decision, the court must specifically place on the record the factors that justify any custody arrangements not agreed to by both parents.

A joint custody decision may consist of either legal custody or physical custody.[10] It must include provisions for residential arrangements specifying whether a child will reside solely with one parent or alternatively with each parent in accordance with the needs of the parents and the child. In addition, a decision must include specific provisions for consultation between the parents in making major decisions regarding the child's health, education, and general welfare.

The court may award joint custody if the children are likely to benefit, if the parents are physically and psychologically capable

---

9. *Id.*
10. *Id.*

of such an arrangement, if it is practical, and if the parents show a potential for cooperation in matters of child rearing.[11] The court also has the power to award custody to a third party such as a grandparent or aunt, even without a specific finding of parental unfitness or abandonment.[12]

A parent not granted custody of the child almost always is entitled to reasonable visitation rights, unless this would be likely to endanger the welfare and best interests of the child:[13]

> Post-divorce custody determinations seek to some extent to provide the children with access to both parents and avoid alienation from either one. Hence, sole custody decrees almost invariably grant visitation rights to the non-custodial parent. Moreover, our courts have imposed a duty on the custodial parent to be active in aiding and encouraging the sincere efforts of the non-custodial parent "to enhance the mutual love, affection, and respect between himself and the child." *Sheehan v. Sheehan,* 51 N.J. Super. 276, 291 (App. Div.), *certif. den.* 28 N.J. 147 (1958).

The court will consider the same factors as those used in the custody determination to determine reasonable visitation rights; there are no preset formulas or guidelines. Visitation rights also extend to the grandparents and siblings, provided that they are in the best interests of the child.[14]

Mental Health Evaluations

Where the parents cannot agree on custody or any other issue, requiring the court to make the determination, the court in its discretion may order any person to be examined by a psychiatrist, psychologist, or other mental health professional designated.[15] The court may appoint the expert independently, or experts may be selected by the mutual consent of the parties. The court may direct who shall pay the cost of such examination. In addition, either party may engage the services of experts of their own choosing. The parties are entitled to have their own attorneys and/or experts present during any examination by a court-appointed expert.

In addition, the court may also order an investigation to be made by the county probation office, which may evaluate the "character and fitness of the parties, the economic condition of the

---

11. Beck v. Beck, 86 N.J. 480, 432 A.2d 63 (1981), *rev'g* 173 N.J. Super. 33, 413 A.2d 350 (App. Div. 1980).
12. S.M. v. S.J., 143 N.J. Super. 379, 363 A.2d 353 (1976).
13. Beck v. Beck, *supra,* at 86 N.J. 495, 432 A.2d 70.
14. N.J.S.A. 9:2-7.1.
15. R. 5:3-3.

family, and the financial ability of the party to pay alimony or support."[16] Such investigation may include a mental health evaluation by an MHP who is affiliated with the county probation department. The court is not bound to accept the opinions of either the probation investigation or an appointed independent expert in arriving at a legal determination.

Confidentiality and Privileged Communications

In most examinations, the information obtained by a psychologist, marriage counselor, or psychiatrist is confidential (see Chapter 4.2) and privileged (see Chapter 4.3). Where these MHPs participate in a custody evaluation as an employee of the county, or at the request of the court or a party, such confidentiality and privilege would not be expected to apply. In one such case, the judge ruled that the constitutional right to a fair trial and the best interests of the children outweighed the psychologist–client privilege.[17] However, an in camera (i.e., private) review of the information by the judge was granted to screen unnecessary information. Because the law is not completely clear, it is good practice to obtain from the party being evaluated a written authorization to release any information pertaining to the evaluation that was ordered by the court.

A second situation arises when the information sought was communicated to an MHP in private counseling or therapy under the belief that it was confidential and privileged. Despite privileged communications laws, the courts are sometimes reluctant to apply these statutes to custody disputes when the information sought is vital to the court to determine a just resolution of a case. Consequently, judges have ordered the "piercing of professional privilege" in several cases.[18] In one case, in which a psychiatrist attempted to assert the marriage counselor's privilege, the judge ruled that the privilege was an unconstitutional interference with the child's constitutional right to "due process of law" and to a fair trial based on all relevant evidence.[19]

---

16. R. 5:8-1.
17. Fitzgibbon v. Fitzgibbon, 197 N.J. Super. 63, 484 A.2d 46 (Ch. Div. 1984).
18. For a detailed legal discussion of this and other issues pertaining to New Jersey divorce law, see E. N. Skoloff and L. J. Cutler. (1990). *New Jersey family law practice* (6th ed.). Newark, NJ: New Jersey Institute for Continuing Legal Education.
19. M. v. K., 186 N.J. Super. 363, 452 A.2d 704 (1982).

Although privileged communication statutes offer different degrees of protection, with psychiatrists having the weakest privilege, psychologists having a stronger one, and marriage counselors the strongest (see Chapter 4.3), it is clear that even the most emphatic language will not always result in the protection of privileged information in a custody dispute. Since there is no statutory privilege pertaining to other MHPs, they can be subpoenaed to testify regardless of the circumstances of the consultation.

5A.7

Reporting of Adult Abuse

The law requires certain individuals who have reasonable cause to believe that an elderly person is being abused or exploited in an institution, nursing home, or other specified facility to make a report. Unlike the child abuse reporting law (see Chapter 5A.8), there is no legal duty upon any person to report probable adult abuse in domestic settings, although such abuse or neglect is a crime.

Institutionalized Elderly Persons

Definitions

Abuse is defined as "the willful infliction of physical pain, injury or mental anguish; unreasonable confinement; or, the willful deprivation of services which are necessary to maintain a person's physical and mental health."[1]

Exploitation is defined as "the act or process of using a person or his resources for another person's profit or advantage."[2]

Who Must Report

The law concerning abuse or exploitation of institutionalized elderly persons applies a duty to any caretaker, social worker, physician, registered or licensed practical nurse, or other professional. Any other person is permitted but not required to make a report.[3]

---

1. N.J.S.A. 52:27G-2 and 30:1A-3.
2. *Id.*
3. N.J.S.A. 52:27G-7.1.

When Must a Report Be Made

A report must be made in a timely manner, soon after the caretaker or professional develops reasonable cause to believe that an institutionalized elderly person (age 60 or over) is being or has been abused or exploited.

How a Report Must Be Made

The duty to report is fulfilled by contacting the Ombudsman for the Institutionalized Elderly or a representative. The report should include "the name and address of the elderly person, information regarding the nature of the suspected abuse or exploitation and any other information which might be helpful in an investigation of the case and the protection of such elderly person."[4] The name of the reporting person will not be disclosed without such individual's request, except if a judicial proceeding follows.[5]

Immunity From Liability

Any person who makes a report or who testifies in a subsequent proceeding is granted immunity from liability except if the person has acted in bad faith or with malicious purpose.[6] In addition, any reporter is protected legally against job action of a discriminatory, disciplinary, or retaliatory nature, which is a crime.[7]

Confidentiality and Privilege

Physicians, attorneys, and psychologists are shielded from the duty to report, to the extent that their confidentiality and privileged communications laws apply (see Chapter 4.3).[8] Such confidentiality laws do not extend to situations in which a client is imminently dangerous to another individual.

Failure to Report

Each failure to report will result in a fine of not more than $5,000. The penalty is collected and enforced in summary proceedings through the Penalty Enforcement Law.[9] Such penalties are then sent to any relevant licensing boards, which may take further actions against the individual.

---

4. N.J.S.A. 52:27G-7.1(b).
5. N.J.S.A. 52:27G-7.1(d).
6. N.J.S.A. 52:27G-7.1(e).
7. N.J.S.A. 52:27G-14.
8. N.J.S.A. 52:27G-7.1(g). Although psychologists are not specifically cited, their privilege extends to the same extent as the attorney–client privilege, which statute is referred to here.
9. N.J.S.A. 52:27G-7.1(f).

Residential Health Care and Other Facilities

Who Must Report

Any person who has reasonable cause to suspect that a resident of a residential health care facility, rooming house, or boarding house is suffering or has suffered abuse or exploitation has a duty to make a report.[10]

When Must a Report Be Made

A report must be made in a timely manner, soon after a person develops reasonable cause to believe that a resident is being or has been abused or exploited.[11]

How a Report Must Be Made

The duty to report is fulfilled by contacting the Commissioner of the Department of Human Services or the designee.[12] The report should include the name and address of the resident, information regarding the nature of the suspected abuse or exploitation, and any other information that might be helpful in an investigation of the case.[13]

When the report involves an elderly person, the commissioner is required to promptly notify the Ombudsman for the Institutionalized Elderly, who must be notified also of any findings and recommendations following an investigation. The county prosecutor must be notified by the commissioner of any determination of abuse or exploitation.[14]

Immunity From Liability

Any person who makes a report or who testifies in any subsequent proceeding is granted immunity from any liability except if the person has acted in bad faith or with malicious purpose.[15] The name of any person who makes a report will not be disclosed involuntarily, except if there is a subsequent judicial proceeding.[16]

---

10. N.J.S.A. 30:1A-3(b).
11. *Id.*
12. *Id.*
13. N.J.S.A. 30:1A-3(c).
14. N.J.S.A. 30:1A-3(f).
15. N.J.S.A. 30:1A-3(e).
16. N.J.S.A. 30:1A-3(d).

Confidentiality and Privilege

There is no statutory inclusion or waiver of confidentiality or professional privilege (see Chapter 4.3). Therefore, it is unclear whether the courts would rule that the requirements of this act supercede professional privilege or not. Even under statutes of professional privilege, a licensed MHP is required to break confidentiality if a client is imminently dangerous to another person.

Failure to Report

There are no statutory penalties for failure to report. However, such failure could be the basis of an action of a professional board against an MHP.

5A.8

Reporting of Child Abuse

New Jersey law requires MHPs as well as lay persons to report known or suspected incidents of child abuse. Although the initial duty to report is discharged once the report is properly filed, the MHP may also have to appear in family court proceedings as a witness on this issue (see Chapter 5A.10).

Who Must Report

The law requires that "any person" who has a reasonable cause to believe that a child has been subjected to child abuse is legally obligated to report such abuse.[1] A recent court case ruled, "[The] duty to make reports of suspected child abuse is not limited to professional persons, friends or neighbors, who are persons ordinarily more apt to observe and detect evidence of child abuse, but is required of every citizen."[2]

When Must a Report Be Made?

The duty to report begins immediately upon the recognition that child abuse probably has occurred, or is about to occur. An "abused child" refers to anyone under the age of 18 years whose parent, guardian, teacher, or other custodian[3]

---

1. N.J.S.A. 9:6-8.10.
2. State v. Hill, 232 N.J. Super. 353, 356, 556 A.2d 1325, 1327 (1989).
3. N.J.S.A. 9:6-8.9(a).

Inflicts or allows to be inflicted upon such child physical injury by other than accidental means which causes or creates a substantial risk of death, or serious or protracted disfigurement, or protracted impairment of physical or emotional health or protracted loss or impairment of the function of any bodily organ.

The definition of child abuse goes on to include the "substantial or ongoing risk of physical injury" in the future, rather than proof by past abuse alone.[4] Abuse includes any child whose physical, mental, or emotional condition has been impaired as the result of the failure (when financially able) to provide adequate food, clothing, shelter, education, or medical care.[5]

Sexual abuse is specifically defined as an act of child abuse.[6] The term sexual abuse includes the following acts against a child (i.e., any individual who is under 18 years of age):[7]

1. the employment, use, persuasion, inducement, enticement, or coercion of any child to engage in, or having a child assist any other person to engage in, any sexually explicit conduct (or any simulation of such conduct) for the purpose of producing any visual depiction of such conduct; or

2. the rape, molestation, prostitution, or other such form of sexual exploitation of children, or incest with children, under circumstances that indicate that the child's health or welfare is harmed or threatened thereby.

In addition, the infliction of "excessive corporal punishment or using excessive physical restraint" when the child's behavior is not harmful to himself, herself, others, or property is considered child abuse.[8] Likewise, willful abandonment by a parent or other adult exercising custodial control is considered child abuse.

Child abuse also can include (1) inappropriate placement in an institution (other than a day school) by a parent or other custodial adult who knows that the placement has resulted in harm to the child's physical or mental well-being and (2) willful isolation from ordinary social contact, in an institution, under circumstances that indicate emotional or social deprivation.[9]

The reporting requirement does not distinguish between events caused by parents and those caused by others acting in a custodial relationship to the child. More important, the fact that a parent is seeking treatment for the child does not absolve the professional of the duty to report.

---

4. N.J.S.A. 9:6-8.9(b).
5. N.J.S.A. 9:6-8.9(d).
6. N.J.S.A. 9:6-8.9(c).
7. N.J.A.C. 10:129-2.2.
8. N.J.S.A. 9:6-8.9(c).
9. N.J.S.A. 9:6-8.9(f).

How a Report Must Be Made

The duty to report is fulfilled by notifying the Division of Youth and Family Services (DYFS) by telephone or otherwise. The report, where possible, should contain the names and addresses of the child and his or her parent(s), guardian(s), or other person(s) having custody of the child. The report should also include the child's age, the nature and possible extent of the injuries or mistreatment, any evidence of previous mistreatment, and any other relevant information that the reporter believes may be helpful.[10]

DYFS will then determine whether it needs to perform an investigation and offer services. If DYFS determines that there is suspected criminal conduct on the part of a parent, caretaker, or any other person, the caseworker is obligated to report the case to the prosecutor for a review of possible prosecution.[11] Reports of child abuse must be kept confidential, except for agencies investigating an abuse claim or treating one of the parties: courts, police, grand juries, and physicians or hospitals involved in treatment of a child who may be abused.[12] However, whenever information is disclosed, the identity of the referrer and any other person must be protected and not disclosed where it would be likely to endanger the life or safety of the referrer or another person or result in job discrimination or discharge.

Immunity From Liability

Any person who makes a report under this law shall have immunity from any liability, civil or criminal, that might otherwise be imposed.[13] For example, the individual cannot be sued on grounds of breaking confidentiality or making a false or malicious report.[14] Such immunity shall also extend to any testimony that may arise as the result of the report. However, it does not extend to immunity from prosecution if the reporting person has been charged with or is suspected of harming the children in question.[15] Also, there is no immunity for persons who make a report without reasonable cause to believe that the child has been subjected to child abuse.[16]

---

10. N.J.S.A. 9:6-8.10.
11. N.J.A.C. 10:129-1.3.
12. N.J.A.C. 10:129-2.1.
13. N.J.S.A. 9:6-8.13.
14. Rubinstein v. Baron, 219 N.J. Super. 129, 529 A.2d 1061 (1987).
15. State v. Hill, 232 N.J. Super. 353, 556 A.2d 1325 (1989).
16. F.A. by P.A. v. W.J.F., ___N.J. Super. ___, ___A.2d ___(App. Div. 1991).

If a person is discriminated against or discharged from his or her job as the result of a report of child abuse made in good faith, the individual may sue in superior court for reinstatement with back pay plus other equitable relief.

Confidentiality and Privilege

Most services provided by an MHP are confidential, either through law or the ethics of the profession (see Chapter 4.2). However, the child abuse law not only requires all persons to report suspected cases, but also exempts them from liability for breaking confidentiality. Furthermore, MHPs have a duty to break confidentiality when a client is likely to harm a potential victim (see Chapter 4.2). Therefore, in most cases of suspected child abuse, the courts would be likely to rule that the duty to prevent child abuse takes precedence over the duty of professional confidentiality.

Regarding privileged communications statutes (see Chapter 4.3), such laws would normally prevent psychologists, marriage counselors, and psychiatrists from testifying in court regarding confidential matters between themselves and their clients. Although formerly the child abuse reporting law created an exception to privileged communications, the privilege was restored in 1977.[17] Consequently, MHPs may assert the privilege against testifying in child abuse cases, although courts may rule that the privilege has been waived where a report has been made to prevent imminent harm by the client to the child.

Failure to Report

A knowing failure to report an act of child abuse subjects such an individual to a "disorderly person" violation.[18]

---

17. N.J.S.A. 9:6-8.46.
18. N.J.S.A. 9:6-8.14. A violation is an offense punishable by no more than 6 months in prison and is not considered a "crime."

5A.9

Abused and Neglected Children

Procedures for handling child abuse and neglect cases typically involve three stages: taking the child into temporary custody, holding a fact-finding hearing, and holding a dispositional hearing. It is generally a hierarchical process that may stop at any point if the allegations are unfounded or upon a showing that the parents are currently capable of raising their children in a responsible manner. Each stage may involve a mental health evaluation of the child and/or parent. In addition, the MHP may be called to testify as an expert witness (see Chapter 5A.10).

Definitions

Parent or guardian refers to any natural parent, adoptive parent, foster parent, stepparent, or any other person who has assumed responsibility for the care, custody, or control of a child, or upon whom there is a legal duty for such care:[1]

> Parent or guardian includes a teacher, employee or volunteer, whether compensated or uncompensated, of an institution who is responsible for the child's welfare and any other staff person of an institution. . . . Parent or guardian also includes a teaching staff member or other employee, whether compensated or uncompensated, of a day school. . . .

An abused or neglected child refers to a child under 18 years of age whose parent or guardian[2]

---

1. N.J.S.A. 9:6-8.21.
2. *Id.*

1. inflicts or allows to be inflicted upon the child physical injury by other than accidental means that creates a substantial risk of death or serious disfigurement, or protracted impairment of physical or emotional health, or protracted impairment of any bodily organ;
2. creates or allows a substantial risk of physical injury to the child that would be likely to cause serious disfigurement or impairment of a bodily organ;
3. commits or allows an act of sexual abuse against the child;
4. allows the physical, mental, or emotional condition of the child to become impaired or endangered as the result of the failure to exercise a minimum degree of care

   a. in supplying the child with adequate food, clothing, shelter, education, or medical or surgical care although able to do so; or
   b. in providing the child with proper supervision by unreasonably inflicting or allowing (the risk of) harm, including the infliction of excessive corporal punishment or similar serious acts;

5. willfully abandons the child; or
6. uses excessive physical restraint when the child is not harmful to himself or herself, others, or property.

In addition, an abused or neglected child includes a child who is in an institution (other than a day school) and has been either placed there inappropriately with the knowledge that the placement may cause harm or willfully isolated from ordinary social contact indicating emotional or social deprivation.

An appellate case has held that parental failure to provide normal intellectual stimulation does not constitute educational neglect within the meaning of the abuse and neglect statute.[3] Rather, neglect must involve the encouragement to truancy or other serious interference with normal educational processes. Likewise, substandard, dirty, and inadequate sleeping conditions that are the consequences of poverty do not constitute abuse or neglect.

Temporary Custody

If a child's continuance in a residence under the care of a parent or a guardian presents an imminent danger to his or her life or

---

3. Doe v. G.D., 146 N.J. Super. 419, 370 A.2d 27 (App. Div. 1976), aff'd, 74 N.J. 196, 377 A.2d 626 (1977).

health, the child may be removed on an emergency basis, without court order, by a police or probation officer, an employee of the Division of Youth and Family Services (DYSF), or a physician.[4] The removal must be reported immediately to DYFS, and the temporary custodian then must bring the child to a place that DYFS designates and inform the parents if possible.

DYFS must immediately inform the parents about the emergency removal and the location of the child (except if he or she is staying in a foster home). DYFS must advise both the parents and the temporary custodian to appear in superior court the next court day when a complaint will be filed.[5] DYFS is authorized in such situations to arrange for and consent to medical care. Any person acting in good faith in the examination of or provision of care and treatment to the child has immunity from any legal liability.

Upon the receipt of any report of child abuse, the Division of Youth and Family Services is empowered to take action immediately to ensure the safety of the child.[6] State and local law enforcement officials are required to provide assistance. If investigation determines that immediate protective custody is required, DYFS may provide such custody while applying for a court order to place the child under its care and supervision.

If the parents refuse to consent to the temporary removal of a child from the home, the superior court may issue a preliminary order directing the removal, before a complaint is filed and preliminary hearing held, if the child appears to be suffering from abuse or neglect and his or her immediate removal is necessary to prevent imminent danger to life and health.[7] The order must specify the facility where the child is being held. The court also may order emergency medical or surgical procedures if necessary.

In any case where the child has been removed without court order, the court is required to hold a preliminary hearing on the next court day.[8] At that time a formal complaint will be filed, and the court will determine whether the child's interests require continued protection prior to the full dispositional hearing. If the court finds that continued removal is necessary to avoid a risk to the child's life or health, it shall continue the removal and ensure custody with a suitable person. The court may also issue a preliminary order of protection. The judge is required to order an examination of the child by a physician designated by DYFS, who will forward results to the court. The court may also order the return of the

---

4. N.J.S.A. 9:6-8.29 and 8.16.
5. N.J.S.A. 9:6-8.30.
6. N.J.S.A. 9:6-8.11 and 9:6-18.
7. N.J.S.A. 9:6-8.28.
8. N.J.S.A. 9:6-8.31. However, if the child initially has been taken into custody by a physician or hospital, a hearing must be held within 3 court days.

child to the custody of his or her parent or guardian pending the final dispositional hearing.

Adjudication of Alleged Child Abuse or Neglect

The New Jersey Superior Court, Chancery Division, Family Part, has jurisdiction over all noncriminal proceedings involving alleged cases of child abuse or neglect, even though any possible criminal proceedings against the parent or guardian must be referred to the county prosecutor for consideration.[9] Any child who is the subject of an abuse or neglect hearing must be represented by a law guardian, appointed by the judge, who will represent the child's interests in court.[10] A legal proceeding may be originated by a parent, agency, DYFS, police officer, county prosecutor, or any person with convincing information that a child is abused or neglected.[11] DYFS is entitled to attempt an adjustment of the dispute in a preliminary conference with parents and complaining parties, prior to the formal filing of a complaint.[12]

DYFS may request all confidential records pertaining to the care of the child from private practitioners and private and public agencies.[13] All those who release such information to DYFS have immunity from legal action against them.[14] A psychologist, psychiatrist, or marriage counselor may assert before a judge that such information is confidential and privileged (see Chapters 4.2, 4.3, and 5A.8). However, the law is not clear as to whether the judge would rule that the abuse and neglect statute "pierces the shield" of such statutory professional privilege. In any case, the MHP would be required to break confidentiality to prevent a client from causing imminent harm to self or others.

The resolution of a complaint of child abuse or neglect occurs during two hearings: A "fact-finding hearing" determines whether the child's circumstance meets the legal standards of abuse or neglect.[15] A "dispositional hearing" then determines what orders the

---

9. N.J.S.A. 9:6-8.36a. Child abuse or neglect is a crime of the fourth degree. N.J.S.A. 9:6-3.
10. N.J.S.A. 9:6-8.23.
11. N.J.S.A. 9:6-8.34.
12. N.J.S.A. 9:6-8.35.
13. N.J.S.A. 9:6-8.40.
14. *Id.*
15. N.J.S.A. 9:6-8.44.

judge will make.[16] In a fact-finding hearing, any determination that the child is abused or neglected must be based upon a preponderance of the evidence.[17] MHPs may participate as expert witnesses in both the fact-finding and the dispositional hearings. If asked to testify regarding confidential communications, psychologists, marriage counselors, and psychiatrists may assert their statutory right of privileged communications, a right that was restored in child abuse and neglect hearings in 1977.[18]

Dispositional Alternatives

If the court rules that the child is abused or neglected, the judge is required to make a finding that includes grounds for the decision.[19] Prior to a final disposition, the judge may make preliminary orders for suitable custody and medical care and orders of protection. The court may suspend a final dispositional order indefinitely by referring any aspect of the matter to DYFS, ordering that DYFS provide whatever services are appropriate to protect the child and rehabilitate the family, with periodic reports to the court.[20]

Following the fact-finding hearing, a final dispositional hearing is required.[21] At that time, the judge may[22]

1. suspend judgment for 1 year, while ordering the parents or guardians to comply with any necessary terms and conditions;[23]
2. release the child to the custody of the parents or guardians; such release may include placing the child under the supervision of DYFS, with any necessary conditions, for a period of 1 year;[24]
3. place the child in the custody of a relative, DYFS, or other suitable person for an initial period of 18 months, renewable yearly upon court hearing, up to age 18;[25]
4. make an order of protection, requiring conditions of behavior for a parent or guardian, such as staying away from the home, other spouse, or child; permitting child visitation at certain times; or abstaining from offensive conduct;[26]

---

16. N.J.S.A. 9:6-8.45.
17. N.J.S.A. 9:6-8.46.
18. N.J.S.A. 9:6-8.46(a)(5).
19. N.J.S.A. 9:6-8.54(a).
20. N.J.S.A. 9:6-8.54(e).
21. N.J.S.A. 9:6-8.44 and 8.45.
22. N.J.S.A. 9:6-8.51.
23. N.J.S.A. 9:6-8.52.
24. N.J.S.A. 9:6-8.53.
25. N.J.S.A. 9:6-8.54.
26. N.J.S.A. 9:6-8.55.

5. place the parents or guardian under the supervision of the probation department, with conditions, for a period of up to 2 years, with a possible 1-year extension through the court;[27]

6. require that an individual found to have abused or neglected a child accept therapeutic services, such as psychotherapy, homemaker services, functional education, and group self-help programs;[28] or

7. find that the child was abandoned by his or her parents or guardian and discharge the child to the custody of DYFS.[29]

---

27. N.J.S.A. 9:6-8.56.
28. N.J.S.A. 9:6-8.57.
29. *Id.*

5A.10

Termination of Parental Rights

There are three separate statutory paths governing the termination of parental rights in New Jersey. The first, general termination, may arise if the child is under custody of the Division of Youth and Family Services (DYFS) and requires guardianship, or if the parents have been convicted of child abuse or neglect.[1] The second, adoption termination, arises during any adoption proceeding if the parents' rights have not been terminated.[2] The third, surrender termination,[3] arises after a parent has executed a voluntary surrender of custody to an approved adoption agency, which then may initiate a termination action and represent the child in a hearing.[4]

Although termination is a frequent and necessary action in a voluntary adoption case, involuntary termination is an extreme measure that infrequently occurs, particularly if it is the first allegation of wrongdoing. Parents must be afforded a range of procedural rights that must be strictly complied with. They must receive notice of the proceedings. Indigent parents are entitled to the assignment of an attorney.[5] Likewise, children are entitled to the appointment of independent counsel.[6] The standard of proof required to be met is that of clear and convincing evidence. Because

---

1. N.J.S.A. 30:4C-11 et seq.
2. N.J.S.A. 9:3-37 et seq.
3. The terms for the three types of termination are taken from Boskey and McCue, *Alternative Standards for the Termination of Parental Rights*, 9 SETON HALL L. REV. 1 (1978).
4. N.J.S.A. 9:2-16 et seq.
5. Crist v. N.J. Div. of Youth and Family Servs., 135 N.J. Super. 573, 343 A.2d 815 (App. Div. 1975).
6. New Jersey Div. of Youth and Family Servs. v. Wandell, 155 N.J. Super. 302, 382 A.2d 711 (1977).

such a decision inevitably involves consideration of the child's emotional well-being and of the parent–child relationship, MHPs are frequently called upon to undertake individual and family evaluations to assist the court in its decision.

General Termination

Any person or agency interested in a child (usually DYFS) may file a petition for termination of parental rights with the superior court whenever[7]

1. parents or guardian have been convicted of abuse, abandonment, neglect, or cruelty to a child;
2. any child has been adjudicated as a delinquent;
3. the best interests of a child under the care or custody of DYFS require guardianship; or
4. a parent or guardian has failed substantially and continuously or repeatedly for a period of more than 1 year to maintain contact with and plan for the future of a child whose care or custody has been transferred to DYFS or other authorized agency.[8]

These statutory standards have been clarified further by the courts to require that in any proceeding involving the termination of parental rights, the trial court must determine whether[9]

1. the child's health and development have been or will be seriously impaired by the parental relationship;
2. the parents are unable or unwilling to eliminate the harm, and whether the delay of permanent placement will add to the harm;
3. there are no alternatives to termination; and
4. termination of parental rights will do more harm than good.

Termination will be ordered by the trial court only if it finds that all four of the requirements have been met.

The court is empowered to issue an interlocutory order in a special summary hearing, terminating parental rights and committing a child to the guardianship of DYFS prior to the final disposition if necessary.[10] Even if DYFS did not bring the complaint,

---

7. N.J.S.A. 30:4C-15.
8. *Id.* and N.J.S.A. 30:4C-11 and 12. DYFS is specifically authorized to initiate a termination complaint when it has received custody of the child.
9. New Jersey Div. of Youth and Family Servs. v. A.W., 103 N.J. 591, 512 A.2d 438 (1986).
10. N.J.S.A. 30:4C-17.

it is authorized to investigate the circumstances of alleged parental unfitness to aid the court in its determination.[11] Hearings are conducted in private.[12] Children do not attend the hearing except when testimony is necessary, and then the child's testimony may be taken privately in the judge's chambers.[13] At the completion of the termination hearing the court may terminate parental rights and commit the child to the guardianship of DYFS for all purposes including the placement of the child for adoption.[14]

If the parents choose not to contest the termination proceedings or if they otherwise decide that it would be in the best interests of their child, such parents may make a voluntary surrender of the child's custody to DYFS for the purpose of adoption.[15] Such surrenders must be signed before a notary public and are considered binding and irrevocable except at the discretion of DYFS or upon court order. The procedures and safeguards that must be followed are identical to those for normal adoption termination proceedings (infra).[16]

Adoption Termination

Most terminations of parental rights originate with birth mothers who voluntarily surrender their child to an adoption agency shortly after delivery (see Chapter 5A.14). There must be a signed document before a notary public that relinquishes parental rights and consents to an adoption of the child.[17] An approved adoption agency may accept the surrender of a child for adoption only after determining that the birth parents or legal guardians are not acting under duress.[18] The agency cannot require the prospective birth mother to sign a document regarding a plan for the child in order to obtain any services, including medical care. The agency must give the father an opportunity to exercise his rights, including the denial of paternity or a surrender of the child. Before accepting surrender of the child, the agency must document that the birth parents were offered counseling which fully explored alternative plans for the child. The parents must also be referred to other community resources when the agency cannot provide needed services.

---

11. N.J.S.A. 30:4C-12.
12. R. 5:12-3(b).
13. Id.
14. N.J.S.A. 30:4C-20.
15. N.J.S.A. 30:4C-23.
16. N.J.A.C. 10:121A-5.4.
17. N.J.S.A. 9:3-40.
18. N.J.A.C. 10:121A-5.4.

The birth parents must be given the opportunity to state any preferences affecting the selection of adoptive parents, although the agency must act in the best interests of the child, in a nondiscriminatory manner.[19] The child must be 72 hours old before a surrender agreement may be executed. The agency must document that birth parents who cannot read English fully understand the meaning of surrender. A child must be returned to the parents if the sole reason for surrender was inability to pay medical and other expenses. The agency must request that the court terminate parental rights if it is in the best interests of the child. The agency must provide at least one counseling visit to the birth parents upon request after the baby is freed for adoption.

The parents must be informed that the agency may contact them in the future if the adult adoptee or adoptive family requests information or wishes to meet the birth parents.[20] The parents must be advised that they may sign a written agreement at any time indicating their willingness to be contacted or provide information. However, without written consent, the parents' identity will remain confidential, and sealed adoption records will be released by the courts only under exceptional circumstances for "good cause."[21] The parents must be requested to update their current address and medical information. The agency must explain to the birth parents that the agency will assume custody and will have the right to consent to adoption of the child pursuant to law.

In adoption proceedings, if the parental rights have not yet been terminated, termination will occur in a preliminary hearing, unless there is an objection.[22] Notice to the parents must be given according to strict guidelines.[23] The law states,[24]

> Any parent who has not executed a surrender . . . and whose parental rights have not been terminated by court order shall have the right to object to the adoption of his child. No judgment of adoption shall be entered over an objection of such parent . . . unless the court finds that such parent has substantially failed to perform the regular and expected parental functions of care and support of the child, which shall include maintenance of an emotional relationship with the child.

Although parental unfitness or abandonment are almost always a requirement of termination absent consent, the "parens

---

19. *Id.*
20. N.J.A.C. 10:121A-5.5.
21. N.J.S.A. 9:3-52 and Backes v. Catholic Family and Community Servs., 210 N.J. Super. 186, 509 A.2d 283 (Ch. 1985).
22. N.J.S.A. 9:3:48.
23. N.J.S.A. 9:3-45 and R. 5:10-5.
24. N.J.S.A. 9:3-46.

patriae" inherent power of the court to determine the best interests of the child may weaken such requirements in extreme cases. Thus, the *Sorentino* case held that the proved duress of the natural mother in the inducement of her to give up a child for adoption at birth did not automatically entitle her to the return of her child already placed with adoptive parents for 31 months. Rather, the case was remanded to the trial court to determine if serious psychological injury would occur if custody were returned to the natural mother.[25]

Parents may not contract to terminate their parental rights either after the conception of a child, or in a surrogate parent contract prior to conception.[26]

Surrender Termination

Any approved adoption agency that is providing supervision of a child as the result of a voluntary surrender of the child may institute an action in the superior court seeking the termination of parental rights and the transfer of custody to the agency, without invoking the adoption process.[27] The court must find that the parents intended to surrender the child, as evidenced officially by a formal document relinquishing custody and acknowledging the termination of parental rights.[28]

The termination of one parent's rights does not affect the rights of the other parent.[29] The judge may find that the other parent's rights are terminated if that parent is dead, mentally incompetent, or has forsaken parental obligation. The court may also negate the control and authority of any neglectful custodian or guardian.

When the court finds that the parents of the child have no further rights to custody, a judgment terminating such rights and transferring the custody of the child to the agency is issued.[30] The only remaining duty of the parents is to support the child financially until an adoption occurs.

---

25. Sorentino v. Family and Children's Serv. of Elizabeth, 72 N.J. 127, 367 A.2d 1168 (1976) (Sorentino I); *but see* Sorentino v. Family and Children's Soc'y, 74 N.J. 313, 378 A.2d 18 (1977) (Sorentino II), in which the New Jersey Supreme Court reviewed the appeal after remand and struggled to find "forsaken parental obligations" in the actions of the natural parents.
26. Matter of Baby M, 537 A.2d 1227, 109 N.J. 396 (1988), *on remand*, 225 N.J. Super. 267, 542 A.2d 52 (1988).
27. N.J.S.A. 9:2-18.
28. N.J.S.A. 9:2-17.
29. N.J.S.A. 9:2-15.
30. N.J.S.A. 9:2-20.

5A.11

Guardianship for Minors

A guardian may be appointed for a minor in situations where the custodial parent(s) is (are) unable to care for the child owing to death, legal termination of parental rights, or other circumstances. In some states, guardians are appointed to undertake parental responsibilities, whereas conservators (see Chapter 5A.12) are appointed to manage the estate (e.g., money, property, and business enterprises). In New Jersey, guardianship law includes appointment of the guardianship of the person, guardianship of the estate, or guardianship of the person and estate if such powers are given to one individual.[1] MHPs are likely to become involved in a guardian selection process and follow-up treatment, if any, for the children.

Application for Guardianship

There are two methods of appointing a guardian of a minor. The first is by testamentary appointment in which either parent indicates in a will who is wished to be guardian of the children, including those in utero.[2] The parent may request separate guardians of the person and of the estate, or one guardian of both person and estate. The children must be under the age of 18 and unmarried at the time of the parent's death.

If one parent survives the other, the appointment of a guardian will be effective only if the surviving parent gives written consent.[3] The appointment of a testamentary guardian is effectual against

---

1. N.J.S.A. 3B:12-1 et seq.
2. N.J.S.A. 3B:12-13.
3. N.J.S.A. 3B:12-14.

anyone else claiming the guardianship.[4] However, anyone may bring an action in the superior court to inquire into the present custody of a minor, and the court may make an order affecting the testamentary guardianship to conform to whatever "may be for the best interest and welfare of the minor."[5]

The second method of appointment is by a formal court hearing that has been convened because a person interested in the child's welfare has petitioned the court requesting that it appoint a guardian. This could occur at any time, including at the death of a parent who has not made a testamentary appointment.[6]

The Guardianship Hearing

The surrogate court, or superior court upon inquiry, has jurisdiction in guardianship hearings. The court may appoint either or both parents, their survivor, or their heirs to be guardian of the person, estate, or person and estate. If none of these will accept the guardianship, the court may appoint any other person it sees fit.[7] If the child is of an age and capacity to form a rational judgment, the court should give consideration to the child's choice of guardian.[8] In making its determination, the court is guided by the principle of best interests of the children.[9]

After the appointment of a guardian, final authority over the ward remains with the court, although the guardian is given considerable discretionary powers.[10] In general, a guardian of the person has the same powers and responsibilities as a parent, except that a guardian is not legally obligated to provide for the ward from his or her own funds.[11] More specifically, the guardian of the person must[12]

1. take reasonable care of the ward's personal effects;

2. apply periodic receipts of money (from the estate or other sources) to the ward's current needs for support, care, and education;

3. exercise due care to conserve any excess funds for the ward's future needs; and

---

4. N.J.S.A. 3B:12-18.
5. N.J.S.A. 3B:12-17.
6. *Id.*
7. N.J.S.A. 3B:12-21.
8. *In re* Guardianship of Hoppe, 32 N.J. Super. 460, 108 A.2d 664 (1954).
9. Albert v. Perry, 14 N.J. Eq. 540 (1862).
10. N.J.S.A. 3B:12-36 and 37.
11. N.J.S.A. 3B:12-51.
12. N.J.S.A. 3B:12-52.

4. facilitate the ward's education and social and other activities and authorize medical or other professional care, treatment, or advice.

The guardian of the estate is vested with title as trustee to all the property of the ward.[13] He or she may distribute as much or all of the income or principal of the ward's estate as necessary for the support, maintenance, education, general use, and benefit of the ward and the ward's dependents, to the extent that the guardian reasonably deems it suitable and proper.[14] However, expenditures for housing, clothing, maintenance, and general welfare can normally only be made out of the income of the estate and not the principal, unless the income is insufficient for such purposes.[15] The guardian of the estate is required to consider the recommendations made by the guardian of the person, and there is no penalty for funding such recommendations unless they are clearly not in the best interests of the ward.[16]

Termination of the Guardianship

The authority and responsibility of a guardian of the person or estate terminates upon the death, resignation, or removal of the guardian or upon the minor's death, adoption, or marriage or when the child reaches age 18.[17] At that time the guardian is required to distribute all funds and properties to the former ward as soon as possible.[18] The court is empowered to substitute one guardian for another on the application of the ward or for any other reason that would be in the best interests of the child.[19]

---

13. N.J.S.A. 3B:12-38.
14. N.J.S.A. 3B:12-43.
15. Strawbridge v. Strawbridge, 35 N.J. Super. 125, 113 A.2d 199 (1955).
16. N.J.S.A. 3B:12-44.
17. N.J.S.A. 3B:12-55.
18. N.J.S.A. 3B:12-54.
19. N.J.S.A. 3B:12-21 and Albert v. Perry, *supra.*

5A.12

Conservatorship for Minors

In some states, guardians are appointed to undertake parental responsibilities, whereas conservators are appointed to manage the estate (e.g., money, property, and business enterprises). In New Jersey, guardianship law includes appointment of the guardianship of the person, guardianship of the estate, or guardianship of the person and estate if such powers are given to one individual.[1] There is no separate conservatorship law for minors (see Chapter 5A.11).

---

1. N.J.S.A. 3B:12-1 et seq.

5A.13

Foster Care

Foster care provides residential housing and support, under the supervision of the Division of Youth and Family Services (DYFS) or private adoption agencies, for children who are not able to live in their own homes. The person may be placed in a foster home for as little as one night or as long as several years. MHPs may be involved in the approval of a home and in providing assessment and therapeutic services to those placed in them.

Licensing Requirements

In some states, foster parent applicants must be licensed. In New Jersey, foster parent applicants must meet the written criteria of an approved adoption agency, usually DYFS.[1] The agency must ensure that foster parents[2]

1. submit written reports of recent medical examinations of all household members, indicating that all are free of communicable diseases or other medical impediments to foster placement;

2. submit a physician's written statement attesting that the foster parents are physically capable of providing foster care services;

3. submit three written references;

4. allow a social worker from the agency (see Chapter 1.5) to conduct a home visit and make a written assessment before the

---

1. N.J.A.C. 10:121A-5.5.
2. *Id.*

home is used; if a foster home has not been used for a year, an updated assessment is required; and

5. sign an agreement that specifies the terms of service and financial remuneration.

In addition to meeting other requirements of the Department of Human Services and DYFS, all those wishing to become foster or adoptive parents, as well as any other adults in their homes, must undergo an investigation of their state and federal criminal records.[3] If there is a criminal history, the Department of Human Services must review the record and determine whether the person is suitable to become a foster or adoptive parent, or whether the home is suitable to place a foster child.

Placement of Children in Foster Homes

Whenever a child's needs cannot be adequately met in his or her own home, the Division of Youth and Family Services may place him or her in a foster home, group home, or institution.[4] DYFS is obligated to try to make a placement of the same religious faith as the parents if possible. DYFS's custody of children in foster homes is considered complete for all purposes and includes the responsibility to administer all real and personal property of the child.[5] Municipalities are prohibited from any single-family zoning laws that discriminate between natural children and foster children or children in a group home (see Chapter 2.8).[6] DYFS may remove a child from a foster home and also discharge any child from its care and custody if such action is in the best interests of the child.[7] However, such action is subject to review by the superior court and the court-appointed placement review board (infra).[8]

A foster home is defined as a private residence, group home, or institution in which a child is placed under the care, custody, or guardianship of DYFS for temporary or long-term care, including private residences where a child may be placed for adoption.[9] The term also includes child care shelters that are authorized to be established throughout the state for the temporary care and supervision of children before placement in a suitable foster home.[10]

---

3. N.J.S.A. 30:4C-26.8.
4. N.J.S.A. 30:4C-26.
5. N.J.S.A. 30:4C-24.
6. N.J.S.A. 30:4C-26(d).
7. N.J.S.A. 30:4C-28.
8. N.J.S.A. 30:4C-61.1.
9. N.J.S.A. 30:4C-26.1.
10. N.J.S.A. 30:4C-26.3.

A foster parent is defined as any person with whom a child in the care of DYFS is placed for temporary or long-term care, except for any person with whom a child is placed for the purpose of adoption.[11]

Foster parents cannot be prohibited by contract with DYFS from seeking adoption of foster children in their care.[12] They may apply for adoption of a child after 2 years of foster care. Foster parents are given statutory preference and first consideration over all other adoption applicants.

DYFS may provide payment for the reasonable and proper cost of maintenance of children in foster homes, including board, lodging, clothing, medical, dental, and hospital care, or any similar or specialized items.[13] Whenever a medical or psychological evaluation is required, the cost must be borne by state and county funds from available appropriations in their maintenance budget. However, any parent, guardian, or other person legally responsible for the child, if financially able, is liable for the full costs of maintenance of the child by DYFS.[14]

Placement Review

Within 5 days of a voluntary placement into a foster home, DYFS is required to notify the superior court and specify what efforts were made to avoid such placement.[15] Additional placement changes, including permanent placement or return home, also require immediate notice. Within 15 days the court is required to determine, on the basis of the received written information and any supplementary materials it requests, whether or not reasonable efforts have been made to prevent the placement and whether or not the continuation of the child in his or her home would be contrary to the welfare of the child.[16] The court may hold a summary hearing if necessary. The court must then either approve the placement or order the return of the child to his or her home.

The superior court in every county is required to establish child placement review boards, consisting of appointed volunteers familiar with child placement to review all placement decisions in the county.[17] Within 15 days of a voluntary foster care placement, DYFS is required to submit a placement plan to the board.[18] The

---

11. N.J.S.A. 30:4C-26.4.
12. N.J.S.A. 30:4C-26.5 and 26.7.
13. N.J.S.A. 30:4C-27.
14. N.J.S.A. 30:4C-29.1.
15. N.J.S.A. 30:4C-53.
16. N.J.S.A. 30:4C-54.
17. N.J.S.A. 30:4C-57.
18. N.J.S.A. 30:4C-58.

board must then review the plan within 45 days of placement, evaluating such factors as[19]

1. the appropriateness of the goal and objectives of the placement plan;
2. the appropriateness of the services provided to the child, the parents, and the temporary caretaker;
3. whether the child has siblings outside the home;
4. whether the wishes of the child were considered regarding the placement and development of the placement plan;
5. whether DYFS, the parents, and the temporary caretaker are fulfilling their respective responsibilities in accordance with the placement plan;
6. whether the parents or legal guardian have been encouraged and provided the opportunity to visit the child regularly;
7. whether there are obstacles that hinder or prevent placement plan objectives; and
8. the circumstances surrounding the placement.

DYFS, the child (except if waived by the court), the parents, legal guardians, temporary caretakers, and any other interested parties must receive notice of the review and are entitled to attend and submit written information to the placement review board.[20]

The review board must submit a written report to the superior court and DYFS. It must find either[21]

1. that continued placement of the child outside of the home is not in the child's best interest and that the child should return home within 2 weeks;
2. that continued placement on a temporary basis is in the child's best interest but that the board needs more information to make a recommendation; or
3. that continued placement is in the child's best interest on a temporary basis until the achievement of a specific long-term goal, which may include the return of the child to the parents, adoption, permanent placement with a relative, long-term foster care, independent living, or institutionalization.

The board is required to give priority to the goal of returning the child to its parents during the first year of placement unless such goal is not in the best interests of the child. After 1 year, the

---

19. *Id.*
20. N.J.S.A. 30:4C-59.
21. N.J.S.A. 30:4C-60.

board may give priority to permanent placement with a relative or adoption, unless they are not in the best interests of the child.

The New Jersey Superior Court, Family Part, is required to review the placement review board's report within 21 days and issue an order consistent with its recommendations or else develop a new plan.[22] The court may order a summary hearing if necessary.

In cases where DYFS proposes to return a child home, although the return is either prohibited by the approved placement plan or contingent upon certain unfulfilled conditions in the placement plan, DYFS is required to promptly notify the review board and the superior court in writing.[23] The review board must then conduct a special evaluation to determine if the proposed action is in the best interests of the child. The court must then review the board's recommendations and either order the return of the child to the parents or otherwise.

---

22. N.J.S.A. 30:4C-61.
23. N.J.S.A. 30:4C-61.1.

Adoption

New Jersey law provides that persons who wish to adopt a child must meet certain minimum requirements (described in the following section). So, too, the adopted child and natural parents, if any, may have rights and responsibilities that must be fulfilled for the adoption to be valid. MHPs may contribute to this process by providing evaluations of prospective adoptive parents and children and treatment to the adopted children, if necessary.

Adoption Requirements

Birth Parents

New Jersey law requires that parental rights must be terminated before an adoption can occur. Either there must be a voluntary surrender of the custody of the child that follows carefully prescribed legal guidelines, or there must be a court-ordered termination (see Chapter 5A.10).

Adoptive Parents

Any person may institute the process for adoption, provided that he or she is at least 18 years old and 10 years older than the child to be adopted.[1] However, a married person may seek adoption only with the consent of the spouse, or jointly with the spouse, except if there has been at least an 18-month separation.

All applicants must undergo a home study evaluation by an approved adoption agency. The agency is required to inform the

---

1. N.J.S.A. 9:3-43.

applicant of all information regarding the child's development, medical history, personality, and temperament, as well as any health information about the birth parents that may affect the child.[2] If the adoption is private rather than an agency adoption, the court will appoint an adoption agency to perform such an evaluation.[3] All home study evaluations must be performed by agency social workers (see Chapter 1.5).

The home study process must consist of at least three in-person contacts including joint and individual interviews with married applicants, interviews with all members of the household, and at least one visit to the applicant's residence.[4] The agency must review three personal references, one current job reference (if applicable), and one neighbor's reference.[5] In addition, the adoption agency must give careful consideration to any parental history of abuse and neglect as well as to any criminal records to determine whether such past conduct would pose a threat to the child.

The home study must obtain and assess identifying information:[6] a description of each adoptive applicant's awareness and sensitivity to adoption issues; applicants' interests, hobbies, child caring skills, strengths and weaknesses; philosophies on child rearing, discipline, parental roles, and experience with children; emotional stability and maturity; state of the marital relationship; attitudes of other family members; each parent's family life history; and written medical reports.

The home study evaluation must also review any present or previous marriages and divorces;[7] the location and description of the physical environment of the residence and neighborhood; a statement of income and financial resources; a description of the types of children the adoptive applicants can accept (including age, racial or ethnic background, sex, sibling groups, and disabilities); a description of any birth family background problems including medical, hereditary, incest, mental illness, or drug abuse; and a description of the applicant's capacity to make viable child care arrangements if employed.

Thirty days after completion of the home study, the social worker and the supervisor must write a joint letter to the applicants, either accepting or rejecting the application.[8] When an applicant is not accepted, the agency must explain its reasons, offer a counseling session, and explain the agency grievance procedure. For

---

2. N.J.S.A. 9:3-41.1.
3. N.J.S.A. 9:3-48.
4. N.J.A.C. 10:121A-5.6(e).
5. Id.
6. N.J.A.C. 10:121A-5.6(f).
7. Id.
8. N.J.A.C. 10:121A-5.6(g).

applicants who have been on a waiting list for more than 1 year after acceptance, the agency must update the home study prior to placement of the child.

The adoption agency must document the reasons for placing a child with an applicant.[9] If siblings are to be separated, the attempts made to avoid such a separation must also be documented. Upon placement of a child, the agency must give the adoptive parents a written explanation of their rights and responsibilities during the minimum 6-month supervision period before the court finalizes the adoption.

The adoption agency must provide to the adoptive parents a written history of the child including developmental and medical history and an assessment of any special needs and disabilities along with support services.[10] In addition, the agency must explain to the adoptive parents that the adoptee may ultimately wish to seek information in the permanent record about the birth family and that the agency may convey updated information about the birth family to the adoptive parents in the future.

During the 6-month supervisory period between placement and adoption, the agency must provide regular postplacement services.[11] It must counsel the adoptive parents; ensure that there are proper child care and educational arrangements; and document how the parents, the adoptee, and each member of the adoptive family are adjusting to the placement. The placement may be terminated either by the request of the applicant or by the agency if it believes that the child's needs are no longer being served by the placement. Counseling must be offered following the removal.

Following legal adoption, an adoption agency must provide postadoption services, including the storage of updated information concerning birth parents, adoptive parents, and child and providing nonidentifying information to clients upon request.[12] It may also provide counseling to the adoptive family if anyone is having difficulty adjusting to the adoption.

Adoptive Child

The adoption agency must complete a comprehensive study for each child evaluated for adoption. The study must include[13]

1. a medical examination when the agency assumes custody and prior to placement,

---

9. N.J.A.C. 10:121A-5.7.
10. *Id.*
11. N.J.A.C. 10:121A-5.8.
12. N.J.A.C. 10:121A-5.9.
13. N.J.A.C. 10:121A-5.5.

2. information about the child's birth family to determine hereditary factors or pathology that may affect development,

3. information on any prior placements,

4. any specialized evaluations for a physically and/or mentally handicapped child,

5. the child's involvement in the adoption, and

6. a careful evaluation of the advisability of placing the child with siblings.

In addition, the agency must provide foster care services, as necessary, to ensure the health and safety of children awaiting adoptive placement (see Chapter 5A.13).

Complaint for Adoption

The family part of the superior court has jurisdiction over adoption proceedings.[14] Court rules govern the manner of filing complaints and notice.[15] Any prospective adoptee age 10 years or older is required to be present at an adoption hearing, and the court must solicit and give consideration to the child's wishes if he or she can form an intelligent preference.[16]

If the child to be adopted has been received from an approved agency, the prospective parent is required to file a complaint with the court for adoption after the child has been in the home for at least 6 months.[17] The complaint must be accompanied by a consent to the adoption by the authorized agency, if the agency approves. The agency is then required to file a two-part report with the court, one part of which must describe the circumstances surrounding the surrender of the child, and the second part of which shall[18]

> set forth the results of the agency's evaluation of the child and of the plaintiff and his spouse, if any, and the agency's assessment of the care being received by the child and the adjustment of the child and the plaintiff as members of a family.

If the agency does not consent to the adoption, the court may appoint another approved agency to perform a separate evaluation. The court may appoint a guardian ad litem to represent the best interests of the child in a contested proceeding.

If the adoption is private, the law requires that an approved adoption agency be appointed to investigate and report to the court[19]

---

14. N.J.S.A. 9:3-42.
15. R. 5:10 and 12.
16. N.J.S.A. 9:3-49.
17. N.J.S.A. 9:3-47.
18. *Id.*
19. N.J.S.A. 9:3-48.

the facts and circumstances surrounding the surrender of custody by the child's parents and the placement of the child in the home of the plaintiff and an evaluation of the child and of the plaintiff and the spouse of the plaintiff . . . provided, however, that whenever the plaintiff is a stepparent of the child, the court may dispense with the agency investigation and report.

If the prospective parent is a close relative of the child, the court may limit the investigation to an inquiry regarding the status of the parent and child and an evaluation of the prospective parent.

Approved Agency Adoption

The Department of Human Services regulates and approves adoption agencies in New Jersey.[20] The agencies are prohibited from discriminating in the selection of adoptive parents with regard to age, sex, race, national origin, religion, or marital status. However, "these factors may be considered in determining whether the best interests of a child would be served by a particular adoptive placement."[21]

The adoption hearing is held in camera, not open to the public. Strict guidelines govern the notification of the parents in any adoption proceeding.[22] If a parent of the child has made an objection to the adoption, the court must hear any evidence and decide to terminate the parent's rights (see Chapter 5A.10) before it can permit an adoption.[23] If the court decides that the proposed adoption is in the best interests of the child, it will enter a judgment of adoption. Otherwise, the court will deny the adoption and make whatever order concerning the custody and guardianship of the child that it considers to be proper. All records of the proceeding must then be sealed[24] and must only be opened in exceptional circumstances for "good cause" (see Chapter 5A.10).[25]

Private Adoption

Only the parent, guardian, or an approved adoption agency can place a child for adoption, or assist in such placement, except if the child is placed with a close relative.[26] Parents and anyone acting

---

20. N.J.S.A. 9:3-40 and N.J.A.C. 9:102-1.1 et seq.
21. *Id.*
22. N.J.S.A. 9:3-45.
23. N.J.S.A. 9:3-47.
24. N.J.S.A. 9:3-52.
25. Backes v. Catholic Family and Community Servs., 210 N.J. Super. 186, 509 A.2d 283 (1985).
26. N.J.S.A. 9:3-39.

as their agents, finders, or intermediaries in arranging a private adoption can be found guilty of a crime for violating this law. The payment of any money for such services is also a crime.[27]

Prospective parents in a private adoption must file a complaint as soon as possible after the child is placed. The court is then required to declare the child a ward of the court and grant preliminary custody to the prospective parents.[28] The court then must appoint an approved adoption agency to perform an investigation of parents and child and to make recommendations (supra). If the agency recommends the removal of the child, the court is required to appoint a guardian ad litem to represent the best interests of the child in the court proceeding.

The court then holds a closed preliminary hearing to determine the circumstances under which the child was relinquished by his or her parents and received into the home of the plaintiff, the status of the parental rights of the parents, the fitness of the child for adoption, and the fitness of the plaintiff to adopt the child and to provide a suitable home.[29]

Upon completion of the preliminary hearing, if the court finds that the adoption would not be in the best interests of the child, the complaint will be denied and the court will order other arrangements for guardianship and custody.[30] The court may also make a finding terminating parental rights if they have not been terminated previously (see Chapter 5A.10). Finally, the court may find that the child is fit for adoption and the plaintiff is fit to adopt the child. In that case, a final hearing will be arranged in 6 to 9 months, and the approved adoption agency will be required to perform a final evaluation of the placement after visiting the home from time to time and making any other inquiries.

The final hearing is also in camera (i.e., private). At that time, the court will make a final order of adoption if it believes such a decision to be in the best interests of the child. Otherwise, the court is required to make any other orders concerning custody and guardianship that are proper. As in agency adoptions, all records of the proceeding shall then be sealed and only opened for "good cause."

Adoption Subsidies

Adoption subsidy is a program that provides monetary assistance and special services for children who otherwise may not be

---

27. N.J.S.A. 9:3-54.
28. N.J.S.A. 9:3-48.
29. *Id.*
30. *Id.*

adopted, making it possible to secure adoptive homes with people who meet all but the financial standards for adoptive parents. Children adopted under this program must be difficult to place for adoption because of physical or mental condition, race, age, membership in a sibling group, or any other reason.[31] A mental condition is further defined as a "diagnosed emotional or behavioral problem, psychiatric disorder, serious intellectual incapacity or brain damage which seriously affects the child's ability to relate to his peers or authority figures, including but not limited to a developmental disability."[32]

The adoptive family must be capable of providing the needed permanent family relationships. Except in adoption by the child's foster parent, there must have been prior reasonable efforts to place the child for adoption without providing subsidies.

Payments must be made by the Division of Youth and Family Services, although qualifying adoptees placed with other approved agencies are eligible for benefits. Required payments must cover maintenance costs, medical expenses, and other costs necessary for the care, training, and education of the child.[33] The amount of monthly payment for care and maintenance is 100% of the applicable foster care board rate, except that families who adopted prior to January 17, 1984, must continue to receive 80% of the board rate unless there is a dramatic decrease in their financial circumstances.[34] Any person aggrieved by an adoption subsidy decision by DYFS may appeal and receive an administrative hearing by the Office of Administrative Law.[35] No payments are permitted for any child whom DYFS determines was brought into the state for the sole purpose of qualifying for subsidies.[36]

---

31. N.J.S.A. 30:4C-46.
32. N.J.A.C. 10:121A-2.1.
33. N.J.S.A. 30:4C-47.
34. N.J.A.C. 10:121A-2.2 and 2.3.
35. N.J.A.C. 10:121A-2.4.
36. N.J.S.A. 30:4C-48.

5A.15

Delinquency and Juvenile–Family Crisis

The New Jersey Superior Court, Family Part, has the responsibility for hearing complaints about juveniles who are alleged to be delinquent or in a "juvenile-family crisis." Children who appear before the court may see an MHP as part of the process. While this generally occurs during the dispositional phase, MHPs may also contribute at other stages.

Terms and Definitions

Before considering how the law operates, it is important to understand the terms it employs and their legal meanings. Juvenile means an individual who is under the age of 18 years.[1] Delinquency means the commission of an act by a juvenile that if committed by an adult would constitute[2]

1. a crime;

2. a disorderly persons offense or petty disorderly persons offense; or

3. a violation of any other penal statute, ordinance, or regulation.

However, violations by juveniles of pedestrian, bicycle, and motorized bicycle offenses do not constitute delinquency and are within the jurisdiction of the municipal courts.

Juvenile-family crisis means behavior or a condition of a juvenile, parent, or other family member that results in[3]

---

1. N.J.S.A. 2A:4A-22.
2. N.J.S.A. 2A:4A-23.
3. N.J.S.A. 2A:4A-22(g).

1. a serious threat to the well-being and physical safety of a juvenile;
2. a serious conflict between a parent and a juvenile regarding rules of conduct that has been demonstrated by repeated disregard for lawful parental authority by a juvenile, or misuse of lawful parental authority by a parent;
3. unauthorized absence by a juvenile for more than 24 hours from his or her home; or
4. a pattern of repeated unauthorized absences from school by a juvenile required to attend classes.

Complaint

Any person who has direct or indirect knowledge of delinquency may sign a delinquency complaint.[4] The signed complaint must include the names and addresses of the juvenile and the parents and a citation of the law or ordinance allegedly violated. It also must describe the date, time, manner, and place of the alleged acts.

A petition alleging that a juvenile-family crisis exists must be signed by the court intake services.[5] It must include the names and addresses of the juvenile and parents, as well as the date, time, manner, and place of the alleged condition or behavior.

A juvenile charged with delinquency has the right to be represented by counsel at every critical stage of the proceeding that may result in institutional commitment.[6] All defenses available to an adult charged with a crime, offense, or violation are available to a juvenile charged with delinquency. The juvenile is entitled to all state and federal constitutional rights except the rights to indictment, trial by jury, and bail.[7]

Detention Hearing

A juvenile may be taken into short-term custody for up to 6 hours if a police officer believes that the juvenile's health and safety are in danger, if the juvenile is believed to have left home or a supervisory agency without consent, if the juvenile is arrested for delinquency, or if the officer acts pursuant to court order.[8] The parents must be notified immediately.[9]

---

4. N.J.S.A. 2A:4A-30 and R. 5:20-1.
5. Id.
6. N.J.S.A. 2A:4A-39.
7. N.J.S.A. 2A:4A-40.
8. N.J.S.A. 2A:4A-30 and 31.
9. N.J.S.A. 2A:4A-33.

Detention is defined as the temporary care of juveniles in physically restricting facilities pending court disposition of delinquency charges.[10] Where it will not adversely affect the juvenile's health, safety, or welfare, the juvenile must be released without detention pending the disposition of the case.[11] However, a juvenile charged with delinquency may be placed in detention if it is necessary to ensure his or her presence at the next hearing, or if the physical safety of persons or property would be seriously threatened and the juvenile is charged with a serious offense. The judge or court intake officer must consider other alternatives first, such as release to parents with conditions or placement in a shelter. The State Department of Corrections must specify placement for juvenile detention, and the Department of Human Services must specify the placement of a shelter.[12]

When a juvenile is taken into custody, a complaint must be filed immediately.[13] The court must determine whether the detention meets statutory criteria. Notice must be given to the juvenile and the parents, although the parents are not required at the hearing if they have been properly notified. If the judge determines that detention is not necessary, the juvenile may be released with or without conditions. If the judge continues detention after the hearing, there must be a second hearing within 2 days at which the juvenile must be represented by counsel. At that time, probable cause of the juvenile's delinquency must be demonstrated to continue detention. Additional detention review hearings must be held every 2 weeks prior to the dispositional hearing.

Dispositional Hearing

Before making a disposition, the court may refer the juvenile to an appropriate individual, agency, or institution for examination and evaluation.[14] The court may also consult any individuals, schools, agencies, or other knowledgeable parties. A parent who wished to present the results of a private, independent examination by an MHP would be able to do so under the right to call witnesses on the child's behalf. A dispositional hearing, with notice to all parties, must be held within 60 days of an adjudication and within 30 days if the juvenile is in detention.[15]

---

10. N.J.S.A. 2A:4A-22.
11. N.J.S.A. 2A:4A-34.
12. N.J.S.A. 2A:4A-37.
13. N.J.S.A. 2A:4A-38.
14. N.J.S.A. 2A:4A-42.
15. N.J.S.A. 2A:4A-41.

In determining the appropriate disposition for a delinquent juvenile, the court must weigh the following factors:[16]

1. the nature and circumstances of the offense;
2. the degree of injury to persons or damage to property;
3. the juvenile's age, previous record, prior social service received, and out-of-home placement history;
4. whether the disposition supports family strength, responsibility, and unity, as well as the well-being and physical safety of the child;
5. whether the disposition provides for reasonable participation by the child's parents;
6. whether the disposition recognizes and treats the unique physical, psychological, and social characteristics and needs of the child; and
7. whether the disposition contributes to the developmental needs of the child, including the academic and social needs where there is mental retardation or learning disabilities.

If the juvenile is adjudicated as delinquent, the court may order incarceration or any of the following dispositions:[17]

1. adjournment for 12 months in contemplation of dismissal;
2. release of the child to the supervision of parents or guardian;
3. probation for up to 3 years;
4. transfer of custody to any relative or other person;
5. placement under the responsibility of the Division of Youth and Family Services (DYFS) for the purpose of providing services in or out of the home;
6. services from the Division of Mental Retardation, if the child is eligible;
7. commitment for hospitalization under the Division of Mental Health and Hospitals;
8. a fine levied against the juvenile according to the law;
9. an order of restitution for any injuries or property damages;
10. community service under the supervision of the probation department or other agency or individual;
11. participation in a work program to provide job skills and employment training;

---

16. N.J.S.A. 2A:4A-43.
17. *Id.*

12. participation in a self-reliance program (such as Outward Bound);

13. participation in a program of academic or vocational education or counseling;

14. placement in a residential or nonresidential program for treatment of alcohol or narcotics abuse;

15. parental participation in appropriate programs;

16. placement in a nonresidential agency program for education, counseling, or family counseling;

17. postponement, suspension, or revocation of the juvenile's driver's license and/or registration, for up to 2 years, if an automobile was used in the act of delinquency; or

18. any other conditions reasonably related to rehabilitation of the juvenile.

If, after weighing all mitigating and aggravating factors, the court determines that the juvenile must be incarcerated, it must state the reasons and commit the youngster to a suitable institution maintained by the Department of Corrections.[18] The sentence may vary from months to 4 years for crimes of the first degree, and up to 20 years for some murders. The court may add an additional sentence for certain repeat offenders. The period of confinement must continue until it is decided that the person can be paroled; however, the total time of confinement plus parole cannot exceed the maximum allowed by law for a particular sentence. Early parole for crimes of a serious nature must be approved by the court.

Disclosure of Mental Health Information

Social, medical, psychological, legal, and other records of the court and probation department and records of law enforcement agencies must be safeguarded from public inspection. They can be made available only to courts, the probation department, the juvenile's parents and attorney, DYFS, an institution where the juvenile is committed, or to others by court order.[19] Law enforcement records may be disclosed to any law enforcement agency in the state.

Information as to the identity of a juvenile, and the adjudication and disposition of the case, must be disclosed to the victim or victim's family, involved law enforcement agencies, the principal of the juvenile's school (on a confidential basis), or a party in subsequent legal proceedings for impeachment purposes. In addition,

18. N.J.S.A. 2A:4A-44.
19. N.J.S.A. 2A:4A-60 and R. 5:19-2.

unless the judge finds that disclosure would be harmful to the juvenile, such information may be disclosed to the public when delinquent acts occurred that would be serious crimes if committed by an adult. The court may permit public attendance during delinquency proceedings where it determines that a substantial likelihood of specific harm to the juvenile would not result.

Upon the motion of an adjudicated delinquent, the court may seal all case records and vacate its order and findings, if the individual has not been convicted of a crime or adjudged delinquent for 2 years after final discharge and there are no pending proceedings in any case.[20]

Diversion and Juvenile-Family Crisis

Each county is required to maintain a court intake service that must screen all juvenile delinquency complaints and juvenile-family crisis referrals.[21] The intake service may make referrals to appropriate agencies, monitor referrals for the development and implementation of family service plans, and review and approve alternative living arrangements as provided by law. The court intake service has the responsibility of monitoring all admissions of alleged delinquents to detention or shelter care on a 24-hour per day basis.

Every complaint must be reviewed by the court intake service for recommendation as to whether it should be dismissed, diverted, or referred for court action.[22] If the complaint alleges a crime of the fourth degree or higher, or a repetitive disorderly persons offense, the case must be referred for court action, unless the prosecutor consents to diversion. Other complaints can be recommended for diversion on the basis of the seriousness and circumstances of the alleged offense, the age and maturity of the juvenile, the dangerousness of the juvenile, family circumstances including drug or alcohol use, the history of prior contacts, the availability of referral sources, and recommendations of the victim and prosecutor.

If the court intake services recommend diversion, the presiding judge and prosecuting attorney must be notified within 5 days, and a hearing may be ordered.[23] The court may divert a complaint to a court intake conference or a juvenile conference committee appointed by the court.[24] In either arrangement, notice is sent to

---

20. N.J.S.A. 2A:4A-62.
21. N.J.S.A. 2A:4A-70 and R. 5:15-2 et seq.
22. N.J.S.A. 2A:4A-71.
23. N.J.S.A. 2A:4A-72.
24. N.J.S.A. 2A:4A-73.

the juvenile and the parents as well as the victim.[25] All pertinent medical, psychological, social, and school records are requested. In considering relevant factors, the goal is to prevent future misconduct by obtaining the cooperation of the juvenile and the family in complying with conference recommendations.

The conference resolution may include counseling, restitution, referral to appropriate community agencies, or other appropriate recommendations (not including confinement or removal from the family). The presiding judge must approve the resolution, and if the juvenile objects at any time to the agreement, the matter shall be referred to the judge for a hearing. At the end of the 6-month diversion period, the court intake service may recommend that the judge dismiss the original complaint if the juvenile has complied with all agreements. Otherwise, the judge may order further obligations or a court hearing regarding the initial complaint.

Each county is also required to have a juvenile-family crisis intervention unit, which functions as part of the court intake service.[26] The unit must be staffed with master's level counselors, and it must provide 24-hour continuous short-term crisis intervention to juveniles and their families.[27] The crisis intervention unit must take referrals from police officers who take a juvenile into short-term custody and who believe that the youngster should not return home, that the juvenile is a runaway, or that the juvenile needs immediate emergency services such as medical or psychiatric care.[28] The crisis intervention unit may also receive referrals from a juvenile or parent or from an agency or institution.[29] The unit may provide short-term counseling to stabilize the family situation, but if necessary, a petition may be filed with the court for further processing by the court intake service.[30]

Whenever the court intake service determines that a juvenile-family crisis may exist, it will present its findings and recommendations to the court, which is then required to hold a hearing.[31] Notice must be given to the juvenile, the family, and the victim. The juvenile may present witnesses and evidence on his or her behalf at the hearing to rebut the intake service recommendations. The court must determine if there is a juvenile-family crisis as defined by statute (supra) and then may require the juvenile and any family members to participate in appropriate programs and services.

---

25. N.J.S.A. 2A:4A-74 and 75.
26. N.J.S.A. 2A:4A-76.
27. N.J.S.A. 2A:4A-77.
28. N.J.S.A. 2A:4A-80.
29. N.J.S.A. 2A:4A-81.
30. N.J.S.A. 2A:4A-83.
31. N.J.S.A. 2A:4A-86.

If, after crisis intervention, the juvenile refuses to return home, the parents refuse to permit a return to home, or it is necessary for the juvenile's care or safety, the court intake services may arrange an out-of-home placement of the juvenile with a relative, neighbor, or other suitable person.[32] There is no need for a court hearing unless there is a lack of agreement regarding the plans. In such case, temporary placement may be arranged in a family setting, shelter, foster home, or group home.[33]

A court hearing must be held after proper notification has been given both the juvenile and the parents.[34] The juvenile must have an attorney, provided by the court if necessary. The court may approve the temporary placement if there is a serious conflict between the juvenile and the parents that cannot be resolved by the delivery of services while the juvenile stays at home, or if the physical safety and well-being of the juvenile would be endangered. If the court orders temporary placement, it will direct DYFS or other agency to submit a family service plan to resolve the crisis. There must be an additional hearing at which the court will endorse or modify the family service plan and make a disposition. The court may order the Department of Human Services or other agency to be responsible for the case, and it may arrange parental visitation rights and transfer selected parental powers to the department. If the situation is severe enough to warrant long-term placement, the court may order such an arrangement, subject to review of the child placement review board (see Chapter 5A.13).[35]

---

32. N.J.S.A. 2A:4A-87.
33. N.J.S.A. 2A:4A-88.
34. N.J.S.A. 2A:4A-89.
35. N.J.S.A. 2A:4A-90.

5A.16

Competency of Juveniles to Stand Trial

Children who appear before the superior court on delinquency charges have most of the procedural protections available to adult defendants (see Chapter 5A.15), including the right to be aware of and participate in any proceedings against them.[1]

A juvenile found to be incompetent by the court may not waive any right.[2] A guardian ad litem must be appointed, who may waive rights only after discussion with the juvenile and the juvenile's attorney. Where there is a question regarding the competence of a juvenile to stand trial, the court must follow the procedure for adult criminal defendants (see Chapter 5D.5).

---

1. N.J.S.A. 2A:4A-40. *See, e.g.,* State in the Interest of R.G.W., 135 N.J. Super. 125, 342 A.2d 869 (App. Div. 1975), *aff'd,* 70 N.J. 185, 358 A.2d 473 (1976).
2. N.J.S.A. 2A:4A-39.

Non-Responsibility Defense

All defenses available to an adult charged with a crime, offense, or violation are also extended by statute to juveniles charged with delinquency.[1] This includes the insanity defense.[2] The legal standard for an insanity defense is the same for juveniles as for adults (see Chapter 5D.9). Proof of insanity does not limit the jurisdiction of the court over a minor; nor does it prevent a finding of delinquency despite the fact that the insanity defense would be a complete defense in an adult court.[3] A finding of insanity precludes penal sanctions but permits rehabilitative measures such as psychotherapy and psychiatric hospitalization.[4]

---

1. N.J.S.A. 2A:4A-40.
2. State in the Interest of R.G.W., 135 N.J. Super. 125, 342 A.2d 869 (App. Div. 1975), aff'd, 70 N.J. 185, 358 A.2d 473 (1976).
3. *In re* State in Interest of H.C., 106 N.J. Super. 583, 256 A.2d 322 (1969).
4. *Id.*

5A.18

Transfer of Juveniles to Stand Trial as Adults

Under certain circumstances (to be discussed below), the law allows a case to be transferred from a juvenile delinquency proceeding to an adult criminal proceeding. This is likely to occur either when the juvenile has a history of contacts with the juvenile court and further treatment is not likely to be beneficial, or when the crime is so serious that the child is likely to be incarcerated beyond his or her eighteenth birthday. The court, the prosecuting attorney, or the juvenile's attorney may request an evaluation by an MHP to provide evidence at the transfer hearing.

Initiation of Transfer Proceedings

A juvenile 14 years of age or older or a juvenile under 14 years charged with murder has the right to have a delinquency case transferred to the appropriate court having jurisdiction over the criminal offense.[1] Upon motion of the prosecutor, the court may also waive jurisdiction and transfer the case without the juvenile's consent, on the basis of its findings at a transfer hearing.[2]

Transfer Hearing

The juvenile court may waive jurisdiction and transfer the case for criminal prosecution if it finds after a hearing that the juvenile was

---

1. N.J.S.A. 2A:4A-27.
2. N.J.S.A. 2A:4A-26.

14 years old or older at the time of the alleged delinquent act and that there is probable cause to believe that the act (or attempt) if committed by an adult would constitute[3]

1. criminal homicide, robbery, aggravated sexual assault, aggravated assault, kidnapping, or aggravated arson;

2. a crime committed after the juvenile had previously been adjudicated delinquent or had been convicted of offenses listed (supra);

3. a crime committed after the juvenile had been sentenced and confined in an adult penal institution;

4. an offense against a person committed in an aggressive, violent, and willful manner, or the unlawful possession of a weapon, or arson;

5. an offense involving death by auto if the juvenile was operating the vehicle under the influence of alcohol or drugs;

6. crimes in concert with two or more persons that indicate a criminal livelihood; or

7. a crime involving the illegal distribution of drugs for profit within 1,000 feet of any school property.

The state must show that the nature and circumstances of the charge or the prior record of the juvenile are sufficiently serious that the interests of the public require waiver. However, the court will not order a transfer if the juvenile can show that "the probability of his rehabilitation by the use of the procedures, services and facilities available to the court prior to the juvenile reaching the age of 19 substantially outweighs the reasons for waiver."[4] Whatever testimony the juvenile may provide at the transfer hearing cannot be admissible in court to determine delinquency or guilt of any crime.[5]

---

3. *Id.*
4. *Id.*
5. N.J.S.A. 2A:4A-29.

5A.19

Voluntary Admission and Civil Commitment of Minors

Minors, who are defined as persons under 18, generally are covered under the same psychiatric hospitalization laws as adults (see Chapters 5E.3 and 5E.4), with a few special provisions.[1] MHPs may become involved in the process by recommending that a minor be hospitalized, by treating a hospitalized minor, or by participating in a commitment hearing.

Involuntary Civil Commitment

The commitment of minors must follow the court rules established for adults.[2] However, an order of commitment need not be based upon a finding that the patient is mentally ill and dangerous to himself or herself or others, but merely that the patient "is in need of intensive psychiatric therapy which cannot practically or feasibly be rendered in the home or in the community or on any outpatient basis."[3]

Any minor who is served with a commitment notice must be appointed a guardian ad litem to represent his or her interests in court and until the minor is released or reaches age 18.[4] In the occasional instances where the appointee is not an attorney, counsel must also be provided. If the minor is committed, the court must review the commitment every 3 months until discharge or the minor reaches his or her majority (at age 18).

---

1. N.J.S.A. 30:4-23 et seq. and R. 4:74-7.
2. R. 4:74-7(j).
3. R. 4:74-7(b)(2).
4. R. 4:74-7(c)(3).

Voluntary Admission of Minors 14 Years or Older

A minor 14 years or older may request a voluntary commitment regardless of the wishes of the parents or guardian.[5] If the court grants this request, the youngster would be treated the same as adults who voluntarily commit themselves. Consequently, the minor may demand discharge after 72-hours' notice, which must be granted unless involuntary commitment procedures are immediately instituted.[6] The court must review the voluntary commitment every 3 months, but the review can be in a summary proceeding.

Limited Admission of Minors by Parents

Parents or guardians may arrange for the admission of a minor for the evaluation or diagnosis of a mental condition for up to 7 days without court proceedings.[7] If further hospitalization is then required, normal involuntary commitment procedures must be followed, or voluntary commitment if the minor is 14 years or older and makes such a request.

5. R. 4:74-7(j).
6. *In re* Application of John Williams, 140 N.J. Super. 495, 356 A.2d 468 (1976).
7. R. 4:74-7(j).

5A.20

Education for Gifted and Handicapped Children

New Jersey law provides that all children, regardless of their intellectual level or learning ability, must be afforded an education that meets their needs.[1] MHPs may become involved in this process through evaluations of the children and consultations with special education personnel.

Terms and Definitions

Before discussing the process by which a child may be deemed eligible for special education services, it is helpful to understand the terms in the law.[2]

1. *Special education* means specially designed instruction to meet the educational needs of educationally handicapped pupils including, but not limited to, subject matter instruction, physical education, and vocational training.

2. *Related services for educationally handicapped pupils* means counseling for pupils and parents, speech-language services, recreation, occupational therapy, physical therapy, transportation, and any other appropriate service necessary to fulfill a student's individualized education program.

3. *Consent* means that the parent has been fully informed of all information relevant to the proposed activity, agrees in writing

---

1. N.J.S.A. 18A:46-1 et seq. and N.J.A.C. 6:28-1.1 et seq. State-mandated support services for handicapped students in New Jersey colleges are outside the scope of this chapter. *See* N.J.S.A. 18A:72H-1 et seq.
2. N.J.A.C. 6:28-1.3 and 3.5 and N.J.S.A. 18A:46-2.

to its implementation, and understands that such consent may be revoked at any time.

4. *Educationally handicapped pupil* means a student who has been determined to be eligible for special education and/or related services:

a. *Auditorily handicapped* means an inability to hear within normal limits because of physical impairment or a dysfunction of auditory mechanisms that impairs the processing of linguistic information.

b. *Communication handicapped* means a severe speech or language disorder that interferes with the ability to use oral language or to communicate. It may also refer to a mild to moderate disorder in language, articulation, voice, or fluency that makes one eligible for speech-language instruction by a speech correctionist or speech-language specialist.

c. *Emotionally disturbed* means the presence of seriously disordered behavior over a period of time, which affects educational performance and is characterized by (1) an inability to build or maintain satisfactory interpersonal relationships or (2) inappropriate behavior, depression, psychosomatic symptoms, or irrational fears.

d. *Mentally retarded* means cognitive, social, and academic functioning that is seriously below age expectations, comprehensive in nature, and demonstrated in home, school, and community settings: (1) educable mentally retarded refers to a mentally retarded person who is moderately below age expectations and scores within a range of two to three standard deviations below the mean in a standardized intelligence test; (2) trainable mentally retarded refers to a mentally retarded person who is severely below age expectations, needs direct and close supervision in all settings, and scores three standard deviations below the mean on intelligence tests; (3) eligible for day training refers to a mentally retarded person who functions at a level profoundly below age expectations, requiring significant personal care and supervision, demonstrates a significant deficit in the ability to understand and respond to simple verbal or nonverbal communication, and is unable to make known basic wants or needs.

e. *Multiply handicapped* means the presence of two or more educationally handicapping conditions that interact in such a manner that programs for individual handicaps will not be able to meet educational needs.

f. *Neurologically impaired* means a specific impairment or dysfunction of the nervous system that adversely affects the education of a pupil. An evaluation by a physician trained in neurodevelopmental assessment is required.

g. *Perceptually impaired* means a specific learning disability manifested in a disorder in understanding and learning, which affects the ability to listen, think, speak, read, write, spell, or compute.

h. *Orthopedically handicapped* means a condition that necessitates special education and/or related services because of malformation, malfunction, or loss of bones, muscle, or body tissue.

i. *Socially maladjusted* means a consistent inability to conform to the standard for behavior established by the school. Such behavior is seriously disruptive to self or others but is not due to emotional maladjustment (supra).

j. *Chronic illness* means a condition such as tuberculosis, cardiac condition, leukemia, asthma, seizure disorder, or other medical disability.

k. *Visually handicapped* means either blindness or partial sight.

1. *Preschool handicapped* means children ages 3 through 5 who have an identified handicapping condition and/or a measurable developmental impairment and would benefit from special education and related services.

Referral and Special Education Evaluation

The boards of education for every school district are responsible for the development and implementation of special education services for children between the ages of 3 and 21 who may be educationally handicapped.[3] Such services are mandatory for handicapped public school students, but they are provided only upon the consent of the parents of private school students.[4] In order to secure special education services, the child must first be evaluated to determine his or her need for it. The parents may request an evaluation, or the school may make a referral to the Child Study Team in the district after documenting efforts to alleviate the problem in the regular classroom.[5] Before the Child Study Team begins

---

3. N.J.A.C. 6:28-3.2.
4. N.J.S.A. 18A:46-19.5.
5. N.J.A.C. 6:28-3.3.

an evaluation, the parents must receive written notice and give consent. Parents have the right to appeal any action, including the proposed evaluation (infra).

The nature of the evaluation that will be conducted depends on the reason for the referral and the type of services sought. All assessments are conducted by a multidisciplinary Child Study Team that must include a school psychologist, a learning disabilities teacher-consultant, and a school social worker.[6] For children ages 3 to 5, the study team must also include a speech correctionist or language specialist.

A comprehensive health evaluation must be performed by a physician employed by the board of education or by a private physician. The Child Study Team must consult with a school physician when considering medical diagnostic services and with other professionals deemed appropriate. Pertinent information from the parents, teachers, and other school personnel must also be considered. In addition to performing its own psychological, social, and educational-learning disabilities assessment, the Child Study Team may agree to review private evaluations conducted by MHPs and other professionals outside of the educational system.[7]

Placement in a Special Education Program

When an initial evaluation is completed, a meeting must be convened to determine whether the pupil is eligible for special education and to determine a classification category of impairment or disability.[8] A pupil in need of special education may be mentally retarded, orthopedically handicapped, communication handicapped, visually handicapped, neurologically or perceptually impaired, chronically ill, emotionally disturbed, socially maladjusted, auditorily handicapped, or preschool handicapped.[9]

The parents must be given notice and invited to attend the classification conference.[10] Notice must include a statement of the action proposed, the reasons for the proposal, a description of any procedures, records or tests used in the decision, and a review of parental rights to appeal. The meeting shall include[11]

---

6. N.J.A.C. 6:28-3.1.
7. N.J.A.C. 6:28-3.4.
8. N.J.A.C. 6:28-3.5.
9. N.J.S.A. 18A:46-2.
10. N.J.A.C. 6:28-2.3.
11. *Id.*

1. the parents,
2. teachers having knowledge of the pupil's educational performance,
3. at least one member of the Child Study Team,
4. the referring certified school personnel, and
5. the school principal or his or her designate.

An individualized education plan will then be developed for the child and will form the basis by which future progress is measured. Educational program options include the following:[12]

1. instruction in school that complements regular or special class programs through supplementary instruction, speech-language services, modification of a normal program, and a resource room that provides individual and small-group instruction;
2. a special class in the pupil's local school district;
3. a special education program in another school district, a vocational school, a county special services district, or other approved program;
4. programs in hospitals or convalescent centers;
5. a program operated by a department of the New Jersey state government;
6. vocational rehabilitation facilities;
7. an approved private school for the handicapped, if other services are not appropriate, after prior approval from the Department of Education; and
8. individual instruction at home or elsewhere, with the prior written approval of the Department of Education.

The individualized education program shall consist of a basic plan and an instruction guide.[13] The basic plan shall be developed with the participation of the Child Study Team and the parents and shall be written upon completion of the Child Study Team's evaluation.

The basic plan of the individualized education program must include a statement of the pupil's[14]

1. eligibility for special education and/or related services,
2. current educational status,

---

12. N.J.A.C. 6:28-4.2.
13. N.J.A.C. 6:28-3.6(a). However, mentally retarded pupils who are eligible for day training are the responsibility of the Department of Human Services, which will prepare educational programs and administer day training centers. N.J.S.A. 18A:46-18.1.
14. N.J.A.C. 6:28-3.6(d).

3. annual educational performance goals,

4. educational objectives that provide measurable steps toward the performance goals, and

5. a description of the proposed educational program.

The educational program description must include[15]

1. a rationale for the type of program and placement chosen;

2. an explanation of why the program and placement are the least restrictive environment appropriate to the pupil's needs;

3. a description of the extent to which the pupil will participate in regular educational programs;

4. a description of exemptions from regular education program options including testing programs;

5. reasons why the individualized education program goals and objectives do not include the proficiencies measured by the High School Proficiency Test;

6. a statement of the alternate requirements for each exemption from state and local high school graduation requirements;

7. consideration of the preparation of the pupil for postsecondary education, work, or independent living;

8. a discussion of the length of time the pupil is expected to be in the special education program;

9. a statement of the language of the proposed instruction;

10. a description of the special education and related services, such as counseling and transportation, including their frequency and duration;

11. a description of the responsibilities and roles of school personnel; and

12. the criteria, procedure, and schedule for determining if the pupil's goals and objectives are being met.

Following the development of the basic plan, the member of the Child Study Team who has been designated the case manager must coordinate the development of the instructional guide.[16] The guide must be developed jointly by the case manager and the teachers of the pupil. Parents and other school personnel may also participate. The instructional guide must include instructional strategies, responsibilities, and time schedules of all teachers, as well as techniques and activities for the social and personal development of the pupil. An annual review of the placement clas-

---

15. N.J.A.C. 6:28-3.6(e)(5).
16. N.J.A.C. 6:28-3.6(f).

sification, the basic plan, and the instruction guide must be held with the case manager, parents, teachers, and pupil when appropriate. In addition, a full reevaluation of the pupil must be completed every 3 years.[17]

Parental Rights

Before the Child Study Team begins an evaluation, the parents must receive written notice and give consent.[18] Parents have the right to appeal any action, including the proposed evaluation. They have the right to attend meetings that determine the pupil's educational classification and eligibility for special education and/or related services. Notice to the parents and communications during meetings must be in a language understood by the parents, if it is feasible.[19] If the parents cannot be identified or located or if the child is a ward of the state, the board of education must appoint surrogate parents who will represent the educational interests of the student.[20]

Evaluation procedures are required to be individually administered by qualified personnel who sign a written report that interprets the information considering the pupil's sociocultural background as well as his or her adaptive behavior in the home and community.[21] Parents may request an independent evaluation if they disagree with the Child Study Team. The board of education must arrange for such evaluation to be performed by another school district at no cost to the parents, unless it initiates a due process hearing that finds the evaluation to be appropriate.

When disputes occur between the parents and the school district regarding a special education issue, the state is obligated to provide mediation if the parties agree to such services.[22] If mediation cannot resolve the issue, either party may request a due process hearing with regard to the referral, classification, evaluation, or educational placement of a pupil and/or the provision of a free appropriate public education for the pupil.[23]

A due process hearing may be initiated by a written request to the Director of the Division of Special Education, New Jersey

---

17. N.J.A.C. 6:28-3.7.
18. N.J.A.C. 6:28-2.3.
19. N.J.A.C. 6:28-2.4.
20. N.J.A.C. 6:28-2.2.
21. Id.
22. N.J.A.C. 6:28-2.6.
23. N.J.A.C. 6:28-2.7.

Department of Education.[24] Within 7 days of receiving such a request, the Department of Education must hold a conference at which the parties will either reach a settlement, withdraw, or transmit the case to the Office of Administrative Law for a hearing. The hearing must be held within 2 weeks by a judge from the Office of Administrative Law, and his or her decision is final.

---

24. *Id.*

5A.21

Consent, Confidentiality, and Services for Minors

Whenever a minor requests services or receives services without the parents' knowledge or consent (see Chapter 6.1), legal issues arise concerning the minor's capacity to give informed consent and the scope of the confidential relations between the minor and the MHP. Because failure to obtain consent from the appropriate person before providing services and failure to maintain confidential information are grounds for loss of licensure or for a malpractice suit or other type of civil liability for MHPs (see Chapters 6.5 and 6.6), it is important to know who the client is from a legal perspective—the minor or the parent. Unfortunately, New Jersey law does not broadly address these issues. This chapter discusses those circumstances that the law does address.

Confidentiality of Services From MHPs

Parents and guardians are generally responsible for providing the food, clothing, shelter, medical, and professional care of children. In that regard, they also have the right to select MHPs and to receive all relevant information about their children's diagnosis and treatment. This principle is recognized by implication in the licensing statutes governing psychologists and marriage counselors, which legally protect the minor's confidentiality only in discussions about venereal disease and abortion (see Chapters 1.3 and 1.8).[1] This exception is not extended statutorily to other MHPs.

---

1. N.J.A.C. 13:42-4.1 and 13:34-2.1.

Treatment for Narcotic Addiction

The law authorizes minors to give consent for treatment of drug addiction:[2]

> When a minor believes that he is suffering from the use of drugs or is a drug dependent person . . . , his consent to treatment under the supervision of a physician licensed to practice medicine shall be valid and binding as if the minor had achieved his or her majority, as the case may be. Any such consent shall not be subject to later disaffirmance by reason of minority.

Although it is clear that a minor would have the legal right to treatment from a licensed psychiatrist (see Chapter 1.1) or MHPs under the psychiatrist's supervision, it is unclear whether the law would be interpreted to include independent treatment from licensed psychologists (see Chapter 1.3).

This law may represent a "pregnant negative," that is, a law that allows action under certain conditions implicitly prohibits the action at all other times. To state it another way as it pertains to this law, a physician's treatment of a minor is consensual even without a parent's consent only when the child is suffering from drug abuse or dependence; this implies that treatment for any other condition requires parental consent.[3]

Although the minor has the right to obtain treatment for drug abuse without parental consent, the confidentiality of such treatment is in question. Although neither the minor nor the physician is obligated to report such treatment to anyone, the physician is legally permitted to inform the parents or guardian about any treatment given or needed regardless of the minor's wishes.[4]

Voluntary Admission of Minors 14 Years or Older

A minor 14 years or older may request a voluntary commitment to a hospital for psychiatric treatment regardless of the wishes of the parents or guardian (see Chapter 5A.19). If the court grants

---

2. N.J.S.A. 9:17A-4. This law also extends to treatment of a minor who believes he or she has venereal disease.
3. However, the United States Supreme Court has held that a minor has a constitutional right to receive medical treatment for an abortion (and perhaps other conditions) without parental consent (see Chapter 5A.22).
4. N.J.S.A. 9:17A-5.

this request, the youngster would be treated the same as adults who voluntarily commit themselves. Consequently, the minor may demand discharge after 72 hours' notice, which must be granted unless involuntary commitment proceedings are immediately instituted.[5] The court must review the voluntary commitment every 3 months, but the review can be in a summary proceeding.

---

5. *In re* Application of John Williams, 140 N.J. Super. 495, 356 A.2d 468 (1976).

5A.22

Consent for Abortion

Although it is constitutionally forbidden for the state to give parents a veto power over a mature minor woman's informed consent to an abortion,[1] some states have imposed constitutionally permissible parental notification requirements.[2] However, New Jersey has not enacted such a law at this time.

When a guardian of an incompetent person wishes to have the ward's pregnancy terminated, the court must apply a three-pronged test.[3] First, the court must decide whether the incompetent lacks the capacity to make a decision. If not, the court must decide what decision the incompetent would have made if she were able to choose, on the basis of available evidence. If the court is unable to make a substitute judgment, then it must determine whether the abortion is in the incompetent's best interests. Expert testimony by MHPs may be relevant in the determination.

1. Planned Parenthood of Central Missouri v. Danforth, 428 U.S. 52, 96 S.Ct. 2831, 49 L.Ed. 2d 788 (1976); Bellotti v. Baird, 428 U.S. 132, 96 S.Ct. 2857, 49 L.Ed. 2d 844 (1976); Matter of Grady, 170 N.J. Super. 98, 405 A.2d 851 (1979).
2. Hodgson v. Minnesota, 110 S.Ct. 2926, 111 L.Ed.2d 344 (1990).
3. D.R. by A.F. v. Daughters of Miriam Center for the Aged, 247 N.J. Super. 464, 589 A.2d 668 (1990).

Evaluation and Treatment of Children at the Request of a Noncustodial Parent

MHPs may be asked to provide services to children at the request of noncustodial parents. If they complied with this request, would they be liable for malpractice for failing to obtain consent from the custodial parent?

Some state laws provide that where one parent has custody, that person exercises exclusive authority concerning the care and upbringing of the child; the noncustodial parent does not have authority to give legal consent to evaluation or treatment decisions regarding the child. Although New Jersey does not have such a statute, it is probable that the courts would uphold such a principle in individual cases. The noncustodial parent might only circumvent this by obtaining joint custody, by securing an agreement from the custodial parent that the noncustodial parent will be allowed to make decisions in this area, or by filing a motion in the superior court alleging that the child's emotional development will be significantly impaired unless the noncustodial parent can have the child provided with the services of an MHP.

The law also makes it a crime of the third degree to interfere with custody by knowingly taking or enticing a child under the age of 18 from the custody of the parent or guardian when he or she has no privilege to do so, or if done in violation of a court order.[1] Crimes of the third degree are punishable by 3 to 5 years imprisonment, a fine of up to $7,500, or both. Defenses against such charges are the following:

1. that the person reasonably believed that the taking was consented to by the other parent or by a state agency;

---

1. N.J.S.A. 2C:13-4.

2. that the child was at least 14 years old and was taken away at his or her own volition, without purpose to commit a criminal offense;

3. that the parent reasonably believed that the child was in imminent danger and so notified the police or Division of Youth and Family Services within 24 hours; or

4. that a parent having custody reasonably believed that he or she was fleeing from imminent physical danger from the other parent, and notified the police or began a legal action affecting custody.

In conclusion, MHPs who provide services at the request of a noncustodial parent without first obtaining the permission of the custodial parent may be vulnerable to a malpractice claim on the basis that consent to the services was not given (see Chapter 6.1).

Other Civil Matters

5B.1

Mental Status of Licensed/Certified Professionals

State laws governing the licensure of professionals are increasingly including provisions concerning the mental status of these persons. Such provisions generally pertain to disciplinary procedures involving possible suspension and revocation of licensure, rather than license application screening. MHPs may be asked to evaluate and testify before the credentialing board and/or a court concerning the professional's mental status and its effect on job performance.

Attorneys

Although other professions are governed by state licensing boards, the regulation of attorneys rests with the state judiciary. Court rules specify the circumstances under which the mental status of attorneys can affect their authority to practice. The rules state that when a practicing attorney has been judicially declared incompetent or involuntarily committed to a mental hospital, the New Jersey Supreme Court must enter an order transferring him or her to "disability inactive" status.[1] That status must be reversed upon a judicial finding that the attorney has been restored to competency.

In addition, whenever the Director of the Office of Attorney Ethics presents evidence questioning the capacity of an attorney to practice law, owing to mental or physical infirmity or to addiction, the Disciplinary Review Board must direct that the attorney submit to appropriate medical examinations to make a determination regarding incapacity.[2] If the board concludes that the attorney lacks

---

1. R. 1:20-9.
2. R. 1:20-9(b).

the capacity to practice law, it must recommend to the supreme court that the attorney be transferred to "disability inactive" status until further order of the court. No disciplinary proceedings against the attorney shall be delayed unless the court finds that he or she is temporarily incapable of assisting counsel in defense of any ethics proceedings.

The investigation of an attorney's competence may be raised and investigated by the Disciplinary Review Board, independent of ethical concerns or violations. The standard of proof at a board hearing is "clear and convincing evidence." The attorney must submit to appropriate medical examinations, and the board may recommend "disability inactive" status due to incapacity. The Supreme Court of New Jersey makes the ultimate finding. The disability finding precludes the practice of law, and the disabled attorney must follow rules governing suspended attorneys. An attorney may apply periodically for reinstatement, which has to be approved by the supreme court.

In any investigation by the Disciplinary Review Board, the attorney must waive the physician–patient privilege. The attorney must disclose the name of every psychiatrist, psychologist, physician, and hospital by whom the attorney has been examined or treated. In addition, the board may review all examination and treatment records.

Other Licensed Professionals

The general licensing law governs the conduct of accountants, architects, barbers and hairstylists, chiropractors, electrical contractors, dentists, morticians, engineers and land surveyors, marriage counselors, physicians, nurses, optometrists, opticians, pharmacists, professional planners, psychologists, master plumbers, shorthand reporters, veterinarians, radiologic technicians, acupuncturists, and social workers (see Chapter 1.0).[3] The law provides that any of these professionals may be denied a license or have a license suspended or revoked if the person "is incapable, for medical or any other good cause, of discharging the functions of a licensee in a manner consistent with the public's health, safety and welfare."[4] This provision allows for the psychological evaluation of any licensed professional and the limitation on licensure for emotional impairment that adversely affects practice. In addition, any professional board may "order any person, as a condition for continued, reinstated or renewed licensure, to secure medical or such other

---

3. N.J.S.A. 45:1-3.1.
4. N.J.S.A. 45:1-21.

professional treatment as may be necessary to properly discharge licensee functions."[5] This provision enables a board to order treatment by MHPs for any professional, as a condition of licensure.

In addition to the provisions of the general licensing law, individual licensing statutes sometimes specify or imply mental conditions that affect licensure. Physicians can have licenses revoked if they are adjudicated insane or if they are mentally incapacitated.[6] Nurses may be disciplined for unfitness or incapacity.[7] Professional misconduct by psychologists includes the failure to ensure competence by taking steps to ameliorate personal problems.[8] Acupuncturists can lose their license if they have been adjudicated insane.[9] Furthermore, many specific licensing statutes allow for the loss of licensure for professional incompetence and for drug or alcohol abuse. However, the general licensing law in New Jersey provides for the evaluation and treatment of professionals more effectively and comprehensively than the specific licensing statutes.

---

5. N.J.S.A. 45:1-22.
6. N.J.S.A. 45:9-16.
7. N.J.S.A. 45:11-32.
8. N.J.A.C. 13:42-4.1.
9. N.J.S.A. 45:9B-12.

5B.2

Workers' Compensation

Workers' compensation law provides employees with protection against the treatment costs and income losses resulting from work-related accidents or disease. The employer purchases compensation insurance (or is self-insured) to provide the benefits for its employees. These benefits are awarded regardless of whether anyone, the employee or the employer, is at fault. In return, the employee relinquishes the right to sue the employer.[1] The employee may elect to forego benefits and retain the right to sue only if workers' compensation coverage is rejected by either employer or employee prior to an accident. Otherwise, the employee is presumed to have elected the coverage.

This law pertains primarily to psychologists and psychiatrists; they may become involved in this process in two ways. First, an injured employee may consult one of these professionals for diagnosis and treatment, with the costs for these services paid by workers' compensation insurance. Second, an insurance company may request a psychologist or psychiatrist to conduct an independent evaluation to determine the nature and extent of an employee's injury and testify about the findings at a hearing.

Scope of the Coverage

Workers' compensation benefits are payable for accidents[2] or diseases[3] arising out of and in the course of employment. Com-

---

1. N.J.S.A. 34:15-8.
2. N.J.S.A. 34:15-7.
3. N.J.S.A. 34:15-30 et seq.

pensation is provided without regard to the negligence of the employer, according to a fixed schedule of statutory benefits. In New Jersey, the principles that govern the granting or denial of an award do not differ on the basis of whether a case is labeled an accident or a disease.[4] An accident need not be an external, unlooked-for event; it merely needs to be an accidental injury that arises out of the employment.[5] An accident arises out of employment "when it results from risks reasonably incidental to employment," meaning risks that "belong to" or are "connected with what a workman has to do in fulfilling his contract of service."[6] Statutory exceptions to compensation for an accident include situations where the injury or death is "proximately" caused by[7]

1. intentional self-infliction;[8]
2. intoxication or the use of controlled dangerous substances (drugs);
3. failure to use a personal protective device despite repeated warnings from the employer (except in emergency situations); or
4. recreational or social activities, except if they are a regular incident of employment and produce a benefit to the employer beyond improvement in employee health and morale.

For an occupational disease to be compensable, it must be shown that the disease[9]

1. arose out of and in the course of employment; and
2. is due in a material degree to causes and conditions that are or were characteristic of or peculiar to a particular trade, occupation, process, or place of employment.

Deterioration of a tissue, organ, or part of the body in which the function of such part is diminished owing to the natural aging process is not compensable.

Classification of an injury or an occupational disease is important because an injury that does not meet the requirements for one or the other cannot be compensated.

---

4. Giambattista v. Thomas A. Edison, 32 N.J. Super. 103, 107 A.2d 801 (App. Div. 1954).
5. Ciuba v. Irvington Varnish & Insulator Co., 27 N.J. 127, 141 A.2d 761 (1958).
6. Hammond v. The Great Atlantic & Pacific Tea Co., 56 N.J. 7, 14, 264 A.2d 204, 206 (1970).
7. N.J.S.A. 34:15-7.
8. However, if the suicide is the result of a mental disturbance caused by a work-related injury and its consequences, the suicide is compensable. Kahle v. Plochman, Inc., 85 N.J. 539, 428 A.2d 913 (1981).
9. N.J.S.A. 34:15-31.

Workers' Compensation and Mental Stress/Disorder

Physical accidents that cause psychological disability are compensable in New Jersey case law.[10] Likewise, job-related stress that contributes in a material degree to physical disability including heart attack, stroke, or death is a compensable accident.[11]

There is an "objective" test for determining whether mental illness can be compensated as an occupational disease induced by repetitive work stress. The illness must[12]

> arise out of the employment. That is, it must be due in some realistic sense and material degree to a risk reasonably incidental to the employment; the onset must issue from or be contributed to by conditions which bear some essential relation to the work or its nature.

Processing a Claim

Both statutory and administrative rules of procedure govern workers' compensation claims.[13] The law provides for two claim processes: the formal claim and the informal claim. The informal claim is initiated by filing a petition with the Division of Workers' Compensation in the Department of Labor and Industry to request an informal hearing.[14] At the hearing conference, the parties, with the assistance of the workers' compensation judge, attempt to reach agreement on the extent of disability.[15] Testimony is taken from the claimant and any expert witnesses. It is possible to file a formal claim following the hearing even if the parties enter into a signed agreement.

If a formal claim is filed, each side prepares for trial by arranging medical and MHP evaluations with expert witnesses. If there is no agreement on the extent of disability following a pretrial conference, a formal trial before a workers' compensation judge will be held.[16] The decision becomes a permanent record of the Division of Workers' Compensation, but it may be appealed to the superior court.[17] The judge awards attorneys fees as part of the

---

10. Simon v. R. H. H. Steel Laundry, 25 N.J. Super. 50, 95 A.2d 446 (1953).
11. Van Ness v. Borough of Haledon, 136 N.J.L. 623, 56 A.2d 888 (1948). *See also* Evans v. Lenox, Inc., 121 N.J. Super. 407, 297 A.2d 582 (App. Div. 1972).
12. Williams v. Western Electric Co., 178 N.J. Super. 571, 585, 429 A.2d 1063, 1070 (App. Div. 1980).
13. N.J.S.A. 34:15-1 et seq. and N.J.A.C. 12:235-1.1 et seq.
14. N.J.A.C. 12:235-6.1 et seq.
15. N.J.A.C. 12:235-6.14.
16. N.J.A.C. 12:235-5.1.
17. N.J.S.A. 34:15-66.

decision. If a settlement is reached, it is entered on the record with the right of the employee to reopen the case if necessary. An employer is permitted to offer a "Section 20" settlement, in which a final payment is made in return for the dismissal of the case and the removal of the right to future medical treatment or reopening of the issues.[18]

Notice of an accidental injury must be given to an employer within 90 days,[19] except for an inguinal hernia, which requires 48 hours' notice.[20] The statute of limitations on filing a claim for an accidental injury is 2 years following the date of the accident.[21] However, if medical treatment was received or voluntary payments were made, the 2-year period starts after the last treatment or payment.

If the basis for the claim is an occupational disease, notice must be given to the employer within 5 months after the worker stopped being exposed to the conditions that caused the disease, or 90 days after the worker knew or should have known the relationship between the disability and employment.[22] The statute of limitations on filing a claim is 2 years following the date that the worker knew or should have known the nature of the disability and its relation to the employment.[23]

Following an approved settlement or an adjudicated finding, it is possible to file an application for review or modification of the findings, if a person's condition worsens or if a new impairment is developed as a consequence of the original injury or disease.[24] The statute of limitations is 2 years after the last receipt of payments.

Workers' Compensation Benefits

The employer must provide the worker with medical benefits to care for all necessary treatment of the injury or disease.[25] The worker is required to request treatment from the employer. The employer is entitled to select its own physicians, except if there is an emergency or the employer refuses to provide treatment.

Disability payments cover the loss of income during recuperation and are classified according to the seriousness of the injury (i.e., whether it results in a total or partial loss of income) and its

---

18. N.J.S.A. 34:15-20.
19. N.J.S.A. 34:15-17.
20. N.J.S.A. 34:15-12(c)(23).
21. N.J.S.A. 34:15-51.
22. N.J.S.A. 34:15-33.
23. N.J.S.A. 34:15-34.
24. N.J.S.A. 34:15-27.
25. N.J.S.A. 34:15-15.

duration (i.e., whether it is permanent or temporary).[26] It is possible, however, for an injury to result in more than one classification. For instance, although an injury may initially prevent an employee from working (a temporary total condition), it may eventually subside, allowing the person to return to work part time (permanent partial disability). The rating of the percentage of functional impairment must be in accordance with statute.[27] Disability awards are divided into scheduled and unscheduled benefits. Scheduled benefits concern loss of bodily function such as deafness or loss of a limb; unscheduled benefits concern all other injuries and require a determination of the extent and nature of the impairment.[28]

Death benefits cover burial expenses and payments to the employee's dependents.

---

26. N.J.S.A. 34:15-36.
27. N.J.S.A. 34:15-12.
28. *Id.*

5B.3

Vocational Disability Determinations

The Division of Vocational Rehabilitation Services (DVRS) in the Department of Labor and Industry administers a vocational rehabilitation program funded jointly by the state and federal governments for persons who have a physical or mental disability that currently prevents them from obtaining employment, but who might be able to engage in a gainful occupation if given vocational rehabilitation services.[1] These services include assessment and psychotherapy from psychologists and psychiatrists. Other mental health workers are directly employed by the DVRS as rehabilitation counselors; they provide nonpsychological and nonpsychiatric services in accordance with division policies.

Recipient Eligibility Requirements

To be eligible for services from DVRS, an individual must meet the following criteria:[2]

1. the individual has a physical or mental disability that for that person constitutes or results in a substantial handicap to employment; and

2. vocational rehabilitation services may reasonably be expected to benefit the individual in terms of employability.

---

1. N.J.S.A. 34:16-1 et seq. and N.J.A.C. 12:45-1.1 et seq. Administrative regulations were in the process of revision as this volume went to press.
2. N.J.A.C. 12:45-1.2 and 1.4.

Evaluation and Rehabilitation

Applicants will be accepted first for a preliminary diagnostic study to determine whether they meet recipient eligibility requirements. The study must include[3]

1. an appraisal of the current general health of the individual, on the basis of available medical information;

2. an evaluation by an appropriate medical specialist, when necessary, to determine the current status of the disorder causing the disability;

3. evaluations by qualified personnel of the potential to benefit from rehabilitation engineering services; and

4. in cases of mental or emotional disorder, an examination by a physician skilled in the diagnosis and treatment of such a disorder, or by a licensed psychologist. (In cases of mental retardation, reports from certified school psychologists may be used to document the disability.)

Individuals may select their own physicians and psychologists to conduct the medical examinations provided that they will accept DVRS fees.

After a person is determined to be eligible for DVRS services, a thorough diagnostic study is required to determine the nature and scope of needed services.[4] This must include an evaluation of the individual's functional capacities and limitations, personality, intelligence level, educational achievement, work experience, personal adjustment, vocational and social adjustment, employment opportunities, patterns of work behavior, facility to acquire occupational skill, capacity for successful job performance, employability, need for rehabilitation engineering services, and any other pertinent data.

If the person has a disability that results in a substantial handicap to employment, but DVRS is unable, without an extended evaluation, to determine whether vocational rehabilitation services might benefit the person in terms of employability, DVRS may offer one such evaluation for a maximum period of 18 months.[5]

If the individual is determined to be eligible for rehabilitation services, an individualized written rehabilitation program must be prepared for him or her.[6] It must provide for rehabilitation services, including the evaluation of vocational rehabilitation potential;

---

3. N.J.A.C. 12:45-1.5.
4. N.J.A.C. 12:45-1.6.
5. N.J.A.C. 12:45-1.7.
6. N.J.A.C. 12:45-1.11.

counseling and guidance from DVRS; vocational and training services; maintenance payments; transportation; services to family members when appropriate; interpreter and notetaking services for the deaf; telecommunications and other technological aids; vocational recruitment and training services; placement in suitable employment; postemployment services; occupational licenses; rehabilitation engineering services; any other reasonable goods and services; and physical and mental restoration services necessary to correct or substantially modify a physical or mental condition that is stable or slowly progressive.[7] *Mental restoration services* refers to the diagnosis and treatment for mental or emotional disorders by a physician skilled in the diagnosis and treatment of such disorders or by a licensed psychologist.[8]

All individual records remain confidential.[9] When a client or a representative makes a written request for personal records, the DVRS must make the information accessible.[10] However, medical and psychological information that could be harmful cannot be released directly to the individual but may be provided through the parent, guardian, representative, physician, or licensed psychologist. *Harmful information* refers to information that may be detrimental to the physical or emotional state of the individual or that may cause the individual to pose a threat to self or others.

When a client requests the release of information to other programs or authorities and provides written consent, the DVRS may release only personal information that may be released to the client, and only to the extent that the other organization demonstrates that the information requested is necessary for its program.[11] Medical or psychological information that the DVRS believes may be harmful to the individual may be released only when the other agency assures that it will not be further released to the involved individual. The DVRS will also release personal information if required by federal law, in response to criminal investigations, or for protection if the client poses a threat to self or others.

If a shortage of funds prevents the provision of services to all eligible clients, services must be prioritized. Clients classified as severely handicapped receive first priority, disabled public safety officers next, followed by nonseverely disabled individuals, and then all other clients.[12] Individuals are entitled to a formal administrative review, represented by counsel, if they are dissatisfied

---

7. N.J.A.C. 12:45-1.13.
8. N.J.A.C. 12:45-1.1.
9. N.J.S.A. 34:16-33.
10. N.J.A.C. 12:45-1.16.
11. *Id.*
12. N.J.A.C. 12:45-1.8.

with any action regarding the furnishing or denial of DVRS services.[13]

Psychological and Psychiatric Services

Some states specify particular psychiatric and psychological services and fees in their statutory or administrative codes. DVRS limits such provisions to the requirement that programs designed for psychosocial rehabilitation be staffed with a consulting psychiatrist.[14] Other staffing decisions are made by the executive director of each DVRS evaluation and/or service facility. However, all consulting psychiatrists for DVRS must be board certified.[15] There are no regulatory provisions for staff or consulting psychologists, although facilities must provide such services as necessary.

---

13. N.J.A.C. 12:45-1.17.
14. N.J.A.C. 12:51-7.1.
15. N.J.A.C. 12:51-9.1.

5B.4

Emotional Distress as a Basis for Civil Liability

Emotional distress, also known as mental suffering or distress, may be the basis for a civil tort suit (i.e., a lawsuit alleging physical or personal injury) or be part of a larger claim. The cause of the distress, the nature of the injury, and the motivations of the injuring person determine whether a suit must be part of a larger claim or can stand by itself. MHPs may be asked to evaluate the person who claims to have suffered the distress and to testify as to its etiology, severity, and duration, as well as methods of treating it.

Intentional Infliction of Emotional Distress

New Jersey law provides some protection against vexing harassment (e.g., from dunning creditors or outrageous neighbors) by allowing a person to sue for intentional infliction of emotional distress. Generally speaking, the plaintiff must establish intentional and outrageous conduct by the defendant, proximate cause, and severe distress. More specifically,[1]

1. the plaintiff must prove that the defendant acted intentionally to produce emotional distress, or recklessly in deliberate disregard of a high probability that emotional distress would follow;

---

1. Buckley v. Trenton Saving Fund Soc'y, 111 N.J. 355, 544 A.2d 857 (1988). *See also* Hume v. Bayer, 178 N.J. Super. 310, 428 A.2d 966 (1981).

2. the defendant's conduct must be so outrageous in character and so extreme in degree as to go beyond all possible bounds of decency, and to be regarded as atrocious and utterly intolerable in a civilized community;

3. the defendant's actions must have been the proximate cause of the plaintiff's emotional distress; and

4. the emotional distress must be so severe that no reasonable person could be expected to endure it.

Complaints that amount to nothing more than aggravation, embarrassment, headaches, and the loss of sleep will not be severe enough to warrant a finding of emotional distress.[2]

The court must decide whether as a matter of law such emotional distress can be found, and the jury decides whether it has in fact been proved. There need not be any physical injury except if the intentional conduct is directed at a third party other than the plaintiff, such as a close relative.

Negligent Infliction of Emotional Distress

The law also provides for protection against negligent infliction of emotional distress. An individual can establish such a claim where[3]

1. the death or serious physical injury of another was caused by the defendant's negligence;

2. a marital or intimate, familial relationship existed between the plaintiff and the injured person;

3. the plaintiff observed the death or injury at the scene of the accident; and

4. the plaintiff suffered severe emotional distress.

Thus, a mother who watched her son die in an elevator accident and who later became suicidal was able to sue the elevator company for negligence.[4] However, any recovery for emotional harm must be reduced by the proportion of the injured party's negligence, as well as by any contributory negligence on the part of the plaintiff.

---

2. Id.
3. Portee v. Jaffee, 84 N.J. 88, 417 A.2d 521 (1980).
4. Id.

Emotional Distress as an Element of Damages

Both of the foregoing claims require the presence of emotional distress. There are other claims, however, that do not require emotional distress to prove liability on the part of the defendant (i.e., a suit by a plaintiff who was physically injured by a defendant's negligence). Such a suit may include emotional distress as an element of damages, however.

Psychological problems that are causally connected to the defendant's acts may be considered by the jury when assessing the amount of damages, even when there is no longer an underlying organic basis for the complaints.[5] However, claims for emotional distress as part of a wrongful death action are prohibited by statute.[6] In this type of action, the decedent's spouse, children, and parents have a claim against the defendant for any damages they may have suffered as a result of the defendant's wrongful conduct against the decedent.

Finally, there are other claims that invoke, directly or indirectly, some measure of emotional distress, such as false imprisonment, slander, or invasion of privacy. These are referred to as dignitory torts (i.e., an injury to the person's reputation or personal sense of worth), yet it is clear that the damage is largely to one's emotional well-being. While these claims do not require evidence of emotional harm to the plaintiff in order to prove liability, the size of the damage award may hinge on such proof.

---

5. Buckley v. Trenton Savings Fund Soc'y, *supra*.
6. N.J.S.A. 2A:31-5.

5B.5

Insanity of Wrongdoers and Civil Liability

A person's mental status may affect whether he or she is liable under civil law for injurious behavior caused to another, whether the person can sue another for wrong caused to him or her, and whether any special procedural rights will be provided to ensure a fair trial. Furthermore, and potentially more important, a party's mental status at the time of the conduct may determine whether the person is covered under a liability insurance policy. MHPs may therefore be asked to evaluate the person and testify as to that person's mental status when the injuries occurred and at the time of trial.

The Liability of an Insane[1] Person

In many states, mentally disordered adults are civilly responsible for injuries they cause to others or property.[2] That is, persons who are suffering from a mental disorder that prevents them from either seeing the consequences of their actions or knowing that they are wrong or dangerous will still be liable just as if they were persons with their faculties intact. In the one case in New Jersey that addressed this issue, the court accepted such a rule.[3] The court held that a schizophrenic who failed to take his scheduled shot of an antipsychotic medication and who subsequently became psychotic and damaged his landlord's property was grossly negligent for his failure and was subject to summary eviction for such negligence.

---

1. *Insane* is a legal, not a psychological, term.
2. Restatement (Second) of Torts § 283B.
3. Stuyvesant Associates v. John Doe, 221 N.J. Super. 340, 534 A.2d 448 (1987).

Insanity and Liability Insurance

Despite the potential for personal liability, insurance policies routinely contain exclusionary clauses that deny coverage for personal injuries or property damage intentionally caused by the insured. The exclusion may also extend to the costs of legal representation. However, if the person is mentally ill, it is unclear what criteria would be used to determine if such acts were intentional. Although the New Jersey courts have not dealt with this issue, the New Jersey Supreme Court has upheld the right of automobile insurers to exclude intentional torts from liability coverage.[4]

Procedural Rights of Insane Persons

New Jersey Court Rules provide that a person who is mentally incompetent must be given sufficient procedural protections to protect his or her right to a fair trial. An infant or an incompetent person must be represented in an action by the guardian of either his or her person or property (see Chapters 5A.2, 5A.3, 5A.11, and 5A.12), or if no such guardian has been appointed or if there is a conflict of interest between the guardian and the ward, the court may appoint a guardian ad litem on the motion of a party or on its own motion.[5] As one court stated,[6]

> The function of the guardian ad litem is generally to insure the protection of the rights and interests of a litigant who is apparently incompetent to prosecute or defend a lawsuit. . . . Adjudication of incompetency is not necessary; it is "sufficient if the proof makes it evident that the party from any cause, whether by age, disease, affliction, or extreme intemperance, has become incapable and unfit for the government of himself and his property."

The guardian ad litem does not take responsibility for any other aspect of the person's life except for the suit. He or she may be any person who is capable of the duties. Frequently it is an attorney, but it may also be a lay person who then arranges for legal representation as is necessary.

Incompetency is not defined in the rules. Presumably, if a guardian is appointed, the definition is based on the laws of guardianship (supra). However, if a guardian ad litem is appointed, the person's incompetence may be more narrow in scope, limited to

---

4. Allstate Insurance Co. v. Malec, 104 N.J. 1, 514 A.2d 832 (1986).
5. R. 4:26-2. *See also* R. 4:34-2.
6. *In re* Commitment of S.W., 158 N.J. Super. 22, 25, 385 A.2d 315, 317 (App. Div. 1978); quoting from East Paterson v. Karkus, 136 N.J. Eq. 286, 288, 41 A.2d 332, 334 (1945).

defending one's interests effectively in a lawsuit. The mere fact that a person is a mental patient does not necessarily mean that he or she is incompetent; nor does mental illness automatically warrant the appointment of a guardian ad litem.[7]

---

7. *Id.*

5B.6

Competency to Contract

A person wishing to buy or sell property[1] must have a minimum mental capacity. This is a passive requirement in that everyone is expected to possess it. It can become an issue if one of the parties to the contract (or that person's legal representative, such as a guardian) wishes to be relieved from executing his or her part of the agreement. An MHP may be asked to evaluate the competence of the person and to testify as to the mental status either before or at the time the person entered into the contract.

Legal Test of Competency to Contract

The test of whether a person was competent to enter into a contract is whether he or she had the mental capacity to comprehend and understand it, or whether "he was so bereft of reason that he was incapable of consciously understanding the nature, import, and effect of his act."[2] It is possible, however, that an unusual contract may only become effective upon the occurrence of a specified event. In that case, capacity is at issue also at the time of that event.

The settled rule of law is that[3]

---

1. Competency to contract also pertains to the conveyance of deeds for real property. That is, whereas a contract obligates one or more persons to undertake some action, a deed is the actual document whereby real property is transferred. Where the conveyance of a deed is contested on the basis of incompetency, the party wishes to undo the transfer of property.
2. Hillside Nat'l Bank v. Sansone, 11 N.J. Super. 390, 398, 78 A.2d 441, 445 (1951).
3. Drake v. Crowell, 40 N.J.L. 58, 59 (Sup. Ct. 1878).

[c]ontracts with lunatics and insane persons are invalid, subject to the qualification that a contract made in good faith with a lunatic, for a full consideration, which has been executed without knowledge of the insanity, or such information as would lead a prudent person to the belief of the incapacity, will be sustained.

Thus, if an incompetent person makes a contract and receives full value (i.e., consideration) in return, the effect of the contract will be upheld if the other party did not or should not have known of the incompetent person's incapacity.

A further exception to the rule that contracts made by an insane person are void occurs when the contract was for necessaries (e.g., food and housing). In that case, the contract will be upheld unless the other party had knowledge of the insanity and was deceptive or fraudulent.[4] Even if the contract was not strictly for necessaries, the exception will apply if the contract was fair and reasonable, to the extent that the other party receives restitution for a benefit received by an insane person, but only to the extent that the situation cannot be restored as it existed before the agreement.

Determination of Competency to Contract

The determination of competency is a factual issue for the jury, or for the judge if there is no jury. Although a party may present evidence of long-standing behavior indicating inability to understand the nature and consequences of a contract, the most important consideration concerns the person's behavior at or around the time the contract was signed. The fact that a person has been in a mental institution does not in itself mean that he or she is incapable of understanding the nature and effect of an agreement and of making a valid contract.

---

4. Matthiessen & Weichers Refining Co. v. McMahon's Adm'r, 38 N.J.L. 536 (N.J. 1876). Affirmed in Manufacturers Trust Co. v. Podvin, 10 N.J. 199, 89 A.2d 672 (1951).

Competency
to Sign a Will

Persons who make wills (referred to as testators) or who amend existing ones must meet minimum mental status requirements. If it is later shown that the person did not have the requisite testamentary capacity, the testator's estate will be distributed according to the terms of a previous valid will, if any, or by the intestacy (i.e., without a will) statutes of New Jersey.

Mental health consultation or testimony may be utilized where an MHP treated or evaluated the testator (but see Chapters 4.2 and 4.3 for limitations on the use of such information). Alternatively, an MHP may be asked to provide an opinion of the person's mental status at the time the will was signed based on reports of other witnesses and any other relevant information.

Test of Testamentary Capacity

The test of testamentary capacity provides that "[a]ny person 18 or more years of age who is of sound mind may make a will and may appoint a testamentary guardian."[1] The test of whether the testator is of "sound mind" at the time the will is signed requires proof that the testator is (was) able to[2]

> comprehend the property he is about to dispose of, the [natural] objects of his bounty, the meaning of the business in which he is engaged, the relation of each of these factors to the others, and the manner of distribution set forth in the will.

---

1. N.J.S.A. 3B:3-1.
2. *In re* Heim's Will. Heim v. Bauer, 136 N.J. Eq. 138, 148, 40 A.2d 651, 656 (N.J. 1945).

The right of testamentary disposition is protected carefully by the courts, who are loathe to overturn a reasonable will. There is often considerable flexibility regarding the amount of mental capacity required, in that it must be "equal only to the subject with which it has to deal."[3] Imperfect memory impaired by age or disease, difficulty in recalling relatives' names, childish behavior, disjointed speech, asking idle questions, repeating questions, and jumping abruptly from one subject to another are not necessarily enough to prove testamentary incapacity.[4]

Suicide or attempted suicide does not in itself indicate insanity; nor does it permit a presumption of a fixed or lasting mental aberration.[5] "Lucid intervals" in a mentally ill or psychotic person may result in adequate testamentary capacity regardless of prior and future mental states.[6] Medical "insanity," demonstrated by senile psychosis, loss of memory, and paranoid ideas, does not in itself prove testamentary incapacity.[7] Finally, addiction to alcohol does not prove incapacity,[8] except if it is proved that there is "incapacitating temporary insanity or drunkenness . . . at the very time when the will was made."[9]

Proving Testamentary Incapacity

The decedent (a testator who has died) is presumed to have had testamentary capacity.[10] The party who objects to the admission of the will to probate must prove that the decedent was not of sound mind at the signing of the will. The determination of whether the decedent lacked this capacity is a factual issue, and the decision will not be reversed absent significant error.

Undue Influence

A second way of negating a will is to prove that the testator's autonomy was so dominated by another, that it was impossible to resist such an influence:[11]

---

3. Clifton v. Clifton, 47 N.J. Eq. 227, 21 A. 333 (1891).
4. Id.
5. In re Rein's Will, 139 N.J. Eq. 122, 50 A.2d 380 (1946).
6. In re Coleman's Estate, 88 N.J. Eq. 284, 103 A. 521 (1918), aff'd, 88 N.J. Eq. 578, 103 A. 78 (1918).
7. In re Ratto, 128 N.J. Eq. 15, 15 A.2d 616 (1940).
8. Bannister v. Jackson, 45 N.J. Eq. 702, 17 A. 692 (N.J. Prerog. Ct. 1889), aff'd, 46 N.J. Eq. 593, 21 A. 753 (N.J. 1890).
9. Koegel v. Egner, 54 N.J. Eq. 623, 629, 35 A. 394, 396 (N.J. Prerog. Ct. 1896); cited in In re Petkos' Will, 54 N.J. Super. 118, 127, 148 A.2d 320, 325 (1959).
10. In re Heim's Will, supra.
11. Gellert v. Livingston, 5 N.J. 65, 73, 73 A.2d 916, 920 (1950).

Not all influence is 'undue' influence. Persuasion or suggestions or the possession of influence and the opportunity to exert it, will not suffice. It must be such as to destroy the testator's free agency and to constrain him to do what he would not otherwise have done in the disposition of his worldly assets. The coercion or domination exercised to influence the testator may be moral, physical, or mental, or all three, but . . . of a degree sufficient to turn the testator from disposing of his property according to his own desires by the substitution of the will of another which he is unable to resist or overcome.

In such circumstances the person challenging the will has the burden of proving undue influence from the circumstances surrounding the signing of the will and the conduct of the parties.

Competency to Vote

The right to vote can be denied or revoked on the basis of a person's mental status. MHPs may be asked to evaluate a person in this regard.

Competency to Register

In order to vote in a state or federal election, a person must first register to vote.[1] At the time of registration, "no person shall have the right of suffrage . . . who is an idiot or is insane."[2] Nevertheless, no patient, solely because he or she is in a state institution, may be deprived of civil rights including the right to register and vote.[3] Likewise, no patient in any alcoholic rehabilitation facility can be denied the right to vote while undergoing treatment.[4] It is clear that institutionalization itself is insufficient to meet the ancient legal criteria for one who is an "idiot" or is "insane." Rather, a judicial hearing is necessary.

In the primary case that dealt with this issue, 33 adults residing in a state school for the mentally retarded were denied the right to vote by the town clerk and county board of elections.[5] The director of the institution testified that some of the plaintiffs were of dull normal intelligence, whereas others were mentally retarded but not mentally deficient (see Chapter 5E.7). All of the plaintiffs

---

1. N.J.S.A. 19:4-1.
2. N.J.S.A. 19:4-1(1) and N.J. Const. art. 2, p. 6.
3. N.J.S.A. 30:4-24.2.
4. N.J.S.A. 26:2B-20.
5. Carroll v. Cobb, 139 N.J. Super. 439, 354 A.2d 355 (1975).

were competent to manage their own affairs, and none had court-appointed guardians.

The appellate court ruled that where the plaintiffs had answered the questions on the voter registration form, all that remained to be done by the municipal clerk was to process the forms, and the clerk was without power to subject a class of people to questioning more than any other applicants. The court further held that the fact that individuals were receiving optional services at an institution for the mentally retarded did not create a presumption of idiocy: "A mentally retarded person is not necessarily an 'idiot' and a mentally ill person is not necessarily 'insane' for voter registration purposes."[6]

---

6. *Id.*

5B.9

Competency to Obtain a Driver's License

The Division of Motor Vehicles (DMV) is in the Department of Law and Public Safety. The DMV Director may[1]

> refuse to grant a license to drive motor vehicles to a person who is, in his estimation, not a proper person to be granted such a license, but no defect of the applicant shall debar him from receiving a license unless it can be shown by tests approved by the Director . . . that the defect incapacitates him from safely operating a motor vehicle.

Although this law gives the director the authority to debar a licensee whose mental incapacity prevents him or her from driving safely, there are no administrative regulations or legal precedents on this issue. On the basis of the language of this statute, as well as the "Mental Patient's Bill of Rights" (see Chapter 5E.4), license debarments could not be founded upon a finding of mental illness or psychiatric hospitalization alone; they would also require proof that the particular mental incapacity interferes with safe operation of a motor vehicle.

There are more specific requirements regarding those with an epileptic disorder. The law requires prompt reporting to the director by physicians (and patients) of treatment for[2]

> recurrent convulsive seizures or for recurrent periods of unconsciousness or for impairment or loss of motor coordination due to conditions such as, but not limited to, epilepsy in any of its forms, when such conditions persist or recur despite medical treatment.

---

1. N.J.S.A. 39:3-10.
2. N.J.S.A. 39:3-10.4 et seq. and N.J.A.C. 13:19-5.1 et seq.

A Neurological Disorders Committee, appointed by the director, reviews cases and makes recommendations to ensure that every license applicant has been free of seizures for 1 year and is qualified to operate a motor vehicle.[3] A similar Cardiovascular Committee reviews cases and makes recommendations regarding cardiovascular conditions that may interfere with safe driving.[4]

---

3. N.J.A.C. 13:19-5.4. *See also* Division of Motor Vehicles v. Granziel, 236 N.J. Super. 191, 565 A.2d 404 (1989).
4. N.J.A.C. 13:19-4.1 et seq.

COMPETENCY TO OBTAIN A DRIVER'S LICENSE

5B.10

Product Liability

Product liability is a legal term that describes a theory (claim) for personal injuries or property damages arising out of the use of a product. Although a product liability claim may be based on principles of negligence[1] or warranty,[2] this chapter is limited to the third basis, strict tort liability. The central element of this claim is that the product was unreasonably dangerous to the user. MHPs who have special expertise in human factors[3] may be asked to evaluate the safety of a product and to testify in court as to the results.

Elements of a Product Liability Claim

The law provides that a seller is subject to liability for physical harm to the user or the user's property if the product is in a defective condition at the time it left the seller:[4] not "reasonably suitable, safe and fit for the purposes for which [the] goods have been sold."[5]

---

1. Negligence means that the wrongdoer's conduct fell below what would be expected of the reasonably prudent person in the particular circumstances.
2. A warranty claim alleges that the product did not work as promised or represented by the seller or manufacturer.
3. This is an interdisciplinary field that focuses on the interrelationship of people's abilities and the requirements of a product's design within a specified environment.
4. A *seller* means any person engaged in the business of selling products for use or consumption. It applies to manufacturers, wholesalers, distributors, or retailers. Restatement (Second) of Torts § 402A comment f.
5. Suter v. San Angelo Foundry & Machine Co., 81 N.J. 150, 169, 406 A.2d 140, 149 (1979). This standard is a modification of Restatement (Second) of Torts § 402A, which is generally followed in the New Jersey products liability statute, N.J.S.A. 2A:58C-1 et seq.

A manufacturer's strict liability for product defect consequences can take one of three forms: manufacturing defect, design defect, or inadequate warning.[6] It is not enough that the product is potentially unsafe. For instance, a sharp knife or chain saw can be very dangerous, but their inherent risks are well-known. Products may be made less dangerous by including directions for use and warnings as to misuse.[7] The basic issue is whether the product, taken with available instructions and warnings, fails to meet a reasonable consumer's expectations of product safety.[8]

An alternative standard by which to determine strict liability for a product defect, when its risk varies with the manner of use, is by a risk-utility analysis.[9] The court and jury, with the help of experts, must compare the utility of the product with the risk of injury that it poses to the public. Factors to consider in such an analysis include[10]

1. the usefulness and desirability of the product—its utility to the user and to the public as a whole;

2. the safety aspects of the product—the likelihood that it will cause injury and the probable seriousness of the injury;

3. the availability of a substitute product that would meet the same need and not be as unsafe;

4. the manufacturer's ability to eliminate the unsafe character of the product without impairing its usefulness or making it too expensive to maintain its utility;

5. the user's ability to avoid danger by the exercise of care in the use of the product;

6. the user's anticipated awareness of the dangers inherent in the product and their avoidability, because of general public knowledge of the obvious condition of the product, or of the existence of suitable warnings or instructions; and

7. the feasibility, on the part of the manufacturer, of spreading the loss by setting the price of the product or by carrying liability insurance.

---

6. Feldman v. Lederle Laboratories, 97 N.J. 429, 479 A.2d 372 (1984).
7. Dewey v. Brown & Williamson Tobacco Co., 225 N.J. Super. 375, 542 A.2d 919 (1988).
8. Suter v. San Angelo Foundry & Machine Co., *supra.*
9. O'Brien v. Muskin Corp., 94 N.J. 169, 463 A.2d 298 (1983).
10. Cepeda v. Cumberland Engineering Co., 76 N.J. 152, 386 A.2d 816 (1978).

Defenses to a Product Liability Claim

The statutory law provides several basic defenses to a product liability claim. The manufacturer or seller shall not be liable if[11]

1. there is no practical and technically feasible alternative design that would have prevented the harm without substantially impairing the intended function of the product;

2. the characteristics of the product are known to the ordinary consumer, and the harm was caused by an unsafe aspect of the product that is an inherent characteristic of it that would be recognized by such ordinary consumer; or

3. the harm was caused by an unavoidably unsafe aspect of the product, and the product was accompanied by an adequate warning or instruction.

However, even if there is no practical and technically feasible alternative design for the product, liability may still be found if the court determines that[12]

1. the product is egregiously unsafe or ultrahazardous,

2. the ordinary user or consumer cannot reasonably be expected to have knowledge of the product's risks, and

3. the product has little or no usefulness.

In addition, if the strict liability claim is based on a theory of risk-utility analysis, the defendant may present evidence to support a position of high utility and relatively low risk.[13]

---

11. N.J.S.A. 2A:58C-3.
12. *Id.*
13. Dewey v. Brown & Williamson Tobacco Co., *supra.*

5B.11

Unfair Competition

Business competitors may engage in fierce battles to win a share of the market. They cannot, however, employ tactics that do not serve the public interest or have been judicially declared to be "unfair," such as defaming competitors or their goods, stealing trade secrets, or starting a business with an ex-employer's customer lists. A large area of unfair competition of interest to MHPs, particularly psychologists, is a type of marketing that attempts to confuse the consumer into believing that one business's products or services were produced by another. MHPs may be asked to conduct consumer surveys to determine whether the defendant's business practices resulted in such confusion and to testify in court as to their findings.

Legal Test of Unfair Competition

The courts have long upheld the principle of preventing unfair competition in business practices. An early New Jersey decision defined the grounds for relief:[1]

> Either that the means used are dishonest, or that, by imitation of name or device, there is a tendency to create confusion in the trade, and enable the seller to pass off upon the unwary his goods as those of another, and thereby deceive the purchaser; or that, by false representation, it is intended to mislead the public, and induce them to accept a spurious article in the place of one they have been accustomed to use.

---

1. Vitascope Co. v. U.S. Phonograph Co., 83 F. 30, 32–33 (N.J. Ch. 1897).

The two main types of "confusion in the trade" are trademark confusion and product confusion.

Trademark Confusion

A trademark is any mark, word, letter, number, design, or picture that is used by an entity to designate its goods. It must be affixed to the goods and must not be a common or generic name. Trademarks are typically registered under federal law, but they are protected under New Jersey law: "No merchant, firm or corporation shall appropriate for his or their own use a name, brand, trademark, reputation or goodwill of any maker in whose product such merchant, firm or corporation deals."[2] The major question for the courts, however, is not whether the trademark was registered, but whether it is a generic term or has an established distinctiveness: "The existing generic name of a thing cannot be appropriated as a trademark by one producer."[3]

The leading New Jersey case in this area of law did not involve a dispute over a product name, but rather the name of a church. The Christian Science Board of Directors had disaffiliated the Plainfield Church from their organization, whereupon the latter church reorganized itself under the name "Plainfield Community Church, An Independent Church Practicing Christian Science." The board of directors then sued to prevent the use of such terms as "Christian Science" in the name of the renegade church. The court held that "Christian Science" was a generic name for a religion that could not be appropriated from the public domain for exclusive use by any one church or organization.[4]

Product Confusion

Product confusion occurs when a business sells a product that is very similar in appearance to a competitor's product. However,[5]

> In the absence of a patent, there is nothing to prevent the imitation or reproduction of a product, provided the imitator does not misrepresent to the public that his product is made by others or cause confusion as to whose product it is or that the product has not yet acquired a secondary meaning or an identification coming from appearance.

Secondary meaning refers to the concept that a particular product appearance is indicative of a certain producer and that the

---

2. N.J.S.A. 56:4-1.
3. Christian Science Board of Directors of the First Church of Christ, Scientist v. Evans, 105 N.J. 297, 307, 520 A.2d 1347, 1353 (1987).
4. *Id.*
5. French American Reeds Mfg. Co. v. Park Plastics Co., 20 N.J. Super. 325, 90 A.2d 50 (App. Div. 1952).

public cares about purchasing from that source. In a well-known case, a producer of plastic tomato-shaped catsup dispensers sued another company for product confusion. The court denied relief on the grounds that there was no patent, that the imitator clearly labeled its product without misrepresentation, and that the catsup dispensors had not developed a "secondary meaning" equating a particular shape with a specific company.[6]

---

6. Squeezit Corp. v. Plastic Dispensers, Inc., 31 N.J. Super. 217, 106 A.2d 322 (1954).

Employment Discrimination

The law prohibits employers from engaging in discriminatory employment practices. This applies to professionals who have employees, as well as management consultants who advise employers concerning personnel selection, discharge, and promotion. The law is enforced through the Division of Civil Rights in the Department of Law and Public Safety. MHPs, especially psychologists, should be aware of this law as it pertains to industrial consulting and test construction.

The law states,[1]

> All persons shall have the opportunity to obtain employment . . . without discrimination because of race, creed, color, national origin, ancestry, age, marital status or sex, subject only to conditions and limitations applicable alike to all persons. This opportunity is recognized as and declared to be a civil right.

In addition, unlawful employment discrimination is prohibited against any person because of a past or present handicap, unless the nature and extent of the handicap reasonably prevents the performance of the particular job.[2] *Handicapped* is defined as[3]

> suffering from any physical disability, infirmity, malformation or disfigurement . . . or from any mental, psychological or developmental disability resulting from anatomical, psychological, physiological or neurological conditions which prevents the normal exercise of any bodily or mental functions or is demonstrable, medically or psychologically, by accepted clinical or laboratory diagnostic techniques.

---

1. N.J.S.A. 10:5-4.
2. N.J.S.A. 10:4.1.
3. N.J.S.A. 10:5-5(q).

This statute has been applied to those handicapped with AIDS,[4] alcoholism,[5] and drug dependency.[6]

In a suit to prove employment discrimination in hiring, the plaintiff must prove[7]

1. that he or she belongs to a protected class (e.g., age, race, handicap);
2. that he or she applied and was qualified for a position for which the employer was seeking applicants;
3. that he or she was rejected despite adequate qualifications; and
4. that after rejection, the position remained open and the employer continued to seek applications for persons of plaintiff's qualifications.

In a suit to prove employment discrimination in discharging, the plaintiff must prove[8]

1. that he or she belongs to a protected class (e.g., age, race, handicap);
2. that job performance was at a level that met the employer's legitimate expectations;
3. that he or she was fired nevertheless; and
4. that the employer sought someone to perform the same work afterward.

Although New Jersey law does not address the issue of psychological tests that tend to exclude members of one class or group more than others from employment, it is expected that such tests would be in violation of the employment discrimination laws, unless such exclusions were proven to be related to actual job performance.

---

4. Poff v. Caro, 228 N.J. Super. 370, 549 A.2d 900 (1987).
5. Clowes v. Terminix Int'l, Inc., 109 N.J. 575, 538 A.2d 794 (1988).
6. *In re* Cahill, 245 N.J. Super. 397, 585 A.2d 977 (App. Div. 1991).
7. Anderson v. Exxon Co., 89 N.J. 483, 446 A.2d 486 (1982).
8. Clowes v. Terminix Int'l, Inc., *supra*.

Civil/Criminal Matters

5C.1

Jury Selection

Jury selection is an area of importance to attorneys because the process allows them, to a degree, to "select a jury." In actuality, potential jurors are rejected from serving rather than selected. MHPs may be involved in this process by conducting pretrial surveys, constructing questions to ask the potential jurors, and evaluating jurors on the basis of results of pretrial surveys and/or in-court observations.

Juror Qualifications

The jury selection process begins by a random selection of names from the combination of voter registration and licensed driver rolls.[1] Questionnaires are then sent to potential jurors to determine whether they are qualified to serve. The law requires that each juror must be[2]

1. a New Jersey citizen for at least 2 years;
2. over 18 and under 75 years of age;[3]
3. a resident of the county from which he or she is asked to serve;
4. without a criminal conviction;
5. neither directly nor indirectly connected with the administration of justice through his or her employment;
6. able to read, write, and understand the English language; and

---

1. N.J.S.A. 2A:70-4.
2. N.J.S.A. 2A:69-1.
3. N.J.S.A. 9:17B-1.

7. without any mental or physical disability that would prevent effective functioning as a juror.

Automatic exemptions from jury service are provided for police officers and fire fighters, dentists and physicians, hospital workers, state agency employees, military personnel, telegraph and telephone operators, school teachers in session, and those providing care to a child.[4] A person is also ineligible to serve on a jury for 1 year after completing jury service.[5] Eligible jurors are randomly selected for jury duty for each session of the courts, and panels of potential jurors for a particular trial are then selected from the pool of eligible jurors called on any given day.

Criminal Trials

When a Jury Is Allowed

The state (and federal) constitution provides that criminal defendants have a right to trial by jury.[6] This right applies to most misdemeanor and felony charges, but not to motor vehicle violations, petty offenses, and misdemeanors punishable by less than 6 months in jail.[7] The court has the discretion to grant a nonjury trial to a criminal defendant upon request.[8] In the sentencing phase of a capital murder case, the consent of the prosecutor is also required.[9]

Jury Size

Juries in criminal cases consist of 12 persons.[10] However, the judge may impanel more jurors than that if it is appropriate. At the close of the trial, if more than 12 jurors remain, the number is randomly reduced to the required 12.

Unanimity Requirement

The jury must reach a unanimous verdict in criminal trials. However, in noncriminal aspects of a trial, such as determining the defendant's competency (see Chapter 5D.5), the civil standard of 10 consenting jurors is accepted.[11]

---

4. N.J.S.A. 2A:69-2.
5. N.J.S.A. 2A:69-4.
6. N.J. Const. art. 1, p. 10.
7. State v. Owens, 54 N.J. 153, 254 A.2d 97 (1969); see also State v. French Funeral Home, 185 N.J. Super. 385, 448 A.2d 1037 (1982).
8. State v. Dunne ___N.J. ___, ___A.2d ___(1991).
9. R. 1:8-1.
10. N.J.S.A. 2A:74-2 and R. 1:8-2(d).
11. State v. Gibson, 15 N.J. 384, 105 A.2d 1 (1954).

Change of Venue

Criminal defendants may request to move the place of the trial to another county within the state for good cause[12] (e.g., if the defendant is unlikely to get a fair and impartial trial in the county). The court must determine whether there exists a "realistic likelihood of prejudice" resulting from pretrial publicity.[13] MHPs may be involved in designing and conducting a survey of a sample of potential jurors within a county to determine the level of prejudice or bias toward the particular parties, attorneys, and issues in the case. Their results may then be used in a pretrial motion for a change of venue. In addition, they may be called to testify in a pretrial hearing on the matter.

However, extensive pretrial publicity does not necessarily preclude the likelihood of an impartial jury.[14] There are a number of steps the judge can take, such as delaying the trial and examining additional potential jurors.[15] If potential jurors state that they can lay aside impressions or opinions and render a verdict based upon the evidence presented in court, a fair and impartial jury can often be created.[16]

Voir Dire

Prior to impanelling a jury, the judge interrogates qualified jurors chosen from the list, aided by questions suggested by the parties or their attorneys.[17] The court identifies the parties and their counsel, briefly outlines the nature of the case, and explains the purposes of the voir dire examination. The court will ask any questions that it thinks are necessary with regard to the potential jurors' qualifications to serve on the particular case. The parties may make an unlimited number of challenges "for cause," alleging that a juror is unqualified because of a lack of impartiality. The partiality may stem from individual bias and prejudice, business interests, personal relationships, or any other reasons. The judge then decides whether any jurors must be dismissed for cause.

In death penalty cases, the state is entitled to a "death-qualified" jury of individuals who are willing to impose the death penalty if warranted by the evidence, and those who would refuse to vote for capital punishment may be eliminated for cause.[18] Likewise, the defense is entitled to jurors who would not automatically

---

12. N.J.S.A. 2A:2-13.
13. State v. Williams, 93 N.J. 39, 459 A.2d 641 (1983).
14. State v. Biegenwald, 106 N.J. 13, 524 A.2d 939 (1987).
15. State v. Williams, *supra.*
16. State v. Sugar, 84 N.J. 1, 417 A.2d 474 (1980).
17. R. 1:8-3.
18. State v. Ramseur, 106 N.J. 123, 524 A.2d 188 (1987).

impose the death penalty but who would carefully weigh the evidence.[19]

Both the defendant and the state are also entitled to a number of peremptory challenges, by which an attorney can strike a juror from the panel for any reason, except if the state uses peremptory challenges in a discriminatory manner to eliminate people of a particular class.[20] The defense is entitled to 20 peremptory challenges, and the prosecution is entitled to 10, in serious cases involving homicide, robbery, and sexual assault.[21] In less serious cases, the rules provide for fewer peremptory challenges, with latitude for judicial discretion.

Civil Trials

When a Jury Is Allowed

Whether a party in a civil suit has the right to a jury trial generally depends on whether the action historically was initiated "at law" or "in equity." The former generally pertains to actions in which the party seeks damages (i.e., monetary compensation), and in such cases either party may demand a jury trial, although it is often waived.[22]

Equity cases generally seek nonpecuniary, coercive relief such as injunctions (where a party seeks to force another party to stop doing something), restitution (where the defendant is ordered to return the injured party to his or her original condition), or specific performance of contracts. Although a party in an equitable suit may request a jury, its conclusion would be only advisory to the court. At law, however, the court must abide by the factual determinations of the jury and may reverse only if there were a legal error.

Jury Size

A jury in a civil case consists of 6 people, unless the court, upon a motion by one of the parties, orders a 12-person jury for good cause.[23] As in criminal cases, the court may impanel alternate jurors, and the jury will be reduced to the required size before deliberation.

---

19. State v. Bey (II), 112 N.J. 123, 548 A.2d 185 (1988).
20. State v. Gilmore, 103 N.J. 508, 511 A.2d 1150 (1986).
21. N.J.S.A. 2A:78-7 and R. 1:8-3(d).
22. R. 1:8-1, 4:35-1, and 6:5-3. However, jury trials have been eliminated from the municipal courts. See R. 7:44.
23. N.J. Const. art. 1, p. 9; N.J.S.A. 2A:74-1 and R. 1:8-2.

Unanimity Requirement

The verdict of findings must be by five sixths of the jurors, unless the parties stipulate that a smaller majority shall be taken as the verdict.[24]

Change of Venue

The parties may request to move the place of the trial to another county within the state for "good cause,"[25] more specifically, if "there is a substantial doubt that a fair and impartial trial can be had" in the original county.[26] As was noted in the section on criminal trials, MHPs may be involved in this process by providing information to be used in motions to the court for change of venue or by testifying as expert witnesses on this issue. In both capacities, MHPs may be involved in conducting pretrial surveys, constructing questions to ask the potential jurors, and evaluating jurors on the basis of results of pretrial surveys and/or in-court observations.

Voir Dire

The procedures governing the voir dire examinations in civil suits are similar to criminal trials. Civil parties may make an unlimited number of challenges for cause. Jurors will be excluded by the judge if they potentially lack impartiality because of individual bias and prejudice, business interests, personal relationships, or any other reasons. After these challenges are completed, each party is generally entitled to six peremptory challenges, and more in certain multiparty suits and at the discretion of the court.[27]

---

24. N.J.S.A. 2A:80-2 and R. 1:8-2.
25. N.J.S.A. 2A:2-13.
26. R. 4:3-3(a)(2).
27. R. 1:8-3.

5C.2

Expert Witnesses

MHPs may testify as expert witnesses if they can provide testimony on a topic that is beyond the trier's[1] competence and if this information will permit the trier to rationally decide the case before it. MHPs are frequently called to testify as expert witnesses on a wide variety of issues.

Qualifying as an Expert Witness

Although anyone who has personal knowledge of a matter may testify as a witness, a person will only be "qualified" (allowed by the court to testify) as an expert if he or she has "knowledge, experience, training or education."[2] Such an individual may testify in the form of an opinion based upon scientific, technical, or specialized knowledge "if such testimony will assist the trier of fact to understand the evidence or determine a fact at issue."[3] The three basic requirements for the admission of expert testimony are[4]

1. the intended testimony must concern a subject matter that is beyond the ken of the average juror,
2. the field testified to must be at a state of the art such that an expert's testimony could be sufficiently reliable, and
3. the witness must have sufficient expertise to offer the intended testimony.

---

1. The "trier" refers to the jury or the court if tried without a jury.
2. Evid. R. 19.
3. Evid. R. 56.
4. State v. Kelly, 97 N.J. 178, 478 A.2d 364 (1984).

However, even if expert testimony would meet these criteria, it may still be excluded if its probative value would be too time consuming or create the danger of undue prejudice or confusion.[5]

In determining whether the expert's testimony would be sufficiently reliable, it must be demonstrated that it satisfies the New Jersey courts' standards of acceptability for scientific evidence. That is, the testimony must have "a sufficient scientific basis to produce uniform and reasonably reliable results so as to contribute materially to the ascertainment of the truth."[6]

In an emerging field of research, such as the battered woman's syndrome, there are three ways its general acceptance and reliability can be proven:[7]

1. by expert testimony as to its general acceptance by those in the profession,

2. by authoritative scientific and legal writings that indicate that the scientific community accepts it, or

3. by judicial opinions that indicate the expert's premises have gained acceptance.

When an Expert Witness May Be Called to Testify

If the judge determines that the subject of the expert witness testimony is of such common knowledge that the average lay person could reach a conclusion as intelligently as the witness, expert testimony may be excluded (supra). Thus, no expert testimony was needed to explain the potential harm associated with the display of wild animals, such as leopards.[8] Likewise, an expert is usually not needed to express an opinion as to whether an individual was intoxicated.[9]

Courts have allowed expert witnesses to testify on the battered woman's syndrome,[10] the behavior of sexually abused child victims,[11] custody and visitation issues following divorce,[12] standards of care in malpractice,[13] psychological impairment in workers'

5. Evid. R. 4.
6. State v. Hurd, 86 N.J. 525, 536, 432 A.2d 86, 91 (1981).
7. State v. Kelly, *supra*.
8. Eyrich v. Earl, 203 N.J. Super. 144, 495 A.2d 1375 (1985).
9. Searles v. Public Serv. Ry., 100 N.J.L. 222, 126 A. 465 (1924).
10. State v. Kelly, *supra*.
11. State v. R.W., 104 N.J. 14, 514 A.2d 1287 (1986).
12. Cooper v. Cooper, 99 N.J. 42, 491 A.2d 606 (1984).
13. Buckelew v. Grossbard, 87 N.J. 512, 435 A.2d 1150 (1981).

compensation cases,[14] and multiple other issues when a standard psychological diagnosis is relevant to the case.

However, the scientific reliability of polygraph tests is considered too questionable and potentially prejudicial to allow into evidence, unless there is a stipulated agreement between the parties (see Chapter 5C.5). The results of sodium amytal ("truth serum") tests are also not admissible.[15] Likewise, psychiatric testimony that a defendant did not fit the profile of a typical rapist was excluded for not meeting the test of scientific acceptance and reliability.[16] The ultimate determination of whether to allow testimony is generally within the discretion of the trial court.

Expert witnesses are typically asked by one party in a case to testify on behalf of its client or position. Although a rule specifically authorizing the court itself to appoint its own independent experts has not been established in New Jersey, it is assumed that courts have inherent power to make such appointments.[17] In all family court proceedings, the court is entitled to appoint any necessary medical, psychological, social, and economic experts.[18]

Form and Content of Testimony

An expert witness may testify in the form of an opinion or inference, on the basis of facts perceived by or made known to him at or before the hearing.[19] Such facts need not be admissible in evidence, if they are relied upon by experts in the particular field in forming opinions. For example, a psychologist could presumably use the (hearsay) statements of witnesses and the opinions of records not in evidence in forming an opinion regarding insanity.

An expert witness must disclose the underlying facts or data behind his or her opinion during cross-examination and during pretrial discovery if ordered by the judge. However, there is disagreement as to whether the failure to submit a report in pretrial procedures would otherwise preclude the expert from testifying regarding the factual basis of his or her conclusions.[20]

During cross-examination of an expert witness, the opposition may attempt to impeach (i.e., discredit) the expert's testimony by

---

14. Saunderlin v. E.I. DuPont Co., 102 N.J. 402, 508 A.2d 1095 (1986).
15. State v. Pitts, 116 N.J. 580, 562 A.2d 1320 (1989).
16. State v. Cavallo, 88 N.J. 508, 443 A.2d 1020 (1982).
17. Finn v. Mayor and Council of Norwood, 227 N.J. Super. 69, 545 A.2d 807 (1988).
18. R. 5:3-3.
19. Evid. R. 56.
20. Biunno, R. J. (1990). Current N.J. rules of evidence. Comment to Evid. R. 57. Newark, NJ: Gann Law Books.

referring to passages in treatises in his or her field of expertise that are inconsistent with the testimony so long as the expert either relied on the works or is willing to concede that they are authoritative.[21] In addition, an expert is subject to cross-examination techniques used against nonexpert witnesses such as proof of prior inconsistent statements or facts demonstrating his or her bias or interest in the outcome of the hearing.

The expert's opinion or inference may touch on the ultimate legal issue to be decided at trial so long as it assists the trier to understand the evidence and does not decide the issue for the trier. As the law notes, "Testimony in the form of opinions or inferences otherwise admissible under these rules is not objectionable because it embraces the ultimate issue or issues to be decided by the trier of the fact."[22] Thus, witnesses may testify, within their expertise, as to whether they believe a defendant is competent to stand trial (see Chapter 5D.5) or was insane at the time of the offense (see Chapter 5D.9), but witnesses may not testify that the defendant is guilty of the crime charged.[23]

The standard of proof required for the expert medical opinion is that it "must be couched in terms of reasonable medical certainty or probability; opinions as to possibility are inadmissible."[24]

The opinions of the expert need not be in hypothetical form unless the judge requires it.[25] However, an attorney may still ask an expert a hypothetical question, provided that the facts are supported by the evidence.[26]

The role of the expert witness is to contribute the insights of his or her specialty to the court. In contrast to an attorney, the expert is not supposed to be an advocate for one party in the dispute.[27] In arriving at an opinion, the expert is not required to collect more evidence than necessary. Although the testimony must be adequately documented, costs must be considered to keep the amount of information "within practical and realistic limits."[28]

21. McComish v. Desoi, 42 N.J. 274, 200 A.2d 116 (1964).
22. Evid. R. 56.
23. State v. Odom, 116 N.J. 65, 560 A.2d 1198 (1989).
24. State v. Freeman, 223 N.J. Super. 92, 116, 538 A.2d 371, 384 (App. Div. 1988).
25. Evid. R. 58.
26. Wilsey v. Reisinger, 76 N.J. Super. 20, 183 A.2d 717 (App. Div. 1962), *certif. denied,* 38 N.J. 610, 186 A.2d 308 (1962).
27. *In re* Hyett, 61 N.J. 518, 296 A.2d 306 (1972).
28. Glen Wall Assocs. v. Wall Township, 99 N.J. 265, 280, 491 A.2d 1247, 1255 (1985).

5C.3

Polygraph Evidence

Although some states govern polygraph examinations through the licensure of polygraph examiners, New Jersey does not have such a law. The admission of polygraph evidence in court is determined by judicial case law.

Admissibility of Polygraph Examinations

The New Jersey courts allow the introduction of polygraph test results into a criminal trial if the prosecution and defendant enter into a stipulation (agreement) to have the defendant submit to a polygraph test and have the results introduced in evidence.[1] The stipulation must be "clear, unequivocal and complete, freely entered into with full knowledge of the right to refuse the test and the consequences involved in taking it."[2]

The stipulation must be basically fair to the defendant.[3] It must state all the consequences to the defendant of agreeing to a test, and it must commit the state to the obligation of introducing the evidence in court regardless of the outcome.[4] In addition, the polygraph examiner must be qualified, and the test must be administered in accordance with established polygraph techniques.[5] Although the defendant has the right to an attorney when deciding whether to take a polygraph test, such right may be waived.[6]

---

1. State v. McDavitt, 62 N.J. 36, 297 A.2d 849 (1972).
2. *Id.*
3. State v. Finn, 175 N.J. Super. 13, 417 A.2d 554 (1980).
4. State v. Smith, 142 N.J. Super. 575, 362 A.2d 578 (App. Div. 1976).
5. State v. McDavitt, *supra.*
6. State v. Reyes, 237 N.J. Super. 250, 567 A.2d 287 (App. Div. 1989).

Where polygraph test results are admitted into evidence, the jury must be instructed that they are not direct proof of a defendant's guilt or innocence of the crime. Rather, it is opinion evidence by an expert and tends only to indicate whether or not the person was telling the truth when tested. Then, the jury must decide the weight and effect such evidence should be given.

The stipulation between the defendant and prosecutor may contain provisions regarding other polygraph tests. Unless there is a clear and unequivocal provision barring the use of the results of an independent private polygraph test, such results are admissible in court to refute the results of the stipulated polygraph.[7]

In the one civil case regarding the admission of polygraph tests into evidence, the court accepted the general principle that such evidence would normally be excluded, absent a stipulated agreement.[8] However, the evidence was permitted on a rules technicality, that it was being used to prove an undisputed fact.

---

7. State v. McMahon, 217 N.J. Super. 182, 524 A.2d 1348 (1986).
8. Senders v. CNA Insurance Companies, 212 N.J. Super. 518, 515 A.2d 820 (1986).

Competency to Testify

A witness in a civil or criminal trial must have the mental capacity to testify accurately and reliably in court; any other rule would open the fairness of the trial to question. Thus, whenever there is a reasonable doubt concerning the competency of a witness, the opposing counsel or court should raise the issue. Child witnesses may be questioned by the court to determine their ability to relate facts accurately and to testify in a truthful manner. To ensure justice, MHPs have been asked to aid in this assessment and to testify as to their findings. In this chapter, the mental status evaluation of rape victims is also discussed.

Legal Test of Competency to Testify

The general principle is that all persons are qualified to testify as witnesses, as long as they are competent to do so.[1] The determination of whether a person is competent to serve as a witness lies within the discretion of the court.[2] The operative rule of evidence states,[3]

> A person is disqualified to be a witness if the judge finds that (a) the proposed witness is incapable of expressing himself concerning the matter so as to be understood by the judge and jury either directly or through interpretation by one who can understand him, or (b) the proposed witness is incapable of understanding the duty of a witness to tell the truth.

---

1. Evid. R. 7.
2. State v. Butler, 27 N.J. 560, 143 A.2d 530 (1985).
3. Evid. R. 17.

The first part of the witness competency rule requires that he or she have the ability to "understand questions and to frame and express intelligent answers."[4] Difficulties in memory are a proper subject of cross-examination and thus are not an issue in determinations of competency.[5] The second part of the competency test requires that the witness "understand the difference between right and wrong, that to tell the truth is right and that in some way he will be punished if he lies to the court."[6]

An exception to this requirement occurs in child sex abuse cases when the victim has made an out-of-court statement regarding an act of molestation. The statement will be admitted into evidence, but the youngster must be required to testify and be cross-examined regardless of any predetermined capacity to tell the truth.[7]

Determination of Witness Competency

The two major classes of potentially incompetent witnesses are those who are mentally ill and those who are young children. The court makes a competency determination after questioning the witness and examining the entire record.[8] The court has the power to compel a psychological evaluation to aid in its determination.[9] However, such examinations should be granted "only upon a substantial showing of need and justification."[10] More specifically,[11]

> there must be a showing of some deviation from acceptable norms, such as an identifiable or clinical psychiatric or similar disorder, beyond the realm of those human conditions that ordinary experience would confirm as normal . . . the party requesting the testing must present evidence reasonably indicating something peculiar, unique, or abnormal about the . . . witness that would influence the witness's competence or the court's ability to assess that competence, or raise unusual difficulties in assessing the witness's credibility.

In the quoted case, the court held that a 3-year-old child was competent to testify without a psychological evaluation, absent any evidence suggesting mental disorder, inappropriate behavior, or undue parental influence.

---

4. State v. Grossmick, 153 N.J. Super. 190, 192, 379 A.2d 454, 455 (App. Div. 1976).
5. State in the Interest of R.R., 79 N.J. 97, 398 A.2d 76 (1979).
6. State v. Davis, 229 N.J. Super. 66, 78, 550 A.2d 1241, 1247 (App. Div. 1988).
7. Rule 63(33). *See* State v. D.R., 109 N.J. 348, 537 A.2d 667 (1988).
8. State in the Interest of R.R., *supra.*
9. State v. Butler, 27 N.J. 560, 143 A.2d 530 (1958).
10. *Id.* at 27 N.J. 572, 143 A.2d 536.
11. State v. R.W., 104 N.J. 14, 22, 514 A.2d 1287, 1291 (1986).

Aside from a competency determination, courts may permit a child to testify via closed-circuit television in cases involving sexual assault or abuse, when there is a substantial likelihood of severe emotional distress from testifying in open court.[12] However, the court is encouraged to make such a determination after a personal interview with the child, and to appoint an expert MHP to evaluate the child only if it is unable to make a decision.[13]

In cases involving mental illness, courts have held that psychological evaluations of competency were proper when there was an initial showing of significant disturbance. In one case, "chronic brain syndrome associated with convulsive disorder, with behavior reaction" was demonstrated.[14] A teenage sex assault victim was required to have a psychological evaluation for competency upon a showing of functional encopresis (fecal soiling).[15]

Evidence that a witness had been committed to a mental institution and another court had doubted her competency was also justification for a competency evaluation.[16] In that case, the witness, a chronic alcoholic, was permitted to testify subject to normal cross-examination of her veracity and reliability. Likewise, the court permitted a witness to testify after a competency evaluation diagnosed him as suffering from paranoid schizophrenia and likely to distort and misinterpret questions during testimony.[17] These cases demonstrate that mental disability alone cannot disqualify a witness without a clear finding of incapacity to either communicate adequately or to understand the duty to tell the truth.[18]

Competency of Rape Victims to Testify

Rape "victim-witnesses" are challenged by defense attorneys in some states as incompetent to testify because of their sexual history or personality traits that may affect their veracity. Those attorneys request that the victim undergo a mental status examination to determine whether the person possesses any attributes that would bear on truthfulness. The New Jersey Supreme Court strongly disfavors such challenges, which are not permitted absent any standard demonstrations of incompetency:[19]

---

12. N.J.S.A. 2A: 84A-32.4.
13. State v. Crandall, 120 N.J. 649, 577 A.2d 483 (1990).
14. State v. Butler, *supra*, at 27 N.J. 572, 143 A.2d 536.
15. State v. Hass, 218 N.J. Super. 133, 526 A.2d 1156 (App. Div. 1987).
16. State v. Franklin, 52 N.J. 386, 245 A.2d 356 (1968).
17. State v. Burgos, 200 N.J. Super. 6, 490 A.2d 316 (App. Div. 1985), *certif. denied*, 101 N.J. 304, 501 A.2d 961 (1985).
18. Evid. R. 17.
19. State v. R.W., *supra*, at 104 N.J. 30, n. 4, 514 A.2d 1295, n. 4.

Defendants charged with sexual offenses against female victims of all ages have historically based attacks against witness reliability on unsound stereotypical notions of the nature of women. . . . We totally repudiate such thinking.

In addition, New Jersey has a rape-shield statute that prevents cross-examination of sexual victims regarding previous sexual conduct, living arrangements, or lifestyle, except when the court determines that the probative value of the evidence will outweigh any prejudice, confusion, or invasion of privacy.[20]

---

20. N.J.S.A. 2C:14-7.

Psychological Autopsy

The motivations and mental state of a person prior to death are frequently critical issues in subsequent litigation. For instance, whether a gift was made by the person "in contemplation of death" has significant tax consequences.[1] Similarly, a finding that a person committed suicide rather than died accidently may determine whether there is insurance coverage. MHPs may contribute in this area by providing a retrospective psychological profile of the decedent.

Admissibility of Psychological Autopsies

There has been only one case in New Jersey where the term *psychological autopsy* has been referred to by an appellate court.[2] In that case, a depressed patient may have committed suicide after his new psychiatrist refused to advance the date of the first appointment despite pleas from his spouse. The wife sued for medical malpractice and wrongful death. A psychiatric expert witness testified regarding a "psychological autopsy of the victim's likely state of mind at the time of his demise."[3] The appellate court accepted the testimony without questioning its propriety.

The legal basis for accepting such evidence is clear. New Jersey law provides that the expert must have information that is outside the knowledge of the lay person.[4] The expert's testimony may be

---

1. *See* Shaffer, *The Psychological Autopsy in Judicial Opinions Under Section 2035,* 3 Loy. L. Rev. 1 (1970).
2. Gaido v. Weiser, 227 N.J. Super. 175, 545 A.2d 1350 (App. Div. 1988).
3. *Id.*
4. Evid. R. 19.

based on information that is generally inadmissible in courts, such as hearsay,[5] if such information is routinely used by experts in the field. The expert is required to disclose the fact basis for the opinion at the request of counsel.[6] If these requirements are met, psychological autopsies are likely to be upheld even if challenged on appeal.

---

5. Hearsay is where a witness repeats on the stand a statement by another to prove the matter stated in the hearsay evidence. An example would be where A is asked to tell what B said because the subject matter of B's statement is at issue (e.g., B saw a car run a red light and told A about it at the time).
6. Evid. R. 57.

Criminal Matters

5D.1

Screening of Police Officers

No person can be appointed as a member of a municipal police department unless he or she meets the following qualifications:[1]

1. is a citizen of the United States;

2. is sound in body and of good health sufficient to satisfy the board of trustees of the police and fire fighters' retirement system of New Jersey as to his or her eligibility for membership in the retirement system;

3. is able to read, write, and speak the English language well and intelligently; and

4. is of good moral character and has not been convicted of any criminal offense involving moral turpitude.

Although these requirements provide general authority for police departments to provide psychological screening of police applicants, such routine screening has been instituted primarily in police departments of municipalities that have elected to join the state civil service system.[2] The Department of Personnel regulations allow for psychological testing of applicants,[3] and many such municipalities require it.

A police department may request that an eligible candidate's name be removed from a civil service appointment list owing to disqualification for medical or psychological reasons, which would preclude the person from effectively performing the duties of an

---

1. N.J.S.A. 40A:14-122.
2. N.J.S.A. 11A:9-2.
3. N.J.A.C. 4A:4-2.2.

officer.[4] The request must be supported by a report and recommendations prepared and signed by a New Jersey licensed physician, psychologist, or psychiatrist.

A rejected police applicant has 20 days to file an appeal with the Merit System Board.[5] The appellant (or the lawyer) is entitled to receive all relevant records. The applicant may then submit a report from a physician or psychologist of his or her own choosing. The new psychological report must include[6]

1. the professional's signature and type of license or degree;
2. the length of the examination or interview;
3. a specific diagnosis or statement of behavioral pattern, or the specific reasons for a recommendation;
4. a finding as to the qualifications of the appellant for effective performance of the duties; and
5. a list of all tests that have been administered and all raw data, protocols, computer printouts, and profiles from the tests.

The Merit System Board must either conduct a written review of the appeal or submit psychological appeals to the New Jersey Personnel Medical Review Panel.[7] The appellant may appear before the panel. The panel then makes a written report, which is reviewed by the Merit System Board, before it renders a final written decision.

The New Jersey Supreme Court has held that any psychological tests used to screen prospective police officers must demonstrate some correlation between the psychological traits the tests evaluate and the work the person will be expected to perform.[8] In the *Matter of Vey*, a police applicant had been rejected because the psychological report had described her as bold and suspicious. The court ruled that she was entitled to a new hearing because the record failed to identify personality traits that would make her unfit.

---

4. N.J.A.C. 4A:4-6.5.
5. N.J.A.C. 4A:4-6.5(b).
6. N.J.A.C. 4A:4-6.5(e).
7. N.J.A.C. 4A:4-6.5(f).
8. In the Matter of Vey, ____N.J.____, ____A.2d ____(1991).

5D.2

Competency to Waive the Rights to Silence, Counsel, and a Jury

Persons taken into custody by police for a criminal offense have the option of waiving the rights to silence and counsel that are guaranteed under the United States and New Jersey constitutions. Criminal defendants may also waive these rights and the right to a jury trial at the time of trial. MHPs may be asked to examine criminal defendants and to testify as to whether they were competent to waive these rights in the arrest and investigation stages or at the trial.

Right to Silence

The right to silence is invoked as soon as a person is taken into custody by a police officer. The person must be read his or her Miranda rights,[1] which include a statement about the right to silence, otherwise any statements the person makes cannot be used against him or her at trial. After the rights have been read, the person may waive them and give any information requested by the police, including, but not limited to, a confession. The waiver must be made "voluntarily, knowingly, and intelligently."[2]

Confessions are presumed to be involuntary, and at trial the state must prove beyond a shadow of a doubt that one was freely and voluntarily given.[3] The test is "voluntariness" as determined

---

1. These include the right to silence and counsel (as well as appointment of counsel if the person is indigent) and that any statement made can be used at trial. Miranda v. Arizona, 384 U.S. 436, 86 S.Ct. 1602, 16 L.Ed.2d 694 (1966).
2. *Id.* at 384 U.S. 444, 86 S.Ct. 1612, 16 L.Ed.2d 707.
3. State v. Yough, 49 N.J. 587, 231 A.2d 598 (1967).

by the totality of the circumstances in the particular case. In determining the voluntariness of a confession, courts consider the characteristics of the accused, as well as the details of the interrogation:[4]

> Relevant factors include the defendant's age, education, intelligence, advice concerning his constitutional rights, length of detention, and the nature of the questioning—specifically whether the questioning was repeated and prolonged and whether it involved physical punishment or mental exhaustion.

In applying these principles, the New Jersey Supreme Court has held that two adolescents, ages 13 and 15, did not make a voluntary confession in light of their youthfulness and interrogation in a police station.[5] In another case, an impaired adult with the mental age of a 6-year-old child did not make a knowing waiver.[6] In a third case, confessions made under the influence of drugs (or alcohol) were not per se involuntary, but had to be weighed within the totality of the circumstances.[7]

A voluntary confession cannot be the product of either physical or psychological coercion.[8] However, the use of psychologically oriented principles and techniques to influence a person to change his or her mind and make a statement are not inherently coercive, unless they represent an "overbearing" of the suspect's will.[9]

Right to Counsel

A criminal defendant is entitled to be represented by counsel in any criminal proceeding. This includes indictable offenses,[10] non-indictable offenses,[11] and even municipal court proceedings.[12] This right attaches as soon as feasible after a defendant is taken into custody. The defendant must be read the Miranda rights and voluntarily waive the right to an attorney as well as to silence before making a confession. The attorney not only represents the defendant at legal proceedings, but also acts as a buffer against direct questioning by the police; the state must direct all further com-

---

4. State v. Bey (II), 112 N.J. 123, 134–135, 548 A.2d 887, 892 (1988).
5. *In re* State in the Interest of Carlo, 48 N.J. 224, 225 A.2d 110 (1966). *See also* State in the Interest of S.H., 61 N.J. 108, 293 A.2d 181 (1972).
6. State v. Flower, 224 N.J. Super. 208, 539 A.2d 1284 (1987). *See also* State v. Cook, 47 N.J. 402, 221 A.2d 212 (1966).
7. State v. Wade, 40 N.J. 27, 190 A.2d 657 (1963).
8. State v. Johnson, 42 N.J. 146, 199 A.2d 809 (1962).
9. State v. Miller, 76 N.J. 392, 388 A.2d 218 (1978).
10. R. 3:27-1.
11. R. 3:27-2.
12. State v. Gonzalez [Manuel], 114 N.J. 592, 556 A.2d 323 (1989).

munications concerning the defendant through the defendant's attorney. Thus, the right to counsel is critical both in and out of trial.

Whether the defendant waives the right at trial or at the time of custodial interrogation, the competency test is whether the defendant can make a voluntary, competent, and intelligent waiver of the right.[13] As was stated earlier, a voluntary waiver after being read the Miranda rights depends on the particular facts and surroundings of the case. The age, education, and intelligence of the defendant as well as the conduct of the authorities must be considered.

The New Jersey courts impose a very strict standard of scrutiny when a defendant wishes to waive the right to counsel at trial and to defend himself or herself. The court must make certain that the defendant is aware of[14]

> the nature of the charges, the statutory offenses included within them, the range of allowable punishments thereunder, possible defenses to the charges and circumstances in mitigation thereof, and all other facts essential to a broad understanding of the whole matter.

The judge must consider the particular facts and circumstances of the case including the background, experience, and conduct of the defendant.[15] Although the defendant need not have the skill and experience of a lawyer, he or she should be made aware of the dangers and disadvantages of self-representation, so that the record will establish that the defendant knows what he or she is doing with open eyes.[16] Only after such a "penetrating and comprehensive inquiry" will the court consider a waiver.[17]

Right to Waive a Jury Trial

Criminal defendants have a right to a jury trial unless it is waived with the approval of the court (see Chapter 5C.1).[18] A judge should not withhold a request for a waiver unless the trial judge has determined that[19]

---

13. State v. Kordower, 229 N.J. Super. 566, 552 A.2d 218 (App. Div. 1989).
14. State v. Cole, 204 N.J. Super. 618, 623, 499 A.2d 1030, 1033 (App. Div. 1985).
15. State v. Guerin, 208 N.J. Super. 527, 506 A.2d 743 (App. Div. 1986).
16. State v. Kordower, supra.
17. State v. Guerin, supra.
18. R. 1:8-1.
19. State v. Fiorilla, 226 N.J. Super. 81, 543 A.2d 958 (App. Div. 1988).

1. a defendant has not voluntarily, knowingly, and competently waived his or her constitutional right to jury trial with advice of counsel;

2. the waiver is not tendered in good faith, but as a stratagem to procure an otherwise impermissible procedural advantage; or

3. consequential, overriding, demonstrable, and articulated reasons exist to require a jury trial, which outweigh the reasons and record in support of waiver.

Precharging and Pretrial Evaluations

In some states, the prosecutor may request a mental health evaluation to determine whether to charge a person with a criminal offense or to divert him or her to the mental health system. Although New Jersey does not have such a provision, it does have an elaborate Pretrial Intervention Program (PTI), which does offer rehabilitative program alternatives to prison in selected cases.[1] MHPs may be involved in PTI evaluations or rehabilitation services, either as private consultants or as part of a PTI program.

Rationale of Pretrial Intervention

Participation in PTI, consisting of supervisory treatment in an approved rehabilitation program, is ordinarily limited to persons who have not been convicted previously of any offense, if such treatment[2]

1. provides applicants with opportunities to avoid ordinary prosecution by receiving early rehabilitative services or supervision, when that can reasonably be expected to deter future criminal behavior, and when there is an apparent causal connection between the offense charged and the rehabilitative need;

2. provides an alternative to prosecution for applicants who might be harmed by criminal sanctions, when PTI can serve as a sufficient sanction;

---

1. N.J.S.A. 2C:43-12 et seq. and R. 3:28.
2. N.J.S.A. 2C:43-12(a).

3. provides a mechanism for permitting the least burdensome form of prosecution possible for defendants charged with "victimless" crimes;

4. provides assistance in clearing the criminal court calendars for more serious crimes; or

5. provides deterrence of future criminal or disorderly behavior through PTI.

Admission of an applicant into PTI should be measured according to the person's amenability to correction, his or her responsiveness to rehabilitation, and the nature of the offense.

Criteria for Diversion to PTI

At any time prior to trial but after the filing of a criminal complaint, the assignment judge or designate may postpone all proceedings against an applicant and refer the applicant to a PTI program approved by the Supreme Court of New Jersey.[3] Such referral only requires the recommendation of a PTI program director and the approval of the prosecutor. The program director or the prosecutor must state his or her findings and conclusions regarding the PTI application. A rejected applicant is entitled to appeal the results before the designated judge.[4] A defendant may receive a PTI diversion only one time.[5]

The following criteria must be considered in recommending or approving an applicant's PTI application:[6]

1. the nature of the offense;

2. the facts of the case;

3. the motivation and age of the defendant;

4. the desire of the complainant or victim to forego prosecution;

5. the existence of personal problems and character traits that may be related to the crime and for which services are unavailable within the criminal justice system or that may be provided more effectively through supervisory treatment, and the probability that the causes of criminal behavior can be controlled by such treatment;

6. the likelihood that the crime is related to a condition or situation that could change through participation in PTI;

---

3. N.J.S.A. 2C:43-12(e).
4. N.J.S.A. 2C:43-12(f).
5. N.J.S.A. 2C:43-12(g).
6. *Id.*

7. the needs and interests of the victim and society;

8. the extent to which the applicant's crime constitutes part of a continuing pattern of antisocial behavior;

9. the applicant's criminal record and the extent to which he or she may present a substantial danger to others;

10. whether the crime is assaultive or violent;

11. whether prosecution would exacerbate the social problem that led to the crime;

12. the history of the use of physical violence toward others;

13. involvement with organized crime;

14. whether the crime is of such a nature that the value of PTI would be outweighed by the public need for prosecution;

15. whether the applicant's involvement with other people in the crime charged or other crime is such that prosecution would be recommended;

16. whether participation in PTI would adversely affect the prosecution of defendants; and

17. whether the benefits to society from PTI diversion outweigh the harm from abandoning criminal prosecution.

PTI guidelines have been developed by the New Jersey Supreme Court that further clarify the program and the criteria for acceptance.[7] The guidelines state that PTI is designed primarily for those who need short-term rehabilitation, within the period designated by the program.[8] This would normally exclude those suffering from chronic mental illness.[9] However, because the law has recently been amended to increase the maximum program participation to 3 years (supra), there may be greater flexibility in the selection of applicants.

The guidelines state further that if the crime were part of organized criminal activity or part of a continuing criminal business, or deliberately committed with violence or threat of violence against another person, or such a breach of public trust that admission would deprecate the seriousness of the crime, then the application ordinarily should be rejected.[10]

However, the applicant has the right to present to the program director any facts or materials demonstrating his or her amenability to the rehabilitative process, showing compelling reasons justifying admission, or establishing that a decision against enrollment would

---

7. R. 3:28.
8. R. 3:28, Guideline 1(d).
9. State v. Von Smith, 177 N.J. Super. 203, 426 A.2d 59 (App. Div. 1980).
10. R. 3:28, Guideline 2.

be arbitrary and unreasonable.[11] This right provides the applicant with the opportunity to present to the program director, and to the court if a rejection is appealed, any private assessments by an MHP.[12] The program director, likewise, may draw upon auxiliary MHP evaluations in making the determination.

PTI Treatment Procedure

The terms and duration of the PTI program must be in writing and agreed to by all parties.[13] During the program any criminal charges shall be held in inactive status. The judge may determine the length of the PTI program, which may not exceed 3 years. The time may be shortened upon the recommendation of the program director and consent of the prosecutor.

Upon completion of the program and with the recommendation of the program director and consent of the prosecutor, the charges against the accused may be dismissed, postponed, or reactivated.[14] If the conditions of PTI are violated, the judge may hold a summary hearing to determine whether the participant should be dropped from the program and required to face the charges against him or her.[15] No statement by a participant in a PTI program may be disclosed to the prosecutor or used as evidence in court.

---

11. *Id.*
12. State v. T.A.B., 228 N.J. Super. 572, 550 A.2d 528 (1988).
13. N.J.S.A. 2C:43-13.
14. R. 3:28(c).
15. N.J.S.A. 2C:43-13.

Bail Determinations

Almost all persons charged with a crime have the right to post bail to secure their release from jail pending trial.[1] Bail may not be excessive, however.[2] The sole purpose of the amount imposed and any other attendant conditions is to ensure that the defendant returns to court when required. High bail should not be used for punishment or "preventive detention."[3] MHPs may contribute to the bail determination through consultation with the court or other personnel advising the court, such as police officers and probation officers, regarding the person's mental health and community stability. Note, however, that the law does not require evaluation or consultation.

Determining Whether Bail Is Appropriate

Not every crime is bailable. If the court concludes that no amount of bail is sufficient to ensure that a defendant will probably not flee to avoid trial, bail may be denied.[4] The New Jersey Constitution prohibits bail in capital offenses where the "proof is evident or the presumption great" of the validity of the charge.[5] The Court Rules interpret this by stating,[6]

---

1. N.J. Const. art. 1, p. 11.
2. N.J. Const. art. 1, p. 12.
3. State v. Johnson, 61 N.J. 351, 294 A.2d 245 (1972).
4. *Id.*
5. N.J. Const. art. 1, p. 11.
6. R. 3:26-1.

All persons, except those charged with crimes punishable by death when the prosecutor presents proof that there is a likelihood of conviction and reasonable grounds to believe that the death penalty may be imposed, shall be bailable before conviction on such terms as, in the judgment of the court, will insure their presence in court when required.

In capital cases, the court must determine whether an aggravating factor exists that, if accepted by a jury, would allow it to impose the death penalty.[7] The prosecutor must prove a "fair likelihood" of conviction, beyond an arrest or indictment.[8]

Although bail procedures vary somewhat from county to county, typically bail may be set immediately after arrest by a municipal court judge or clerk, or a superior court judge.[9] Occasionally, arrested persons are committed to jail without bail. Every defendant placed in jail is interviewed the next day by a member of the bail unit of the criminal case management office. Basic information is obtained from each defendant that will assist in the bail determination (infra). When appropriate, family, friends, and arresting officers are consulted, but not about the details of the crime.

The incarcerated defendant is entitled to a "first appearance" before a superior court judge on the day following incarceration, at which time bail will be set or adjusted.[10] One court has held that a bail hearing is a "critical stage" of criminal prosecution, during which both the defendant and attorney are entitled to participate.[11] Bail for imprisoned defendants is reviewed by a superior court judge on a regular basis, or at the request of defense counsel.

Determining Amount and Conditions of Bail

Once it is determined that the circumstances warrant a bail decision, the court has the discretion to decide the amount of bail and any conditions imposed. The defendant must deposit, in cash to the court, 10% of the total amount of bail.[12] However, the judge must set the amount of bail on the basis of the reasonableness of the total, rather than upon the 10%.[13]

---

7. *Id.*
8. State v. Engel, 99 N.J. 453, 493 A.2d 1217 (1985).
9. State v. Fann, 239 N.J. Super. 507, 571 A.2d 1023 (1990).
10. R. 3:4-2.
11. State v. Fann, *supra.*
12. R. 3:26-4.
13. State v. McNeil, 154 N.J. Super. 479, 381 A.2d 1214 (App. Div. 1977).

The court sets an amount of bail sufficient to insure the defendant's presence when required, on the basis of[14]

> background, residence, employment and family status and, particularly, the general policy against unnecessary sureties and detention. In its discretion the court may order the release of a person on his own recognizance and may impose terms or conditions appropriate to such release.

The New Jersey Supreme Court has further elaborated the factors that must be considered in fixing the amount of bail:[15]

1. the seriousness of the crime charged against the defendant, the apparent likelihood of conviction, and the extent of the punishment prescribed by the legislature;

2. the defendant's criminal record and his or her previous record on bail;

3. the defendant's reputation and mental condition;

4. the length of residence in the community;

5. family ties and relationships;

6. employment status, record of employment, and financial condition;

7. responsible members of the community who would vouch for the defendant's reliability; and

8. any other factors indicating lifestyle, ties to the community, or bearing on the risk of failure to appear.

Failure to follow the court-imposed conditions may result in additional conditions, or revocation of the release and forfeiture of the deposit.[16]

---

14. R. 3:26-1.
15. State v. Johnson, *supra.*
16. R. 3:26-1(e).

5D.5

Competency
to Stand Trial

Justice requires not only that a criminal defendant be "sane" at the time of the offense (see Chapter 5D.9), but that the defendant be aware of and able to participate in any criminal proceedings against him or her. This right, originating in common law (case law), is guaranteed under the U.S. Constitution. Only psychiatrists may be appointed to conduct competency evaluations in New Jersey. Presumably, other MHPs may be appointed when necessary to assist the psychiatrist in the assessment.

Legal Determination of Competency to Stand Trial

Test of Competency

New Jersey law states that no person who lacks capacity to understand the proceedings against him or her or to assist in his or her own defense can be tried, convicted, or sentenced for the commission of an offense as long as the incapacity endures.[1] The prosecution must prove competency to stand trial, by a preponderance of the evidence.[2] Proof of competency must establish the defendant's capacity to understand and appreciate[3]

1. his or her presence in relation to time, place, and things;

---

1. N.J.S.A. 2C:4-4(a).
2. State v. Ortero, 238 N.J. Super. 649, 570 A.2d 503 (1989).
3. N.J.S.A. 2C:4-4(b).

2. that he or she is in a court of justice charged with a criminal offense;
3. that there is a judge on the bench;
4. that he or she has a lawyer who will undertake a defense against that charge;
5. that the defendant will be expected to describe his or her role in the charges if he or she chooses to testify, and understands the right not to testify;
6. that a jury may determine guilt or innocence, or if the defendant chooses to enter plea negotiations, he or she comprehends the consequences of a guilty plea and knowingly, intelligently, and voluntarily waives trial rights; and
7. that he or she has the ability to participate in an adequate presentation of the defense.

Note that under this standard, a person may be schizophrenic yet still be competent to stand trial.[4] Medications may be used to restore competency, and the defendant may even be required by the court to take medication to achieve that purpose.[5] Finally, it should be noted that a defendant can be legally "insane" at the time of the offense yet competent to stand trial and vice versa (see Chapter 5D.9).

A special problem arises when a defendant claims to be unable to remember anything concerning the offense. Although even complete amnesia has been held not to prevent a finding of competency,[6] the court should consider these factors:[7]

1. the extent to which the amnesia affected the defendant's ability to consult with and assist the lawyer;
2. the extent to which the amnesia affected the defendant's ability to testify in his or her own behalf;
3. the extent to which the evidence could be extrinsically reconstructed;
4. the extent to which the government assisted the defendant and his or her counsel in that reconstruction;
5. the strength of the prosecution's case, such as to negate all reasonable hypotheses of innocence; and
6. any other facts and circumstances that would indicate whether or not the defendant can receive a fair trial.

---

4. State v. Spivey, 65 N.J. 21, 319 A.2d 461 (1974).
5. State v. Otero, *supra*.
6. State v. Pugh, 117 N.J. Super. 26, 283 A.2d 537 (App. Div. 1971).
7. State v. Jasuilewicz, 205 N.J. Super. 558, 501 A.2d 583 (App. Div. 1985).

Even when the defendant claims that he or she is suffering from multiple-personality disorder, that the nondominant personality committed the crime, and that the dominant personality has no recollection of such event, he or she may be found competent to stand trial.[8]

An additional problem arises when a delusional defendant, who would be otherwise competent to stand trial, refuses to plead that he or she was insane at the time of the offense and insists upon an implausible argument such as self-defense.[9] In that case, a hearing is required to determine whether the choice to waive the insanity defense was knowing, intelligent, and voluntary. The defendant must be aware of his or her rights and alternatives, as well as the possible consequences of failing to assert the defense. The court may find the defendant competent but require that the issue of insanity be argued in the interests of justice, regardless of the defendant's wishes. If the jury does not vote for an acquittal on those grounds, the trial will continue with the alternative argument (e.g., self-defense).

Raising the Competency Issue

The issue of whether a defendant is competent to stand trial is usually raised by the defense attorney owing to difficulties in communicating with the person.[10] But the prosecution and court also have a duty to raise the competency issue whenever there is doubt regarding it. A mental examination will then be ordered, followed by a competency hearing.

Competency Hearing

After the competency evaluations have been completed, the court must determine whether the defendant is competent to stand trial.[11] If no one contests the findings of the court-appointed psychiatrist, the competency determination may be made on the basis of the report. Otherwise, there must be a hearing in which the psychiatrist(s) will testify. A determination of competency is not conclusive. If the defendant's condition deteriorates, or if further doubts about competency arise during trial, another competency evaluation must be ordered.[12]

---

8. State v. Badger, 229 N.J. Super. 288, 551 A.2d 207 (1988).
9. State v. Khan, 175 N.J. Super. 72, 417 A.2d 585 (App. Div. 1980).
10. State v. Spivey, *supra.*
11. N.J.S.A. 2C:4-6.
12. State v. Spivey, *supra.*

Competency Evaluation

Whenever there is "reason to doubt" the defendant's competency to stand trial, the court must appoint at least one psychiatrist to examine and report upon the person's mental condition.[13] The appointed psychiatrist must be from a list agreed upon by the court, the prosecutor, and the defendant. The court may order a 30-day commitment to a hospital or other facility to facilitate the examination. The defense may retain its own expert psychiatrist to perform an evaluation as well.

The competency report must include a description of the nature of the examination, a diagnosis, and an opinion regarding the defendant's capacity to understand the proceedings and to assist in his or her own defense.[14] If the defendant refuses to participate in the competency evaluation, the report must so state, along with an opinion as to whether the lack of cooperation was caused by mental incompetence.[15] The court may then permit an examination without cooperation, may appoint a different psychiatrist, or may commit the defendant for observation for up to 30 days. Any competency reports must be sent to the court, the prosecutor, and defense counsel.[16]

Confidentiality and Privileged Communications

The psychiatrists may ask questions regarding the crime charged, if necessary, to form an opinion regarding competency. Any inculpatory statements may be admitted into evidence only to determine the question of competency, not to determine guilt of the crime charged or any other issue.[17] This rule supercedes any claims of confidentiality (see Chapter 4.2) and privileged communication (see Chapter 4.3) that might otherwise apply, and includes all competency evaluations, whether ordered by the court or arranged through defense counsel.

---

13. N.J.S.A. 2C:4-5(a).
14. N.J.S.A. 2C:4-5(b).
15. N.J.S.A. 2C:4-5(c).
16. N.J.S.A. 2C:4-5(d).
17. N.J.S.A. 2C:4-5(b) and 2C:4-10.

Disposition of Defendants Found Incompetent to Stand Trial

If the court determines that a defendant lacks fitness to proceed (i.e., incompetent to stand trial), the criminal proceedings must be temporarily suspended.[18] The court may then commit the person to the custody of the Commissioner of Human Services. The defendant will be committed to a hospital if he or she is dangerous to self or others. Otherwise, outpatient placement or release will be arranged. No person can be committed to an institution, under this statute, longer than necessary to determine whether it is substantially probable that he or she will regain competence to stand trial in the foreseeable future.

Each defendant's incompetency must be reviewed every 6 months.[19] When competency has been restored, the criminal proceedings must resume. The court may dismiss charges against the defendant at a time when it would be unjust to hold a trial owing to the delay in proceedings, or if it is not substantially probable that competency will be restored in the foreseeable future.[20] The court must balance evidence regarding the prospects for regaining competency, the time period of the incompetency, the nature and extent of institutionalization, the likelihood of prejudice in trial due to the delay, the gravity of the crimes charged, and the public interest in prosecuting the charges. If charges are dismissed, the court may order either a discharge or hospitalization under the civil commitment laws (see Chapter 5E.4).

---

18. N.J.S.A. 2C:4-6(a).
19. N.J.S.A. 2C:4-6(c).
20. N.J.S.A. 2C:4-6(c) and (e) and State v. Gaffey, 92 N.J. 374, 456 A.2d 511 (1983).

5D.6

Provocation

The law[1] provides that persons who have committed murder[2] are entitled to be convicted of the lesser charge of manslaughter if the crime was committed in the heat of passion resulting from a reasonable provocation. There are four separate elements involved:[3]

1. the provocation must be adequate or sufficient to arouse the passions of an ordinary person beyond the power of his or her control,
2. there must not be reasonable time to cool off before killing the victim,
3. the provocation must actually have impassioned the perpetrator, and
4. the perpetrator must not have actually cooled off.

Words alone do not constitute adequate provocation.[4] Neither does a bump and an insult by the victim.[5] Nor does conduct that is alleged to have been sexually frustrating.[6] A threat with a gun or knife or an actual physical assault have been considered enough in the past to submit the issue to the jury.[7]

---

1. N.J.S.A. 2C:11-4.
2. N.J.S.A. 2C:11-3.
3. State v. Mauricio, 117 N.J. 402, 568 A.2d 879 (1990).
4. State v. Crisantos, 102 N.J. 265, 508 A.2d 167 (1986).
5. State v. King, 37 N.J. 285, 181 A.2d 158 (1962).
6. State v. Hollander, 201 N.J. Super. 453, 493 A.2d 563 (App. Div. 1985).
7. State v. Mauricio, *supra.*

Expert testimony regarding a defendant's state of mind at the time of a homicide is permitted under New Jersey law (see Chapter 5C.2) and may be used to support a finding of provocation.[8]

---

8. *See* State v. Pitts, 116 N.J. 580, 562 A.2d 1320 (1989).

5D.7

Mens Rea

The criminal code prescribes that the minimum requirement for criminal liability is a voluntary act (or omission to perform a duty) that caused the criminal result, plus the necessary "culpable mental state," formerly referred to as mens rea.[1] The purpose of determining a mental state is to distinguish between inadvertent or accidental acts and those that are performed with a "guilty mind." MHPs are legally entitled to testify on this issue (see Chapter 5C.2). They most frequently do so when a defendant argues that, owing to mental illness or defect, he or she lacked a culpable mental state required as an element of a crime (see Chapter 5D.8).

Culpable Mental States

The law defines the required mental state for each offense, with the majority of offenses requiring either purpose or knowledge. There are four hierarchical types of culpable mental states:[2]

1. *Purposely* means, with respect to conduct or a result, that a person's conscious object is to engage in such conduct or cause such a result.

2. *Knowingly* means, with respect to conduct or a result, that a person is aware or believes that his or her conduct is of that nature or that such circumstances exist, or he or she is aware of a high probability of their existence.

---

1. N.J.S.A. 2C:2-2.
2. *Id.*

3. *Recklessly* means, with respect to a result or circumstance, that a person consciously disregards a substantial and unjustifiable risk that the result will occur or that the circumstances exist. The risk must be of such a nature and degree that, considering the nature and purpose of the actor's conduct and the circumstances known to him or her, its disregard involves a gross deviation from the standard of conduct that a reasonable person would observe in the actor's situation.

4. *Negligently* means, with respect to a result or to a circumstance, that a person fails to perceive a substantial and unjustifiable risk that the result will occur or that the circumstance exists. The risk must be of such nature and degree that the failure to perceive it constitutes a gross deviation from the standard of care that a reasonable person would observe in the situation.

5D.8

Diminished Capacity

There are two primary versions of diminished capacity law in the United States. In some jurisdictions, the defense reduces the degree of crime for which the defendant may be convicted, even if the defendant's conduct satisfied all the formal elements of a higher offense. However, in most states, including New Jersey, the diminished capacity doctrine allows a criminal defendant to introduce evidence of mental abnormality at trial to negate a mental element of the crime charged, thereby completely exonerating the defendant of that charge.

Test of Diminished Capacity

Statutory law provides that[1]

> evidence that the defendant suffered from a mental disease or defect is admissible whenever it is relevant to prove that the defendant did not have a state of mind which is an element of the offense. In the absence of such evidence, it may be presumed that the defendant had no mental disease or defect which would negate a state of mind which is an element of the offense.

In practice, evidence of mental disease or defect is typically used to disprove that a defendant acted "purposely" or "knowingly" in committing an otherwise criminal act (see Chapter 5D.7). There must be a cognitive impairment that prevents knowing or purposeful behavior, rather than a mere emotional reaction such as rage or impassioned impulse.[2]

---

1. N.J.S.A. 2C:4-2.
2. State v. Carroll, 242 N.J. Super. 549, 577 A.2d 862 (App. Div. 1990).

Although diminished capacity may negate crimes such as murder, which require a purposeful or knowing mental state, the defendant still may be convicted if the behavior meets the statutory criteria for crimes requiring a "reckless" or other mental state, such as in aggravated manslaughter.[3] Regardless of whether the defendant raised the issue, the judge must instruct the jury to consider a "lesser included offense" if the evidence at trial presented a rational basis for such a verdict.[4]

Raising the Diminished Capacity Issue

In cases where the insanity defense is offered, diminished capacity evidence will be admitted as part of that defense, although the court will require the jury to make separate findings as to each issue.[5] In cases where insanity is not a defense, the court must first require the defendant to show[6]

1. that the alleged mental condition is relevant to his or her ability to have formed the requisite mental state;
2. that the medical theory is generally accepted within the scientific community (e.g., an accepted diagnosis); and
3. that the evidence is relevant to the defendant's condition.

If these conditions are met, the evidence will be presented at trial to help the jury in determining guilt or innocence of the particular charge.

Standard of Proof

Although the statute previously stated that evidence of mental disease or defect was an affirmative defense that had to be proved by a preponderance of the evidence,[7] that requirement has been held to be unconstitutional by the federal appeals court.[8] The court held that if the evidence of mental disease or defect creates a reasonable doubt about the required mental state, the defendant must

---

3. State v. Moore, 113 N.J. 239, 550 A.2d 117 (1988).
4. *Id.*
5. State v. Breakiron, 108 N.J. 591, 532 A.2d 199 (1987).
6. *Id.* and Evid. R. 8.
7. N.J.S.A. 2C:4-2.
8. Humanik v. Beyer, 871 F.2d 432 (1989), *cert. denied* by Beyer v. Humanik, 110 S.Ct. 57, 107 L.Ed.2d 25 (1989).

be acquitted of that charge. Consequently, the statutory burden of proof has been amended to conform to this ruling.

Intoxication and Diminished Capacity

The defense of intoxication has a separate statutory basis in New Jersey law.[9] Evidence of voluntary intoxication may be used to negate a crime that requires a "purposeful" or "knowing" mental state, but the evidence may still support conviction for a lesser-included offense requiring a "reckless" state of mind. The intoxication defense requires a condition by which the "mental or physical capacities of the actor, because of the introduction of intoxicating substances into the body, are so prostrated as to render him incapable of purposeful or knowing conduct."[10]

Intoxication is not considered a mental disease or defect that would require expert testimony in most circumstances. However, if the defendant suffered from "pathological intoxication," in which there was an extreme reaction due to a disease or other such condition, an insanity defense would be permitted.

---

9. N.J.S.A. 2C:2-8.
10. State v. Cameron, 104 N.J. 42, 58, 514 A.2d 1302, 1310 (1986).

5D.9

Criminal Responsibility

An early, yet still controversial, contribution of MHP expertise in the courtroom has been the evaluation of criminal defendants who plead not guilty by reason of insanity because of their mental state at the time of the offense. MHPs may evaluate a defendant and testify as to his or her psychological functioning at the time the criminal behavior occurred. The issue is typically raised by the defendant, who privately arranges for an MHP to conduct the evaluation. Once the issue is raised, the prosecution has the right to retain its own expert to perform a separate evaluation.

Legal Determination of Insanity

New Jersey has long adhered to the M'Naghten Rule as the test for criminal insanity.[1] The rule has two elements. To be found not guilty by reason of insanity, the defendant must not have known either (1) the nature and quality of the act or (2) that what he or she was doing was wrong. The test is essentially one of cognitive impairment, in which the purpose is to determine whether the defendant had sufficient mental capacity to understand what he or she was doing when the crime was committed.[2] New Jersey courts have been flexible in admitting any credible expert testimony on the insanity defense.[3] Whether a defendant "knew" the nature

---

1. N.J.S.A. 2C:4-1.
2. State v. Worlock, 117 N.J. 596, 569 A.2d 1314 (1990).
3. State v. Maik, 114 N.J. Super. 470, 277 A.2d 235 (App. Div. 1971), *modified*, 60 N.J. 203, 287 A.2d 715 (1972).

of the act or its wrongfulness has been interpreted to allow testimony as to whether the defendant "appreciated" such information.[4]

An example of the first element of the M'Naghten Rule would be a defendant who thought he was shooting a demon but was actually murdering his spouse. Thus he would not know the nature and quality of his act. A defendant who understood that she was killing her spouse but believed that God had commanded it as a righteous act would not know that what she was doing was wrong.[5]

The etiology of the mental disease or defect is also important. Voluntary intoxication or drug abuse alone is not grounds for an insanity defense (see Chapter 5D.8). However, "pathological intoxication," in which there was an extreme reaction such as a psychosis, would be grounds for a finding of insanity.[6]

Burden of Proof

Criminal defendants are presumed sane.[7] They must prove by a preponderance of the evidence that they were not responsible for their criminal conduct by reason of insanity.[8] In jury trials, the insanity verdict must be unanimous.[9]

Mental Examination

If a defendant intends to claim the insanity defense (or diminished capacity), he or she must serve a written notice upon the prosecutor within 30 days of informing the court whether the plea will be guilty or not guilty.[10] If both the defense and prosecution agree,

---

4. The New Jersey legislature has rejected two other formulations of the insanity test in other jurisdictions. The first, the irresistible impulse test, holds that a defendant might not be criminally responsible if as the result of mental illness, he or she did not have the power to choose between right and wrong—that is, the person acted under an irresistible impulse. The second, the American Law Institute Model Penal Code test, holds that a defendant "is not responsible for criminal conduct if at the time of such conduct as the result of mental disease or defect he lacks substantial capacity either to appreciate the criminality (wrongfulness) of his conduct or to conform his conduct to the requirements of law." Under this test, the incapacity need only be substantial rather than all or nothing, and the question is frequently one of capacity to control behavior rather than to understand it. State v. Worlock, *supra*.
5. Although she may know that it was legally wrong, she might not know that it was morally wrong, which is also encompassed in the New Jersey M'Naghten test. The test is not based on the defendant's own legal and moral beliefs, but on knowledge of the laws and morals of society. State v. Worlock, *supra*.
6. N.J.S.A. 2C:2-8 and State v. Maik, *supra*. *See also* State v. Cameron, 104 N.J. 42, 514 A.2d 1302 (1986).
7. N.J.S.A. 2C:4-2.
8. N.J.S.A. 2C:4-1.
9. State v. Gadson, 148 N.J. Super. 457, 372 A.2d 1143 (App. Div. 1977).
10. R. 3:12.

an independent expert may be appointed to determine the question of insanity. If there is no agreement, the defense may retain experts privately to perform an evaluation. If the defendant is unable to afford an expert evaluation, the state must pay for it.[11] The prosecution also has the right to a psychological examination.[12] Defense experts, but not the defense attorney, have the right to be present at the state's evaluation.

If the defendant is capable of cooperating with prosecution experts but refuses, the judge may order a temporary commitment to a hospital for observation and study.[13] If the defendant continues to be uncooperative, the judge may limit the defense testimony to the same extent as the prosecution testimony. The defense is entitled to copies of the prosecution expert reports, but it must also share the reports of its own experts.

Although it is the defendant's right to raise an insanity defense, a problem arises when a delusional defendant, who would be otherwise competent to stand trial (see Chapter 5D.2), refuses to plead that he or she was insane at the time of the offense and insists upon an implausible argument such as self-defense.[14] In that case, a hearing is required to determine whether the choice to waive the insanity defense was knowing, intelligent, and voluntary. The defendant must be aware of his or her rights and alternatives, as well as the possible consequences of failing to assert the defense. The court may find the defendant competent but require that the issue of insanity be argued in the interests of justice, regardless of the defendant's wishes. If the jury does not vote for an acquittal on those grounds, the trial will continue with the alternative argument (e.g., self-defense).

Finally, note that testimony by mental health experts is not conclusive. The jury may reject such testimony if they do not find it persuasive. The jury may also consider testimony from lay witnesses concerning the defendant's sanity, provided that such opinions are based upon facts within the knowledge of the witness.[15]

Confidentiality and Privileged Communications

In the majority of mental health examinations the information obtained by psychologists or psychiatrists is confidential (see Chapter

---

11. N.J.S.A. 2A:158A-5.
12. State v. Whitelow, 45 N.J. 3, 210 A.2d 763 (1965).
13. *Id.*
14. State v. Khan, 175 N.J. Super. 72, 417 A.2d 585 (App. Div. 1980).
15. State v. Morehous, 97 N.J.L. 285, 117 A.2d 296 (1922).

4.2) and privileged (see Chapter 4.3). This is not generally true when a criminal defendant is ordered to undergo an evaluation for competency to stand trial or for an insanity defense.

If the prosecution psychiatrist or psychologist can evaluate the defendant's insanity without any questioning about the crime, such inquiry should be made.[16] If it is necessary to inquire about the alleged crime, the defendant is required to cooperate fully, without the right to claim a privileged communication. Any inculpatory statements made will be admitted in court only to prove insanity, not to determine guilt or innocence of the crime.[17]

Commitment of Defendants Found Not Guilty by Reason of Insanity

After a defendant is found not guilty by reason of insanity, the court must order that he or she undergo an examination by a psychiatrist of the prosecutor's choice.[18] (The defendant may also arrange for a private psychiatric evaluation.) If the defendant refuses to cooperate, the judge may order a commitment to a state hospital for observation and evaluation.[19]

After the psychiatric evidence is presented in a hearing, the judge must release the defendant without supervision if the person is without danger to self or others.[20] The court may also release the defendant under court-ordered supervision or with specified conditions. However, if the defendant is found to be dangerous to self or others, he or she must be civilly committed (see Chapter 5E.4) to an approved (noncorrectional) hospital or institution, subject to periodic court review.

If the Commissioner of Human Services, the superintendent of the institution, or the committed person believes that he or she may be released without danger to self or others or that the person may be transferred to a less restrictive setting for treatment, an application must be made to the court that committed the defendant.[21] The court may appoint two psychiatrists to conduct an evaluation. If the reports satisfy the court that the committed person is no longer dangerous to self or others, the person may be discharged or released with conditions. Otherwise, the court must hold a civil commitment hearing and make a determination.

---

16. *Id.*
17. N.J.S.A. 2C:4-10.
18. N.J.S.A. 2C:4-8.
19. N.J.S.A. 2C:4-5(c).
20. N.J.S.A. 2C:4-8 and State v. Krol, 68 N.J. 236, 344 A.2d 289 (1975).
21. N.J.S.A. 2C:4-9.

Commitment requires that there be a substantial risk of dangerous conduct within the reasonably foreseeable future.[22] The probability of dangerousness and the seriousness of the potential harm must be considered. Although the determination of dangerousness involves a prediction of the defendant's future conduct, his or her past conduct should be considered an important predictor.[23] Dangerous conduct includes not only illegal behaviors, but also significant physical or psychological injury to persons or substantial destruction of property.

If the court orders a conditional release, its determination must be guided by the adequacy of supervisory controls to ensure public safety.[24] Careful follow-up and long-term psychiatric evaluation and treatment are generally required. Conditional releases may be modified or revoked, depending upon the patient's progress.

The prosecuting attorney has the right to be present and heard at all commitment proceedings.[25] Although the defendant is generally subject to civil commitment law, the continued commitment must be proved by a preponderance of the evidence at any hearing. In addition, the patient is usually not entitled to an in camera (private) hearing.[26] The defendant may be committed under the insanity laws up to the maximum period of confinement that could have been imposed if he or she had been found guilty of any charge.

---

22. State v. Krol, *supra*.
23. *Id.*
24. *Id.*
25. N.J.S.A. 2C:4-8(b) (3).
26. *In re* Commitment of Edward S., 118 N.J. 118, 570 A.2d 917 (1990).

5D.10

Battered Woman's Syndrome

The battered woman's syndrome describes a woman who has been physically abused by her husband or paramour on a regular basis over a period of time. In some states, including New Jersey, the law recognizes a defense to serious physical injury of a husband based on the battered woman's syndrome.

In the principal case regarding the issue, a battered wife killed her angry husband with a pair of scissors. The Supreme Court of New Jersey held that the battered woman's syndrome was relevant to the honesty and reasonableness of the defendant's belief that she was in imminent danger of death or serious injury, and therefore was an appropriate subject for expert testimony.[1] The court held further that the battered woman's syndrome has a sufficient scientific basis to permit the introduction of expert testimony regarding it (see Chapter 5C.2).

In a second case, the court held that expert testimony was permissible to explain why a battered woman remained with her boyfriend for the remainder of the day following an alleged assault. The victim's credibility was under attack and the testimony might have helped the jury assess her credibility not only from her testimony but also from her conduct that day.[2]

---

1. State v. Kelly, 97 N.J. 178, 478 A.2d 364 (1984).
2. State v. Frost, 242 N.J. Super. 601, 577 A.2d 1282 (1990).

5D.11

Rape Trauma Syndrome

Rape trauma syndrome describes behavioral, somatic, and psychological sequela of an attempted or successful forcible rape. In some states, the law allows a party to introduce evidence that a rape victim is suffering from rape trauma syndrome to assist in a prosecution where the defendant acknowledges that sexual intercourse occurred but claims that it was consensual. The presence of rape trauma syndrome tends to disprove that the victim consented. It has also been used as a defense when the raped individual attempts to murder the rapist. In this situation the rape victim attempts to argue "diminished capacity" (see Chapter 5D.8) because he or she was unable to form the necessary intent to commit that crime as a result of the syndrome.

Although there is no statute or case in New Jersey that addresses the rape trauma syndrome in criminal cases, the Supreme Court of New Jersey has recognized the concept in a civil case, in which it held that a woman suffering from rape trauma syndrome was psychologically incapacitated from filing a timely claim with the Violent Crimes Compensation Board.[1] The court permitted the filing of the claim after the expiration of the statutory 1-year period.

The New Jersey Supreme Court has also stated in another case that[2]

> defendants charged with sexual offenses against female victims of all ages have historically based attacks against witness reliability on unsound stereotypical notions of the nature of women. . . . We totally repudiate such thinking. . . . Rape complainants are no less credible than other victims.

---

1. White v. Violent Crimes Compensation Bd., 76 N.J. 368, 388 A.2d 206 (1978).
2. State v. R.W., *supra*, at 104 N.J. 30, n. 4., 514 A.2d 1295, n. 4.

The New Jersey legislature has also enacted a "rape shield" statute, which prevents defendants, in most cases, from attempting to discredit a complainant by challenging the person's past sexual history or lifestyle.[3] In light of the stated policy of the courts and the legislature, along with the admissibility of evidence regarding the battered wives syndrome (see Chapter 5D.10), it is probable that if the admissibility of rape trauma syndrome evidence is challenged in the appellate courts, such expert testimony will be admitted into evidence.

---

3. N.J.S.A. 2C:14-7.

5D.12

Hypnosis of Witnesses

A person who experiences stress or trauma while witnessing a legally important event may be unable to recount the event in sufficient detail to allow the police or attorneys to reconstruct the exact circumstances. Hypnosis may be used to alleviate the stress or other condition to allow for better recall. A legal issue arises regarding the reliability of the hypnotic memory when it is used for a legal purpose, such as in forming the basis for a search warrant or as evidence at a trial.

Hypnotically Induced Information in a Police Investigation

Police departments frequently use MHPs with expertise in hypnosis to obtain greater detail concerning a suspect or the details of the crime. In some states, these hypnotically induced statements may be used as the basis for the issuance of a search warrant only if there is other corroborating evidence. The police must be able to identify some other information that supports the evidence obtained from a person under hypnosis. This issue has not been directly addressed in the New Jersey courts. However, there has been one case in which an arrest was obtained on the basis of hypnosis without corroborating evidence.[1] Although the court did not rule on the validity of this procedure, it did quote with approval the following statement by Dr. Martin Orne:[2]

---

1. State v. Hurd, 86 N.J. 525, 432 A.2d 86 (1980).
2. *Id.* at 86 N.J. 539, 432 A.2d 93.

Hypnosis may be useful in some instances to help bring back forgotten memories following an accident or a crime while in others a witness might, with the same conviction, produce information that is totally inaccurate. . . . As long as this material is subject to independent verification, its utility is considerable and the risk attached to the procedure minimal.

Hypnotically Induced Courtroom Testimony

In the leading case considering the admissibility of hypnotically induced courtroom testimony, the New Jersey Supreme Court permitted its use under strict guidelines.[3] The test for the admission of "scientific" evidence obtained from procedures such as hypnosis or polygraph testing (see Chapter 5C.3) is that the evidence must be considered "reasonably reliable." The court held that testimony enhanced through hypnosis meets that test in a criminal trial if the court finds that the use of hypnosis was reasonably likely to result in recall comparable in accuracy to normal (fallible) human memory. If the testimony enhanced through hypnosis is ruled admissible, the hypnotist may still be cross-examined regarding the reliability of the procedures used in the particular case, but not to prove the general unreliability of hypnosis.

The court established several requirements that must be met before hypnotically refreshed testimony will be permitted in a criminal trial:

1. a psychiatrist or psychologist experienced in the use of hypnosis must conduct the session;

2. the professional conducting the session should be independent of and not regularly employed by the prosecutor, investigator, or the defense;

3. any information given to the hypnotist by law enforcement personnel or the defense prior to a hypnotic session must be recorded, either in writing or another suitable form;

4. before inducing hypnosis, the hypnotist should obtain from the subject a detailed description of facts as the subject remembers them;

5. all contacts between the hypnotist and subject must be recorded; and

---

3. *Id.*

6. only the hypnotist and subject should be present during any phase of the hypnotic session.

Whoever seeks to introduce hypnotically refreshed testimony has the burden of establishing its admissibility by clear and convincing evidence. Where the use of hypnosis results in a subsequent identification of a defendant, the defendant may also challenge the admissibility of the testimony on the constitutional grounds that the identification was so unnecessarily suggestive and conducive to irreparable mistaken identification as to amount to a violation of due process of law. However, such challenges would be expected to fail if the guidelines for admissibility of hypnotic evidence are followed.

Although the Hurd case concerned a prosecution witness, a New Jersey appellate court has held that the same procedures would also apply to defense witnesses, with the added precaution that an in camera pretrial screening of the proposed evidence would be required to determine the reliability of such testimony.[4]

---

4. State v. L.K., 244 N.J. Super. 261, 582 A.2d 297 (App. Div. 1990).

5D.13

Eyewitness Identification

The role of the eyewitness to any event is critical in many trials. The persons may be parties to the action, victims, or bystanders. Their testimony raises the issue of whether their identification at the time of the event, at a subsequent line-up (or other identifying procedure), or during the trial was valid. MHPs can contribute experimental and clinical expertise to aid the jury or court in evaluating the testimony of eyewitnesses.

Admissibility of Expert Testimony on Eyewitness Identification

In the leading case regarding the admissibility of expert testimony (see Chapter 5C.2) on eyewitness identification,[1] the Superior Court of New Jersey, Appellate Division, held that such evidence might be admissible after a trial court's evaluation of evidentiary factors.[2] The trial court must consider whether the testimony would assist the jury without unduly misleading or overwhelming it or impinging upon its exclusive fact-finding province, whether the testimony deals with matters outside the jury's ken or with assertions contrary to common assumptions, whether the testimony is based on reliable predicates and methodology that would yield uniform and reliable results, whether the import of the proffered testimony closely relates to the facts surrounding the eyewitness identification,

---

1. State v. Gunter, 231 N.J. Super. 34, 554 A.2d 1356 (App. Div. 1989), *cert. denied,* 117 N.J. 81, 563 A.2d 841 (1989).
2. Evid. R. 8.

whether the proffered witness has the requisite expertise, and whether the availability of the evidence transcends a single source.

Although the issue has not been fully resolved, the Supreme Court of New Jersey has recognized the fallibility of eyewitness testimony and supported its recognition by citations from the psychological literature.[3] In addition, the fact that the Supreme Court of New Jersey declined to review the *Gunter* decision (supra) demonstrates its implicit support of the appellate court's reasoning.

---

3. State v. Hurd, 86 N.J. 525, 432 A.2d 86 (1981).

5D.14

Competency to Be Sentenced

New Jersey law provides that criminal defendants may not be sentenced while, as the result of a mental illness or defect, they are unable to understand the proceedings against them or to assist in their own defense.[1] This rule and its application are discussed in detail in Chapter 5D.5.

---

1. N.J.S.A. 2C:4-4.

5D.15

Sentencing

After a finding of guilt, many states, including New Jersey, permit the court to request a mental health evaluation prior to reaching a sentencing decision. This information functions as a supplement to the presentence report by a probation officer. This chapter discusses the rules authorizing a mental health evaluation. In addition, special procedures governing sex offenders and death sentences are considered.

Presentence Mental Health Examination

If, after the required presentencing investigation, the court desires additional information concerning an offender before imposing a sentence, it may order that he or she receive a medical or mental examination.[1] Because there are no limitations as to who may undertake a mental health evaluation, it presumably includes all MHPs. The defendant may not be committed to an institution for the purpose of such an evaluation.[2] The examination report must be furnished to the defendant and to the prosecuting attorney.

In determining whether to impose a sentence or whether to impose a stricter or more lenient sentence than the presumptive sentence for a crime of a particular degree, the court must consider specific aggravating and mitigating circumstances. The presentence mental health evaluation will influence the sentencing to the extent

1. N.J.S.A. 2C:44-6.
2. R. 3:21-2.

that such factors are affected. Specific aggravating circumstances include the following:[3]

1. the nature and circumstances of the offense, and the role of the defendant, including whether or not it was committed in an especially heinous, cruel, or depraved manner;

2. the gravity and seriousness of harm inflicted on the victim, including whether the defendant knew or should have known that the victim was particularly vulnerable owing to age, disability, or health;

3. the risk that the defendant will commit another offense;

4. the defendant's betrayal of a position of trust or confidence;

5. the substantial likelihood that the defendant is involved in organized criminal activity;

6. the extent of the defendant's prior criminal record and the seriousness of the offense;

7. the defendant's commission of the offense pursuant to a monetary agreement; and

8. the defendant's commission of the offense against a law enforcement officer or because of the person's status as a public servant.

Specific mitigating factors include the following:[4]

1. the defendant's conduct neither caused nor threatened serious harm;

2. the defendant did not contemplate that the conduct would cause or threaten serious harm;

3. the defendant acted under a strong provocation;

4. there were substantial grounds tending to excuse or justify the defendant's conduct, though failing to establish a defense;

5. the victim of the defendant's conduct induced or facilitated the crime's commission;

6. the defendant has compensated or will compensate the victim or will participate in a program of community service;

7. the defendant has no history of prior delinquency or criminal activity or has led a law-abiding life for a substantial period of time before the commission of the present offense;

8. the defendant's conduct was the result of circumstances unlikely to reoccur;

---

3. N.J.S.A. 2C:44-1(a).
4. N.J.S.A. 2C:44-1(b).

9. the character and attitudes of the defendant indicate that he or she is unlikely to commit another offense;

10. the defendant is particularly likely to respond affirmatively to probationary treatment;

11. the imprisonment of the defendant would entail excessive hardship to the person or dependents;

12. the defendant has displayed willingness in cooperating with law enforcement authorities; and

13. the conduct of a youthful defendant was substantially influenced by another person more mature than the defendant.

Sex Crime Sentences

Whenever a person is convicted of aggravated sexual assault, sexual assault, aggravated criminal sexual contact, or an attempt to commit any of these crimes, the judge must order the person to be referred to the Adult Diagnostic and Treatment Center at Avenel for up to 10 days for a complete physical and psychological examination.[5] Chapter 5D.25 describes sentencing, evaluation, and treatment procedures for sex offenders.

Death Penalty Evaluations and Sentences

When a defendant is convicted of murder, the court must conduct a separate sentencing proceeding to determine whether the sentence should be at least 30 years without parole or death.[6] If there was a jury trial, the same jury that convicted the defendant of murder will determine the sentence, except if the judge orders a new jury for good cause. At the proceeding, the state must unanimously prove that aggravating factors outweigh mitigating factors beyond a reasonable doubt in order to secure a death sentence.[7] The defendant has the burden of producing evidence of mitigating factors, whereas the prosecution has the burden of proving aggravating factors.[8] MHPs are frequently asked to perform evaluations and provide expert testimony regarding such factors. Any reports must be made available to both the prosecution and the defense in advance of testimony.[9]

---

5. N.J.S.A. 2C:47-1.
6. N.J.S.A. 2C:11-3(c) (1).
7. State v. Biegenwald, 106 N.J. 13, 524 A.2d 130 (1987).
8. N.J.S.A. 2C:11-3(c) (2).
9. R. 3:13-4.

The aggravating factors that may be found by the jury or court include the following:[10]

1. the defendant has previously been convicted of murder;
2. the defendant purposely or knowingly created a grave risk of death to another person in addition to the victim;
3. the murder was outrageously or wantonly vile, horrible, or inhuman in that it involved torture, depravity of mind, or aggravated assault and battery to the victim;
4. the defendant committed the murder in expectation of financial gain;
5. the defendant committed the murder for payment;
6. the murder was committed for the purpose of preventing punishment for another offense;
7. the offense was committed while the defendant was attempting to commit (or escape after committing) robbery, sexual assault, arson, burglary, or kidnapping; and
8. the defendant murdered a public servant engaged in the commission of official duties or because of the victim's status as a public servant.

The mitigating factors that may be found by the jury or the court include the following:[11]

1. the defendant was under the influence of extreme mental or emotional disturbance insufficient to constitute a defense to prosecution;
2. the victim solicited, participated in, or consented to the conduct that resulted in his or her death;
3. the defendant was of youthful age at the time of the murder;
4. the defendant's capacity to appreciate the wrongfulness of his or her conduct or to conform his or her conduct to the law was significantly impaired as the result of mental disease or defect or intoxication, but not to a degree sufficient to constitute a defense to prosecution;
5. the defendant was under unusual and substantial duress insufficient to constitute a defense to prosecution;
6. the defendant has no significant history of prior criminal activity; and
7. the defendant rendered substantial assistance to the state in the prosecution of another person for the crime of murder.

---

10. N.J.S.A. 2C:11-3(c) (4).
11. N.J.S.A. 2C:11-3(c) (5).

In addition, the court may consider any other factor that may be relevant to the defendant's character or record or the circumstances of the offense.

5D.16

Probation

A sentencing court may place a defendant on probation following conviction. In this situation, the court must first suspend the imposition of the sentence.[1] This means that if the person does not abide by the terms of probation and the probation is revoked, the court may order the imposition or execution of the sentence. The court may impose conditions of probation on the defendant, including treatment by an MHP, in a specified facility if necessary.[2] MHPs may be required to provide the probation department or the court with treatment reports as a part of this process. The court may revoke probation or modify the terms, following a hearing at which the defendant has the right to counsel and to present witnesses.[3]

---

1. N.J.S.A. 2C:45-1.
2. N.J.S.A. 2C:45-1(b) (3).
3. N.J.S.A. 2C:45-4.

Dangerous Offenders

In some states, the criminal sentencing law has provisions for increasing the term of imprisonment of defendants who pose special risks or who are determined to be "dangerous offenders" because of propensity for future criminal activity. The legal determination of whether a defendant fits this category may depend on psychological characteristics that could be assessed by an MHP.

In New Jersey, a sentence may be increased owing to aggravating circumstances such as the risk of further crime, which might be assessed in a presentence MHP evaluation (see Chapter 5D.15). However, the primary statute governing extended terms of imprisonment for dangerous criminals requires that the defendant be either a persistent offender, a professional criminal, a second offender with a firearm, or a contract criminal.[1] Psychological considerations do not influence that determination.

---

1. N.J.S.A. 2C:44-3.

5D.18

Habitual Offenders

In some states, the criminal sentencing law has provisions for increasing the term of imprisonment of defendants who have a history of criminal offenses. The determination of whether a person is likely to commit additional offenses in the future may depend on psychological characteristics that could be assessed by a mental health professional.

In New Jersey, a sentence may be increased owing to aggravating circumstances such as the risk of further crime, which might be assessed in a presentence MHP evaluation (see Chapter 5D.15). However, the primary statute governing extended terms of imprisonment for habitual criminals requires that the defendant be either a persistent offender, a professional criminal, a second offender with a firearm, or a contract criminal.[1] Psychological considerations do not influence that determination.

---

1. N.J.S.A. 2C:44-3.

5D.19

Competency to Serve a Sentence

The law in several states provides that a criminal defendant must be competent to serve a sentence. New Jersey does not have such a statute. If an inmate suffers from mental illness, his or her problem typically would be covered by the laws governing the treatment of inmates and the transfer of inmates from prisons to mental health facilities (see Chapters 5D.20 and 5D.21).

However, courts are empowered to review postconviction effects of imprisonment on a defendant's physical and mental health.[1] New information about a person's health may result in a decision to release a prisoner because of illness or infirmity. However, the court must weigh the health needs of the inmate against the demands of public security.[2]

In addition, at the time of sentencing (see Chapter 5D.15), the court must consider as a mitigating factor whether imprisonment would entail excessive hardship to a person. A defendant's inability to understand or endure imprisonment must be an important consideration in determining the sentence.[3]

---

1. R. 3:21-10(b).
2. State v. Verducci, 199 N.J. Super. 329, 489 A.2d 715 (App. Div. 1985), *certif. denied,* 101 N.J. 256, 501 A.2d 926.
3. State v. Jarbath, 114 N.J. 394, 555 A.2d 559 (1989).

5D.20

Mental Health Services in Jails and Prisons

Mental health services in prisons and jails are a vital part of an overall health care program for incarcerated persons. MHPs may provide services as employees of these institutions or in a consulting capacity.

Mental Health Services in New Jersey Jails

Although county jails are not expected to assume responsibility for all the inmates' health needs, essential medical and mental health services must be provided.[1] Written standard operating procedures, approved by the assigned physician, must include screening, referral, and care of mentally ill and retarded inmates whose adaptation to the detention environment is significantly impaired. Facility personnel must be trained with regard to the recognition of symptoms of mental illness and retardation.

A social service program must be administered and supervised by a trained person, preferably someone having a master of social work (M.S.W.) degree.[2] Counseling must be provided by qualified, trained counselors, who provide individual and family counseling, crisis intervention, assistance in linking inmates with existing community resources, and discharge planning services. Drug and alcohol counseling and program services are also required.

---

1. N.J.A.C. 10A:31-3.15.
2. N.J.A.C. 10A:31-3.16.

Mental Health Services in New Jersey Prisons

Because of a finding by the New Jersey legislature that the Department of Corrections and the Department of Human Services have failed to coordinate an effective policy for mental health treatment of state prisoners, a law mandating the development of regulations in this area has been passed.[3] The regulations have not been promulgated to date. (For a discussion of the procedures by which inmates are transferred from prison to a mental health facility, see Chapter 5D.21.)

However, there are existing regulations governing the provision of psychological services to inmates by Department of Corrections employees. A Director of Psychological Services is responsible for coordinating and integrating the psychological activities of the department.[4] A licensed psychologist must be appointed Director of Psychology at each state correctional facility.[5] He or she must supervise all other individuals providing psychological services at the institution.

The psychology department of each correctional facility must develop and maintain an operations manual.[6] The manual must include procedures for making appointments, procedures for making recommendations and/or referrals, a flow chart of service delivery, a method of reporting psychological service results, and a method of establishing accountability for obtained results. Timely records of psychological services must be kept.[7] Only the psychology department is authorized to administer psychological evaluation data. Confidentiality of psychological records must be maintained in accordance with Department of Corrections general confidentiality standards. Psychological research must be conducted in accordance with administrative regulations.[8]

Inmate–Psychologist Confidentiality

Specific rules have been established regarding confidential communications between psychology department staff and inmates.[9]

---

3. N.J.S.A. 30:4-82.1 et seq.
4. N.J.A.C. 10A:16-4.1.
5. N.J.A.C. 10A:16-4.2.
6. N.J.A.C. 10A:16-4.5.
7. N.J.A.C. 10A:16-4.6.
8. N.J.A.C. 10A:1.
9. N.J.A.C. 10A:16-4.4.

Although licensed psychologists are bound to professional guidelines (see Chapters 1.3, 4.2, and 4.3), they and other unlicensed psychology staff are required to follow departmental regulations as well.

Communications between psychological staff and inmates are considered confidential and privileged, not to be disclosed to any person except in the following situations that present a clear and imminent danger to the inmate or others:[10]

1. where the inmate discloses planned action that involves a clear and substantial risk of imminent serious injury, disease, or death to the inmate or other identifiable persons;

2. where an escape plan is disclosed;

3. where drug trafficking presents a clear and imminent danger;

4. where the inmate discloses a suicide plan or other life-threatening behavior; or

5. where the inmate discloses a past, unreported murder, aggravated sexual assault, or arson that resulted in a death, under circumstances that present a clear and imminent danger to other identifiable persons.[11]

If a member of the psychology department receives information that may meet the criteria of an exception to confidentiality, the therapist and the chairperson must confer to determine if disclosure is necessary.[12] Relevant considerations include whether

1. it is known that another individual is serving a sentence for the confessed crime,

2. it can be ascertained that the crime was in fact committed but unprosecuted,

3. the inmate is under consideration for parole,

4. the inmate has described the criminal event or plan in credible detail, and

5. consequences of the inmate's past or intended conduct are considered dangerous to the health or well-being of correctional facility residents or personnel.

---

10. N.J.A.C. 10A:16-4.4(b).

11. The superior court has ruled that a former Department of Corrections regulation excepting inmate–patient communications from the psychotherapist–patient privilege when it was believed that disclosure would be more important to interests of substantial justice or safety was invalid as being broader than a situation that presents clear and imminent danger to the inmate or others. Matter of Rules Adoption Regarding Inmate–Therapist Confidentiality (N.J.A.C. 10A:16-4.4), 224 N.J. Super. 252, 540 A.2d 212 (App. Div. 1988).

12. N.J.A.C. 10A:16-4.4(c).

If the therapist and/or the chairperson believes that an exception to confidentiality has occurred, the matter should be reported immediately to the correctional facility superintendent, with the necessary facts and background information.[13] The superintendent may take whatever action is necessary, such as requesting a further investigation by the Internal Affairs Unit, arranging for a polygraph test, informing the prosecutor, initiating disciplinary charges against the inmate, placing the inmate in close custody, and increasing the inmate's custody status from minimum to maximum.

Upon entry into therapy, the inmate must be advised of the limitations on confidentiality, and a standard form describing such limitations must be signed.[14]

---

13. N.J.A.C. 10A:16-4.4(e).
14. N.J.A.C. 10A:16-4.4(h).

5D.21

Transfer From Penal to Mental Health Facilities

Because of a finding by the New Jersey legislature that the Department of Corrections and the Department of Human Services have failed to coordinate an effective policy for mental health treatment of state prisoners, a law mandating the development of regulations in this area has been passed.[1] The regulations have not been promulgated to date. (For a discussion of mental health services in jails and prisons, see Chapter 5D.20.) Nevertheless, when a prisoner becomes mentally ill to the extent that he or she meets the legal standards for civil commitment (see Chapter 5E.4), the person may be committed to a state psychiatric hospital.[2] If the inmate is in custody awaiting trial on criminal or disorderly persons charges, a standard form must be completed by the Department of Corrections.[3] Upon discharge, the department must again take custody of the person within 48 hours of receiving notice.

Prisoners who are under a death sentence may be committed to the Department of Human Services and treated in prison without physical transfer to a Department of Human Services facility, under an agreement between the Department of Corrections and the Department of Human Services.[4] In this regard, such prisoners do not have the full extent of the rights normally guaranteed to mental patients (see Chapter 5E.4).

---

1. N.J.S.A. 30:4-82.1 et seq.
2. N.J.S.A. 30:4-27.1 et seq.
3. N.J.S.A. 30:4-27.22.
4. *In re* Savage, 233 N.J. Super. 356, 558 A.2d 1357 (App. Div. 1989).

Parole Determinations

Parole is a conditional release from imprisonment that entitles the parolee to serve the remainder of the term outside the confines of the prison. It differs from probation in that the convicted person must first serve a period of time in a New Jersey Department of Corrections institution. Although a parole determination is generally made by the Board of Parole (Board) primarily on the basis of information supplied by the department, MHPs in or out of the system may be asked to provide information for the parole hearing. This chapter will describe the procedures and laws that apply to adult criminals. Regulations governing juveniles and youthful offenders, although administered by the Board of Parole, vary somewhat from these requirements.

Eligibility for Parole

Each inmate must receive a written letter by the Board within 90 days of confinement informing him or her of the primary eligibility date for parole.[1] Eligibility generally occurs after serving any statutory or court-ordered minimum term or, if there is no minimum, one third[2] of the sentence imposed less commutation time for good behavior and institutional assignments. The prosecuting attorney or the sentencing court may advise the Board that the punitive aspects of the sentence have not been fulfilled at the time of the

---

1. N.J.S.A. 30:4-123.51.
2. Third or fourth offenders must serve one half or two thirds of their sentences, respectively.

primary eligibility date, in which case the date will be statutorily recalculated and extended.[3]

If a panel of the Board determines that an inmate has seriously or persistently violated institutional rules or has engaged in indictable conduct while incarcerated, the inmate's parole eligibility date may be increased pursuant to a schedule developed by the Board.[4] Likewise, the eligibility date may be decreased by a Board panel if an inmate has made exceptional progress by participation in institutional or community programs.[5]

Board of Parole

The Board consists of seven full-time members with training or experience in law, sociology, criminal justice, or related social sciences, appointed by the governor to terms of 6 years.[6] It is authorized to determine all parole decisions in the state, and it may develop any necessary administrative rules in conjunction with its duties.[7]

The Board chairperson assigns each parole case to a member of the Board, who reviews a preparole report containing all sentencing and correctional records.[8] If he or she determines that there is no basis for denial of parole in the materials, a recommendation for parole will be made to the full Board, which may approve the decision by majority vote. However, if there is a basis for parole denial, the Board member must arrange an informal parole hearing, at which a Board panel will receive any relevant and reliable documents and testimony. The inmate has the right to be aided by a Board representative and may present as well as rebut any evidence, including evaluations from MHPs.[9]

Prior to the hearing, the inmate has the right to receive a copy of the preparole report, which contains preincarceration records; penal conduct records; a complete report on the inmate's social, physical, and mental condition; a report on the inmate's parole plans; and any information bearing upon the likelihood that the inmate will commit a crime if released on parole.[10] Only those documents that have been classified as confidential pursuant to Board regulations will be excluded from the report.

---

3. N.J.S.A. 30:4-123.51.
4. N.J.S.A. 30:4-123.52(a).
5. N.J.S.A. 30:4-123.52(b).
6. N.J.S.A. 30:4-123.47.
7. N.J.S.A. 30:4-123.48 and N.J.A.C. 10A:70-1.1 et seq.
8. N.J.S.A. 30:4-123.55.
9. N.J.A.C. 10A:71-3.11 and 13.
10. N.J.S.A. 30:4-123.54.

The inmate must be released at the time of parole eligibility, unless the evidence from the report and hearing indicates by a preponderance of the evidence that there is a substantial likelihood that the inmate will commit a crime if released at such time.[11] In that case, the Board must issue a new parole eligibility date for the inmate on the basis of a predetermined schedule.[12] The inmate must be released on the new date unless new information indicates that there is a substantial probability that the inmate will commit a crime if released. Any decisions by the panel may be appealed to the full Board.[13] Board decisions will be upheld by the courts unless they are arbitrary and capricious.[14]

Parole Conditions

Each parolee must agree in writing to conditions established by the Board panel.[15] Such conditions must include a requirement that the parolee not commit further crimes, that he or she obtain permission for any changes in residence, and that there be regular meetings with the parole officer. Other conditions may also be imposed, such as a requirement of full or partial restitution to the victim, psychotherapy by MHPs, or hospitalization. The parole officer is obligated to provide assistance to the parolee in obtaining employment, education, or vocational training and in meeting other obligations.

A person subject to parole commits a felony if he or she goes into hiding or leaves the state with the purpose of avoiding supervision. Abandoning a place of residence without prior permission of the supervision system is prima facie evidence of a purpose to avoid such supervision.[16]

Any parolee who has seriously or persistently violated the conditions of parole may have it revoked.[17] Any parolee who is convicted of a crime committed while on parole may have it revoked. Parole may be revoked on new criminal charges upon application of the prosecutor and concurrence by the Board chairperson, when the charges are serious and the parolee poses a danger

---

11. N.J.S.A. 30:4-123.53.
12. N.J.S.A. 30:4-123.56.
13. N.J.S.A. 30:4-123.58.
14. New Jersey State Parole Bd. v. Cestari, 224 N.J. Super. 534, 540 A.2d 1334 (App. Div. 1988), *cert. denied*, 111 N.J. 649, 546 A.2d 558 (1988).
15. N.J.S.A. 30:4-123.59.
16. N.J.S.A. 2C:29-5.
17. N.J.S.A. 30:4-123.60.

to public safety. A Board panel must hold a parole revocation hearing within 60 days after the parolee is returned to custody, and parole can remain revoked only after clear and convincing evidence that the parole was seriously or persistently violated.[18] A new parole eligibility date must then be set.

---

18. N.J.S.A. 30:4-123.63.

5D.23

Competency to Be Executed

Although New Jersey has no statutory law that authorizes or provides for the delay of execution of an "insane" person, the principle that a person must be competent to be executed has been long recognized in common law.[1] New Jersey courts also have upheld the ruling that no person may be executed if he or she is incapable of understanding the nature of the proceedings and his or her impending fate and execution.[2]

1. Solesbee v. Balkcom, 339 U.S. 9, 70 S.Ct. 457, 94 L.Ed. 604 (1950).
2. In re Lang, 77 N.J.L. 207, 71 A. 47 (1908). See also In re Herron, 77 N.J.L. 315, 72 A. 133 (1909).

5D.24

Pornography

The law prohibits a person from selling obscene material to anyone 18 years of age or older.[1] However, a municipality may adopt as part of its zoning ordinances an ordinance permitting the sale of obscene material in a particular location. There is also a statute that prohibits knowledgeable selling of obscene materials to a person under 18, or admitting such a person into an obscene film.[2] Finally, it is prohibited to communicate obscenity in a public place such as a street, shopping mall, or bus.[3]

MHPs may be asked to evaluate and testify whether the dominant theme of a work taken as a whole appeals to a prurient interest in sex, whether a work is patently offensive because it affronts contemporary community standards regarding sexual matters, or whether the work is utterly without redeeming social value.[4] Although expert testimony regarding these issues may be required where the defense argues that a work has serious literary, artistic, political, or scientific value, it is not necessary in cases where there is no such issue.[5]

Whether particular materials are obscene depends on the definitions used in the laws:[6]

1. *Obscene material* means any description, narrative account, display, or depiction of specified sexual activity (infra) or a specified

---

1. N.J.S.A. 2C:34-2.
2. N.J.S.A. 2C:34-3.
3. N.J.S.A. 2C:34-4.
4. Keuper v. Wilson, 111 N.J. Super. 489, 268 A.2d 753 (1970).
5. State v. Wein, 162 N.J. Super. 159, 392 A.2d 607 (App. Div. 1978).
6. N.J.S.A. 2C:34-2 and 3.

anatomical area (infra) contained in a picture, publication, sound recording, live performance, or film, which by means of posing, composition, format, or animated sensual details

a. depicts or describes in a patently offensive way ultimate sexual acts (normal or perverted, actual or simulated), masturbation, excretory functions, or lewd exhibition of the genitals;

b. lacks serious literary, artistic, political, or scientific value when taken as a whole; and

c. is part of a work that, to the average person applying contemporary community standards, as a dominant theme taken as a whole, appeals to a prurient interest.

2. *Obscene film* means any motion picture film or preview or trailer to a film, not including newsreels portraying actual current events or pictorial news of the day, in which a scene, taken by itself

a. depicts a specified anatomical area or specified sexual activity, or the simulation of a specified sexual activity, or verbalization concerning a specified sexual activity; and

b. emits sensuality sufficient, in terms of the duration and impact of the depiction, to appeal to a prurient interest.

3. *Specified anatomical area* means less than completely and opaquely covered human genitals, pubic region, buttock, or female breasts below a point immediately above the top of the areola, or human male genitals in a discernibly turgid state, even if covered.

4. *Specified sexual activity* means human genitals in a state of sexual stimulation or arousal; any act of human masturbation, sexual intercourse, or deviate sexual intercourse; or fondling or other erotic touching of covered or uncovered human genitals, pubic region, buttock, or female breast.

5D.25

Services for Sex Offenders

In some states, including New Jersey, the law provides specialized services for sex offenders through sentencing to a treatment program. MHPs are involved in evaluating the individual, testifying in court, and providing treatment.

Referral to the Adult Diagnostic and Treatment Center

Whenever a person is convicted of aggravated sexual assault, sexual assault, aggravated criminal sexual contact, or an attempt to commit any of these crimes, the judge must order the person to be referred to the Adult Diagnostic and Treatment Center at Avenel for up to 10 days for a complete physical and psychological examination (see Chapter 5D.15).[1] If the examination finds that the offender's conduct was characterized by a pattern of repetitive, compulsive behavior, the court may sentence the offender to the center for psychological treatment, if the center recommends it.[2] Even with this sentence, the court must also establish a sentence within statutory sentencing guidelines. If the recommendation of the center is probation combined with a specific form of treatment, the court may alternatively order such a sentence.

Whenever the court orders an examination at Avenel, the defendant and prosecuting attorney are entitled to a copy of the re-

---

1. N.J.S.A. 2C:47-1.
2. N.J.S.A. 2C:47-3.

port, which will otherwise remain confidential.[3] The defendan has the right to arrange for a private psychological evaluation and to present evidence, as well as contest the findings of the center's report at a hearing prior to sentencing.[4]

Treatment and Parole

The Department of Corrections must provide for the treatment of a person committed to the center at Avenel.[5] The Commissioner of Corrections, on the basis of his or her discretion, may order the transfer of a person out of the center if the treatment is failing.

A Special Classification Review Board (SCRB), appointed by the commissioner, must review the psychological and physical condition of all inmates eligible for parole consideration at least twice per year.[6] Any person at the center at Avenel can be released under parole (see Chapter 5D.22) only after a recommendation by the SCRB.[7] The review board must determine that the person is capable of making an acceptable social adjustment in the community. If, upon the written recommendation of the SCRB, continued confinement is not necessary, the commissioner also may petition the sentencing court for modification of the original sentence.

3. R. 3:21-3.
4. *Id.* and State v. Howard [Charles G.], 110 N.J. 113, 539 A.2d 1203 (1988).
5. N.J.S.A. 2C:47-4.
6. N.J.A.C. 10A:9-8.4.
7. N.J.S.A. 2C:47-5.

5D.26

Services for Victims of Crimes

Some states, including New Jersey, have enacted laws that provide victims of crimes with the services of MHPs and others.[1]

Violent Crimes Compensation Board

The Violent Crimes Compensation Board (Board) is composed of five members, including at least three attorneys, appointed by the governor.[2] It is in the Department of Law and Public Safety, although independent of it. The Board is authorized to hold hearings to determine whether and how much crime victims may be compensated for their injuries.[3]

The Board may order the payment of compensation for the commission or attempted commission of aggravated assault, mayhem, threats to do bodily harm, lewd or obscene acts, indecent acts with children, kidnapping, murder, manslaughter, rape, or any other crime involving violence, including domestic violence, burglary, or tampering with a drug or food product.[4] In addition, compensation may be given for personal injury or death that resulted from an attempt to prevent the commission of crime or to arrest or aid the arrest of a suspected criminal. Finally, compensation may be given for victims of drunk driving offenders.

The Board may order payment of compensation to the victim or to the victim's caretaker to reimburse monetary losses.[5] In ad-

1. N.J.S.A. 52:4B-1 et seq. and N.J.A.C. 13:75-1.1 et seq.
2. N.J.S.A. 52:4B-3.
3. N.J.S.A. 52:4B-7.
4. N.J.S.A. 52:4B-11.
5. N.J.S.A. 52:4B-10.

dition, dependents may be compensated when the victim has died. The Board is authorized to consider the behavior of the victim during the crime and may alter an award on the basis of provocation, consent, or past history. The Board may order compensation regardless of whether there is a prosecution or conviction of a perpetrator. An emergency award may be given prior to the hearing when compensation is likely and the applicant will suffer undue hardship without immediate funding.[6]

Psychotherapy and counseling fees are reimbursable up to $150 per hour for psychiatrists, $110 per hour for psychologists, $90 per hour for licensed marriage and family counselors, and between $80 and $90 per hour for social workers, depending on their qualifications.[7] However, the board is currently reimbursing only 75% of this fee schedule. Current board policy reimburses MHPs up to 50 sessions for a direct victim of crime, and up to 24 sessions for a secondary victim, such as a family member.

The Board may award compensation for[8]

1. reasonable expenses incurred as the result of the injury or death of the victim;

2. loss of earning power as the result of total or partial incapacity of the victim;

3. pecuniary loss to the dependents of the deceased victim; and

4. any other reasonable financial loss resulting from the injury or death of the victim, including medical care, psychotherapy, and rehabilitation.[9]

Prior to a hearing, the applicant must submit reports from all physicians or religious practitioners who have treated or examined the victim.[10] A panel of medical experts created by the Board and the Medical Society of New Jersey will review the materials and conduct an independent examination when appropriate.[11]

The victim must apply for an award within 2 years after the date of injury unless there is good cause for delay.[12] In one case, the psychological effects of rape trauma syndrome in delaying the filing of a claim were held to be a justifiable reason for filing after the 2-year statute of limitations had expired.[13] No compensation

---

6. N.J.S.A. 52:4B-10.1.
7. N.J.A.C. 13:75-1.27.
8. N.J.S.A. 52:4B-12.
9. *Id.* and N.J.A.C. 13:75-1.7.
10. N.J.S.A. 52:4B-14.
11. *Id.*
12. N.J.S.A. 52:4B-18.
13. White v. Violent Crimes Compensation Bd., 76 N.J. 368, 388 A.2d 206 (1978).

can be awarded if it results in unjust enrichment to the offender, or if the victim does not cooperate with the reasonable requests of law enforcement authorities without a compelling health or safety reason.[14] The maximum award is $25,000.[15] Police departments and hospitals are obligated to inform crime victims about the Board and, if the crime is a sexual assault, about the location of nearby rape crisis centers.[16]

Other Victim Services

The Board is also responsible for establishing and maintaining a system of victim counseling services throughout the state.[17] The centers provide free assistance to victims, including information on filing a compensation claim, emergency food and clothing, employment opportunities, and referrals to agencies and attorneys.

Services for victims and potential witnesses in criminal prosecutions are also provided by the Office of Victim-Witnesses Advocacy in the Division of Criminal Justice, Department of Law and Public Safety.[18] The office must provide services upon request for victims and witnesses, including updated information and assistance regarding their role in the trial, information about the defendant's legal status, and advice about the Crime Victim's Compensation Board.[19] The office must provide assistance to victims in submitting a written statement to the county prosecutor about the impact of the crime, before the decision is made whether to file criminal charges. It must also notify victims of the right to make an in-person statement directly to the sentencing court concerning the impact of the crime.

Finally, the curriculum for police training courses throughout the state must include training on responding to the needs of crime victims and on services available to provide assistance.[20] In-service training must be made available to police officers, assistant prosecutors, county detectives, and investigators on specialized needs of crime victims and available services.

---

14. N.J.S.A. 52:4B-18.
15. N.J.S.A. 52:4B-18.1.
16. N.J.S.A. 52:4B-22.
17. N.J.S.A. 52:4B-25.
18. N.J.S.A. 52:4B-43.
19. N.J.S.A. 52:4B-44.
20. N.J.S.A. 52:4B-47.

Voluntary or Involuntary Receipt of State Services

5E.1

Medicaid

Medicaid is the federally supported program whereby the states provide direct payments to suppliers of medical care and services for individuals receiving cash payments in programs such as old-age assistance, aid to needy families with dependent children, aid to the blind, and aid to the disabled. It provides "last resource benefits" only when there are no other funds or services providing payment.[1] In New Jersey, the program is administered by the Division of Medical Assistance and Health Services in the Department of Human Services.[2]

Inpatient Treatment

Psychiatric hospitalization is reimbursed only for treatment in acute care hospitals or in psychiatric institutions if the individual is over 65 or under 21 years old.[3] Medicaid provides scheduled payment for treatment by licensed psychologists and psychiatrists and reimburses for assessment, psychological testing, psychotherapy, and drug prescriptions. Reimbursement for inpatient care is based on the medical necessity of the admission and may not exceed 20 days, unless the provider completes a recertification form for an additional 20-day period of treatment.[4]

---

1. N.J.S.A. 30:4D-2.
2. N.J.S.A. 30:4D-1 et seq. and N.J.A.C. 10:49-1.1 et seq.
3. N.J.A.C. 10:49-1.4.
4. N.J.A.C. 10:52-1.4.

Outpatient Services

Medicaid reimburses outpatient services of licensed psychologists and psychiatrists in private practice, hospital settings, mental health clinics, and narcotic and drug abuse treatment centers.[5] Except in hospital settings, prior authorization is required for psychiatric and psychological services exceeding $300 in any 12-month period.[6] To qualify for reimbursement, the psychologist or psychiatrist must meet the qualifications of an "eligible provider" and receive a provider identification number.[7]

---

5. N.J.A.C. 10:66-1.6.
6. N.J.A.C. 10:54-1.5 and 10:67-1.8.
7. N.J.A.C. 10:49-1.3.

5E.2

Health Care Cost Containment System

Some states have health care cost containment systems that administer medical and other services to indigent persons. However, in New Jersey, the Medicaid Program is administered by the Division of Medical Assistance and Health Services in the Department of Human Services (see Chapter 5E.1).

5E.3

Voluntary Civil Admission of Mentally Ill Adults

The law provides for the voluntary admission of mentally ill persons to state-operated facilities. MHPs are involved in this process, both in evaluating the person for admission and in providing services within the facility.

Evaluation and Admission

The law provides for a screening service to evaluate all potential patients who may be in need of commitment to a psychiatric facility or hospital (see Chapter 5E.4).[1] The screening service is authorized to provide emergency and voluntary treatment to the person, and may transport and detain him or her for up to 24 hours for the purpose of providing treatment and conducting an assessment. If the person is in need of hospitalization, voluntary admission may be agreed upon.

Voluntary admission applies to an adult who is mentally ill; whose mental illness causes the person to be dangerous to self, others, or property; who is willing to be admitted to a facility voluntarily for care; and who needs care at a short-term care or psychiatric facility because other facilities or services are not appropriate or available.[2] A person may also be voluntarily admitted to a psychiatric facility if his or her mental illness presents a substantial likelihood of rapid deterioration in functioning in the near future, there are no appropriate community alternatives, and the psychi-

---

1. N.J.S.A. 30:4-27.5(a).
2. N.J.S.A. 30:4-27.2(ee).

atric facility can admit the person and remain within a rated capacity.

A person may be admitted voluntarily only after being informed orally and in writing of statutory discharge provisions that allow the facility to initiate involuntary commitment proceedings if necessary.[3] If the mental health screener determines that the person is not in need of admission or commitment to a psychiatric facility, the screener must refer the person to an appropriate community mental health center or social services agency, or to appropriate professional or inpatient care in a psychiatric unit of a general hospital.[4]

Within 20 days of a voluntary admission or a request by a patient to convert from involuntary to voluntary status, the court must hold a hearing to determine whether the patient had the capacity to make an informed decision to be voluntarily admitted or converted, and whether the decision was made knowingly and voluntarily. Counsel must be appointed to represent the patient at the hearing.[5]

Discharge

If a voluntary patient requests discharge from a psychiatric facility before the treatment team recommends it, such request must be documented in the patient's clinical record.[6] The facility must discharge the patient as soon as possible, but no later than a maximum of 48 hours or at the end of the next working day from the time of the request, whichever is longer. However, if the treatment team determines that the patient needs involuntary commitment, court proceedings may be initiated (see Chapter 5E.4). In that case, the patient may be detained only after receiving a temporary court order.

---

3. N.J.S.A. 30:4-27.9.
4. N.J.S.A. 30:4-27.5(e).
5. R. 4:74-7(2).
6. N.J.S.A. 30:4-27.20.

Involuntary Civil Commitment of Mentally Ill Adults

The law pertaining to involuntary civil commitment concerns mentally ill adults, as well as minors (see Chapter 5A.19).[1] MHPs are involved in this process by evaluating the person for admission, testifying in court as to their findings, and providing services within the facility to which the person is committed. Physicians must be involved in the evaluation process, although other MHPs may assist.

Terms and Definitions

Before considering the operation of the law, it is important to understand the terms it employs and their legal meanings:[2]

1. *Division* refers to the Division of Mental Health and Hospitals in the Department of Human Services, which administers state psychiatric facilities.

2. *Clinical certificate* means a form prepared by the division that is completed by the psychiatrist who has examined a person. The certificate concludes that the person needs involuntary commitment and describes the facts on which the conclusion is based.

3. *Dangerous to self* means that by reason of mental illness the person has threatened or attempted suicide or serious bodily

---

1. Habilitation and other services for developmentally disabled and retarded persons are discussed in Chapter 5E.7.
2. N.J.S.A. 30:4-27.2.

harm, or has behaved in such a manner as to indicate that the person is unable to satisfy the need for food, essential medical care, or shelter, so that it is probable that substantial bodily injury, serious physical debilitation, or death will result within the reasonably foreseeable future.

4. *Dangerous to others or property* means that by reason of mental illness there is a substantial likelihood that the person will inflict serious bodily harm upon another person or cause serious property damage within the reasonably foreseeable future. The determination shall take into account a person's history, recent behavior, and any recent act or threat.

5. *In need of involuntary commitment* refers to an adult who is mentally ill; whose mental illness causes the person to be dangerous to self, others, or property; who is unwilling to be admitted to a facility voluntarily for care; and who needs inpatient care because other services are not appropriate or available to meet the person's mental health care needs.

6. *Mental health screener* means a psychiatrist, psychologist, social worker, registered professional nurse, or other individual trained to do outreach for the purposes of psychological assessment who is employed by a screening service.

7. *Mental illness* means a current substantial disturbance of thought, mood, perception, or orientation that significantly impairs judgment, behavior, or capacity to recognize reality, but it does not include simple alcohol intoxication, transitory reaction to drug ingestion, organic brain syndrome, or developmental disability unless it results in the severity of impairment described herein.

8. *Patient* means a person over the age of 18 who has been admitted to a psychiatric facility.

9. *Screening service* means a public or private ambulatory care service, designated by the commissioner, that provides mental health services including assessment, emergency, and referral services to mentally ill persons in a specific geographic area.

Admission

The Commissioner of Human Services must designate one or more mental health agencies or facilities in each county as a screening service.[3] The screening service has the responsibility of assessing

---

3. N.J.S.A. 30:4-27.4.

every person who may need psychiatric commitment.[4] The screening may occur at the facility of the screener, or the screening service may need to make a screening outreach visit if the person is unwilling or unable to come to the screening service for an assessment.

The screening service may provide emergency and consensual treatment (see Chapter 5E.3) to the person being assessed, and may transport or detain the individual for up to 24 hours for the purposes of providing treatment and conducting the assessment.[5] When involuntary commitment seems necessary, the screener must report the person's history on a clinical certificate and give reasons why alternative facilities are inappropriate for the person. If the psychiatrist (or designated physician) agrees with these findings after an independent assessment, he or she must complete the clinical certificate.

Upon completion of the screening certificate, the screening service must determine the appropriate facility in which the person should be placed.[6] A person normally would be hospitalized in a short-term care facility, except that a psychiatric hospital should be considered if the individual has been admitted three times or has been an inpatient for 60 days at a short-term care facility during the preceding 12 months. The screening service must arrange for transportation to the appropriate facility.

A law enforcement officer must take custody of a person and transport the individual immediately to a screening service if he or she has reasonable cause to believe that the person is in need of commitment or if a mental health screener has certified on a clinical certificate that the person requires commitment.[7] The officer is authorized to remain at the screening center as long as necessary to protect the safety of the person in custody as well as the safety of the community.

The director of a facility must notify appropriate agencies to arrange for the care of any dependents and to ensure the protection of a person's property while that individual is detained.[8] The facility is authorized to provide assessment, treatment, rehabilitative services, and discharge services. An individual must not be committed unless he or she is "in need of involuntary commitment" (supra). After referral from a screening service, the person may be detained in a facility without court order for no more than 72 hours after the screening certificate was executed. During this period, the facility may initiate court proceedings for involuntary commitment.

---

4. N.J.S.A. 30:4-27.5.
5. Id.
6. N.J.S.A. 30:4-27.5(b).
7. N.J.S.A. 30:4-27.6.
8. N.J.S.A. 30:4-27.9.

Commitment Proceedings

A psychiatric facility initiates commitment proceedings by submitting to the court a clinical certificate completed by a psychiatrist on the patient's treatment team and the screening certificate that authorized admission of the patient to the facility.[9] If the person was not referred by a screening service, commitment may be initiated by the submission of two clinical certificates, at least one of which was completed by a psychiatrist. It is a crime for a relative to execute a clinical certificate or for a certificate to be completed for any purpose or motive other than care and treatment.

If the court, upon review of the records, finds that there is probable cause to believe that the person is "in need of involuntary commitment" (supra), it must issue a temporary order authorizing the retention of the person in the custody of the facility for 20 days, pending a final hearing.[10] In exceptional circumstances, the temporary order may be extended for 10 days by the court for "good cause." The person may be transferred to another psychiatric facility prior to the final hearing if 24-hours' notice is given to both the patient and his or her relatives, but transfers are prohibited less than 5 days before a hearing.[11]

Notice must be given to the patient and his or her next of kin, guardian if any, and attorney, as well as to the psychiatric facility, at least 10 days prior to a court hearing.[12] A psychiatrist from the treatment team usually must testify at the hearing. The court may request a licensed psychologist and others from the treatment team to testify. In addition, the court may appoint an independent psychiatrist, psychologist, or other expert to examine the patient and to testify.[13]

A person subject to involuntary commitment must be represented by counsel.[14] He or she has the right to be present at the court hearing unless the hearing cannot continue because of the patient's inappropriate conduct. The patient has the right to review and copy records, present evidence, cross-examine witnesses, and have the hearing in camera (i.e., private).

The court must find by "clear and convincing evidence" that the patient is "in need of continued involuntary commitment" (supra).[15] In that case, the patient must remain at a psychiatric facility

---

9. N.J.S.A. 30:4-27.10.
10. *Id.* and R. 4:74-7.
11. N.J.S.A. 30:4-27.10.
12. N.J.S.A. 30:4-27.13.
13. R. 4:74-7(d).
14. N.J.S.A. 30:4-27.14 and R. 4:74-7(f).
15. N.J.S.A. 30:4-27.15.

until he or she no longer needs commitment, at which point the person will be administratively discharged by the treatment team.[16] However, the patient has the right to a new hearing every 3 months during the first year of commitment, and annually thereafter.[17] The court may schedule additional review hearings upon request.

If the court finds that the patient is not committable, he or she must be discharged within 48 hours of the court's verbal order or by the end of the next working day, whichever is longer. However, if the patient's history indicates a high risk of rehospitalization because of failure to comply with discharge plans, the court may discharge the patient subject to conditions recommended by the facility and developed with the patient's participation. If the patient does not comply with such discharge plans, the court may determine that rehospitalization is required, pending a hearing within 20 days.

Discharge

A person discharged either by the court or administratively must have a discharge plan prepared by the treatment team at the facility.[18] Both the patient and an outpatient community mental health agency must participate in the formulation of the discharge plan. The mental health agency must arrange for follow-up care to the patient, which may include private treatment by MHPs.

Patient Rights

Subject to other provisions of law, no patient may be deprived of any civil right solely because he or she receives treatment under this law.[19] Such rights include the right to vote and to hold a license, permit, privilege, or legal benefit. No patient may be presumed to be incompetent (see Chapters 5A.2 and 5A.3) because he or she has been examined or treated for mental illness. Psychiatric patients have the right to have evaluations and services provided in their primary means of communication, with the aid of an interpreter if necessary.[20] Each patient has the right to an attorney, including free legal representation if he or she cannot afford to pay for a lawyer.

---

16. N.J.S.A. 30:4-27.17.
17. N.J.S.A. 30:4-27.16.
18. N.J.S.A. 30:4-27.18.
19. N.J.S.A. 30:4-24.2.
20. N.J.S.A. 30:4-27.11.

Every patient has the right to receive treatment.[21] Each patient has the right to participate in treatment planning to the extent that his or her condition permits.[22] Every patient has the right to confidentiality of all treatment certificates, records, and reports, except if requested by a guardian or parent of a minor, if disclosure is necessary to effect the requirements of this law, or if ordered by a court.[23] (However, disclosure of the patient's current medical condition to a relative, friend, physician, or personal attorney is permitted if it appears that it is for the benefit of the patient.)

Each patient in treatment has a number of additional rights, a list of which must be posted in all psychiatric facilities. The following are some of the more important rights related to MHPs:[24]

1. to be free from unnecessary or excessive medication; voluntarily committed patients have the right to refuse medication and other treatment in nonemergency situations; involuntarily committed patients' constitutional rights to an informed refusal may be overridden by the treating physician who, using accepted professional judgment, determines that the patient is dangerous to self or others and is in need of medication;[25] however, the decision is subject to review by the medical director of the hospital, who must perform an independent clinical evaluation and review of the case, in the presence of the patient's attorney if so requested;

2. not to be subjected to experimental research, shock treatment, psychosurgery, or sterilization, without the express and informed consent of the patient after consultation with counsel or an interested party of the patient's choice; if the person has been adjudicated as incompetent (see Chapter 5A.2), a court hearing must be held to determine the need for such procedures, at which the patient must be present and represented by counsel;

3. to be free from physical restraint and isolation; except for emergency situations lasting no more than 1 hour, a patient may be physically restrained or placed in isolation only on a medical director's written order or that of a physician designee that explains the rationale for such action; the order may be entered only after the person signing it has personally seen and eval-

21. State v. Carter, 64 N.J. 382, 316 A.2d 449 (1974).
22. N.J.S.A. 30:4-24.1.
23. N.J.S.A. 30:4-24.3.
24. N.J.S.A. 30:4-24.2(d).
25. Rennie v. Klein, D.C., 476 F. Supp. 1294 (1979), *stay denied in part, granted in part*, 481 F. Supp. 552, *modified and remanded*, 653 F.2d 836, *cert. granted and vacated*, 458 U.S. 1179, 102 S.Ct. 3506, 73 L.Ed.2d 1381, *on remand*, 720 F.2d 266.

uated the patient involved, and its effect is for no more than 24 hours;

4. to be free from corporal punishment; and

5. to have the least restrictive conditions necessary to achieve the purposes of treatment.[26]

Civil Liability

Law enforcement officers, screening services, or screening staff, acting in good faith, who take reasonable steps to assess, take custody of, detain, or transport an individual for the purposes of mental health assessment or treatment under this statute, are immune from civil and criminal liability.[27]

---

26. *See* K.P. v. Albanese, 204 N.J. Super. 166, 497 A.2d 1276 (App. Div. 1985), *cert. denied*, 102 N.J. 355, 508 A.2d 225 (1985).
27. N.J.S.A. 30:4-27.7.

5E.5

Voluntary Admission and Involuntary Commitment of Alcoholics

The law provides for voluntary as well as involuntary treatment of those persons who are seriously disabled by alcoholism, and it alters the focus of the legal intervention from a criminal to a treatment model. MHPs may be part of a multidisciplinary evaluation and treatment team under this law. Alcoholism programs in New Jersey are administered by the Division of Alcoholism in the Department of Health.

Terms and Definitions

Before discussing how the law operates, it is important to understand the terms it employs:[1]

1. *Alcoholic* means any person who chronically, habitually, or periodically consumes alcoholic beverages to the extent that

   a. such use substantially injures his or her health or substantially interferes with social or economic functioning in the community on a continuing basis, or

   b. he or she has lost the power of self-control with respect to the use of such beverages.

2. *Intoxicated person* means a person whose mental or physical functioning is substantially impaired as a result of the use of alcoholic beverages.

3. *Incapacitated* means the condition of a person who

---

1. N.J.S.A. 2B-8.

a. is unconscious as the result of alcohol abuse or has judgment so impaired as the result of alcohol abuse that he or she is incapable of realizing and making a rational decision with respect to the need for treatment,

b. is in need of substantial medical attention, or

c. is likely to suffer substantial physical harm.

4. *Facility* means any public or private place providing services especially designed for the treatment of intoxicated persons and alcoholics, including, but not limited to, intoxication treatment centers, inpatient treatment facilities, outpatient facilities, and residential aftercare facilities.

5. *Treatment* means services and programs for the care or rehabilitation of intoxicated persons and alcoholics, including, but not limited to, medical, psychiatric, psychological, vocational, educational, recreational, and social services and programs.

6. *Authorized persons* means persons who serve as volunteer first aid or ambulance squad members, para-professional medical personnel, and rehabilitated alcoholics.

Admission and Commitment

Any person who is intoxicated and who voluntarily applies for treatment or is brought to a facility by a police officer or other authorized person may be treated at an alcohol treatment facility.[2] Any alcoholic, even if not intoxicated, may apply and receive treatment at a facility. Any such person may be involuntarily detained until he or she is no longer incapacitated, for up to 48 hours. Police officers may remain at the facility at any time to provide adequate security and protection.

If a person is arrested for violation of a municipal ordinance or disorderly persons offense, and not also for a misdemeanor, the court must inform the person that he or she is entitled to request a medical examination to determine if the individual is an alcoholic.[3] If the examining physician reports that the person is an alcoholic who would benefit by treatment, the court must inform the defendant that he or she may request commitment to the Division of Alcoholism. If the physician does not so report, the court may appoint an independent physician for a second opinion.

If the court determines that the defendant is an alcoholic who would benefit from treatment and he or she requests commitment,

---

2. N.J.S.A. 2B-15.
3. *Id.*

the court then may stay the criminal proceeding and commit the defendant to the division for a specified period not to exceed 30 days as an inpatient and 60 days as an outpatient. The administrator of a facility may transfer a patient's status from inpatient to outpatient, and back again. In determining whether to order commitment, the court must consider the report of the physician, the nature of the offense charged, the past criminal record of the defendant, and any other relevant evidence.

At the end of the commitment period, the director of a treatment facility must report to the court on whether the defendant successfully completed the treatment program, together with the reasons for that conclusion. In reaching this determination, the director must consider whether the defendant was cooperative and complied with the terms of the commitment. If the director reports success in completing the program, the court may dismiss the charges pending against the defendant. If the director reports failure, the court may either dismiss the original charges or else reinstate them. If the defendant is then sentenced to a term of imprisonment, the sentence must be reduced by the amount of time spent in the treatment facility.

Confidentiality and Patients' Rights

The administrator of each facility must keep confidential treatment records[4] that can be released only upon court order.[5] Each patient is entitled to receive adequate and appropriate treatment on the basis of a written individualized treatment plan. Any patient has the right to be examined by a private physician, to consult privately with an attorney, to receive visitors, and to send and receive uncensored communications by mail and telephone. No person who has received treatment at a facility or who is an alcoholic can be denied any right or privilege under the laws of New Jersey for those reasons.[6]

Alcohol Education Services

The Division of Alcoholism must provide an ongoing program for the education of police officers, prosecutors, court personnel, judges, probation and parole officers, correctional personnel, and

---

4. N.J.S.A. 2B-20 et seq. and N.J.A.C. 8:42A-15.1 et seq.
5. N.J.S.A. 2B-20.
6. N.J.S.A. 2B-21.

welfare and vocational rehabilitation personnel regarding the causes, effects, and treatment of intoxication and alcoholism.[7]

Repeal of Inconsistent Laws

No state or local law is permitted that renders public intoxication an offense.[8] Any such inconsistent laws are repealed by legislation.[9] However, any laws prohibiting the operation of motor vehicles or other machinery while under the influence of alcohol are not affected.

7. N.J.S.A. 2B-23.
8. N.J.S.A. 2B-26.
9. N.J.S.A. 2B-29.

5E.6

Voluntary Admission and Involuntary Commitment of Drug Addicts

The law in several states, including New Jersey, provides for treatment and commitment of drug addicts. MHPs provide evaluative and therapeutic services, as well as court testimony. The drug treatment programs are administered through the Department of Human Services.

Admission for Treatment

A person over the age of 18 believing himself or herself to be addicted to narcotics or drugs may be admitted to any state or county institution with special facilities for the care and treatment of drug addicts.[1] An unmarried person under this age may be admitted voluntarily upon the application of a guardian, custodian, next of kin, or caretaker.

If the superintendent or physician in charge of any facility certifies that it is in the best interest of any drug addict, the patient may be retained for a period not exceeding 30 days for treatment, and afterward until 15 days after receipt of written notice from the patient or from the caretaker if the person is a minor.[2] However, the patient may be discharged at any time if recovered or if not suitable for treatment in the facility.

---

1. N.J.S.A. 30:6C-5.
2. *Id.*

Treatment and Probation of Criminals

Any individual convicted of being a disorderly person may be placed on probation on condition that the person immediately and voluntarily be admitted to a designated facility for the treatment of drug addiction.[3] The patient must remain confined in the program as long as he or she would have been confined to a correctional facility, unless discharged and returned to probation status. The probationer must then receive special medically oriented aftercare treatment for the remainder of probation.[4] A refusal to continue such treatment will be considered a violation of probation, and the probationer must return to court for further disposition.

Hearings

A person held involuntarily in a drug treatment facility may file a writ of habeas corpus, which is a request for a court hearing on the grounds that the individual is being deprived of liberty without due process of law.[5] If the writ is denied by the court, the person may be remanded to the drug facility until such time as he or she is no longer in need of institutional care and treatment.

---

3. N.J.S.A. 30:6C-6.
4. N.J.S.A. 30:6C-7.
5. N.J.S.A. 30:6C-9.

5E.7

Services for Developmentally Disabled Persons

The law provides various residential and outreach services to developmentally disabled and retarded persons. MHPs aid in the provision of evaluation and treatment. Services are provided by the Division of Developmental Disabilities in the Department of Human Services.

Terms and Definitions

It is important to understand the meanings of several terms used in the laws.

1. *Developmental disability* means a severe, chronic disability of a person that[1]

   a. is attributable to a mental or physical impairment or a combination thereof;

   b. is manifest before age 22;[2]

   c. is likely to continue indefinitely;

   d. results in substantial functional limitation in three or more areas of major life activity, including self-care, receptive and expressive language, learning, mobility, self-direction, and capacity for independent living or economic self-sufficiency; and

---

1. N.J.S.A. 30:6D-3(a). A person who suffers from minimal brain damage and borderline mental retardation does not meet the statutory definition of developmental disability. State in the Interest of A.B., 109 N.J. 195, 536 A.2d 240 (1988).
2. N.J.S.A. 30:6D-31 allows the director to extend services to individuals whose disability was manifested after the age of 22 but before the age of 55.

e. reflects the need for a combination and sequence of special interdisciplinary or generic care, treatment, or other services that are of lifelong or extended duration and are individually planned and coordinated; developmental disability includes, but is not limited to, severe disabilities attributable to mental retardation, autism, cerebral palsy, epilepsy, spina bifida, and other neurological impairments where the above criteria are met.

2. *Mental retardation* means a significant subaverage general intellectual functioning existing concurrently with deficits in adaptive behavior that are manifested during the development period.[3]

3. *Mental deficiency* means that state of mental retardation in which the reduction of social competence is so marked that persistent social dependency requiring guardianship of the person shall have been demonstrated or be anticipated.[4]

4. *Services* means specialized services provided by any public or private agency directed toward the alleviation of a developmental disability or toward the social, personal, physical, or economic habilitation or rehabilitation of an individual with such a disability.[5] The term includes diagnosis, evaluation, treatment, personal care, day care, domiciliary care, special living arrangements, training, education, sheltered employment, recreation, counseling of the individual with such disability and of the family, protective and other social and sociolegal services, information and referral services, follow-along services, and transportation services necessary to assure delivery of services to persons with developmental disabilities.

5. *Functional services* means those services and programs available to provide the mentally retarded with education, training, rehabilitation, adjustment, treatment, care, and protection.[6]

6. *Residential services* means observation, examination, care, training, treatment, rehabilitation, and related services, including community care, provided by the department to patients who have been admitted or transferred to, but not discharged from, any residential functional service for the mentally retarded.[7]

---

3. N.J.S.A. 30:4-25(a) (5).
4. N.J.S.A. 30:4-25(a) (4).
5. N.J.S.A. 30:6D-3(b).
6. N.J.S.A. 30:4-25(a) (3).
7. N.J.S.A. 30:4-25(a) (6).

Admission to Services

An application for admission of an eligible mentally retarded person to functional services of the department may be made by the parent, guardian, person, or agency having care and custody of the individual; by a mentally retarded person himself or herself if over 18 years old; by a juvenile court with jurisdiction over a minor; or by a court during or after criminal proceedings.[8]

The person must then be evaluated, and the commissioner or a designate must issue a statement of eligibility if the person qualifies.[9] The statement must advise the applicant of the particular functional services deemed most appropriate for his or her training, habilitation, care, and protection. The statement should also advise whether such services or alternate services are immediately available. The applicant can then be admitted for functional services, although it may be necessary to be placed on a waiting list before certain programs become available.

The Department of Human Services is required to make diligent efforts to maintain contact with the parent or guardian of each individual receiving functional services and to advise the parent or guardian of any significant changes in the condition of the patient.[10] The department must make reasonable efforts to consult with the parent or guardian concerning recommended changes in a patient's program and to secure prior consent for such changes. However, absent the expressed prohibition of an action by the parent or guardian, the commissioner or the designated agent is free from liability for the consequences of any prudent action taken in the interest of the immediate health or safety of the patient when an emergency arises.

Rights of the Developmentally Disabled

No developmentally disabled person (including those with mental retardation, supra) may be presumed incompetent or may be discriminated against or deprived of any constitutional or legal right solely by reason of the receipt of any service.[11] Such rights include the right to vote, to practice a religion, to receive and send unopened correspondence, to receive private visitations and have private

---

8. N.J.S.A. 30:4-25 and N.J.A.C. 10:46-1.1 et seq.
9. N.J.S.A. 30:4-25.3 and 4.
10. N.J.S.A. 30:4-25.8.
11. N.J.S.A. 30:6D-4.

telephone conversations, to have reasonable opportunities for interaction with members of the opposite sex, and to receive confidential handling of personal and medical records.

In addition, no person receiving services for the developmentally disabled at any facility, including a community residence,[12] can[13]

1. be subjected to any corporal punishment;

2. be administered any medication except upon written authorization by a physician as treatment for a specific condition in conformity with acceptable medical standards;

3. be physically or chemically restrained or isolated, except under strict regulations in emergency situations, for behavior that may or has harmed a person, or may or has caused substantial damage to property;

4. be subjected to shock treatment, psychosurgery, sterilization, or research without the express and informed consent of the person or a guardian ad litem appointed by the court to protect the person's interests, which include the right to a court hearing;

5. be denied a nutritionally adequate diet or regular and sufficient medical care;

6. be denied, if between the ages of 5 and 21, a thorough and efficient education suited to the person's age and abilities; or

7. be denied the right to file a writ of habeas corpus to enforce any of these rights in court.[14]

Each service provided for persons with developmental disabilities must be designed to maximize the developmental potential of such a person and be provided in a humane manner, with full recognition and respect for the dignity and rights of each person, and in a setting and manner that is least restrictive of each person's liberty (see Chapter 6.3).[15] Each agency providing services to a person with developmental disabilities must develop a written individualized habilitation plan within 30 days of admission into a program.[16] The service plan must be developed and revised by the agency, in consultation with the disabled person and the parents or guardian.

Except in emergency situations, whenever an individual may be transferred from one locale or another, whether it be a community residence, an institution, or other facility, the department

---

12. N.J.S.A. 30:6D-17.
13. N.J.S.A. 30:6D-5.
14. N.J.S.A. 30:6D-7.
15. N.J.S.A. 30:6D-9 and N.J.A.C. 10:44A-1.1.
16. N.J.S.A. 30:6D-10 and N.J.A.C. 10:44B-1.1 et seq.

must ensure that an individual habilitation plan is prepared at least 30 days in advance.[17] Before a transfer occurs, persons participating in the development and review of the new plan must be given the opportunity to inspect the site of the proposed transfer. A transfer can be made only when it is consistent with the best interests of the disabled person.[18]

A person who fails to adjust to a community residential facility may return to the original institution or to a more suitable community residential facility.[19] To the maximum extent possible, placement in a community residence should be accessible to those interested in the well-being of the disabled person, and such placement should afford reasonable employment opportunities where applicable.[20]

---

17. N.J.S.A. 30:6D-16.
18. N.J.S.A. 30:6D-21.
19. *Id.*
20. N.J.S.A. 30:6D-18.

5E.8

Hospice Care

Hospice care is a program of psychological and physical support offered to terminally ill persons. The emphasis is on increasing the quality of a person's last days or months through active participation by the family in caring for the person and openly facing the meaning and importance of death. There is continued medical assistance in such matters as the control of pain and other symptoms so as to allow the person to concentrate on other aspects of life. A complete program may consist of three phases: home care with nursing, emotional, and religious support; inpatient care with overnight facilities for the family; and bereavement services for the family. MHPs may be involved in all three phases as a member of the support team.

There is a strong federal interest in hospice care, especially as it pertains to health insurance coverage and the quality of services. Individual states are also considering laws pertaining to hospice care. In New Jersey, a law was recently passed that provides Medicaid reimbursement (see Chapter 5E.1) for hospice care.[1] Before this enactment, the legislature had stated, "There is a need to explore and encourage the development of innovative programs, such as hospices . . . which are designed to make the final days of terminally ill persons more comfortable, dignified and humane."[2] It is clear that New Jersey is moving toward the implementation of hospice care as part of the overall health delivery system for its citizens.

---

1. N.J.S.A. 30:4D-6.
2. N.J.S.A. 52:9Y-1.

Limitations on and Liability for Practice

6.1

Informed Consent for Services

Informed consent should be obtained before administering services, disclosing information concerning the client to a third party, or taking any other action that has an impact on the client. The failure of MHPs to obtain it may be considered professional misconduct by a licensing board (see Section 1), and it renders MHPs liable to a malpractice suit (see Chapter 6.5). This chapter focuses on the duty of informing a patient about the risks of treatment, and the ensuing malpractice liability for failure to obtain informed consent.

Legal Definition of Informed Consent

The standard for MHPs is the same as that imposed upon physicians. The MHP must inform the patient of any inherent and potential hazards of the proposed treatment, the alternatives to that treatment if any, and the results likely if the patient remains untreated.[1] The focus is on what should be disclosed to a prudent patient for that patient to make an informed decision regarding treatment.

In a malpractice suit, the plaintiff must prove not only that the MHP failed to comply with the applicable standard regarding disclosure of information, but also that a prudent person in the patient's position would have decided differently if adequately informed. Although there are few cases involving MHPs in this area, the greatest liability potential would involve the failure to inform the patient about the risks of treatment with a particular drug or

---

1. Largey v. Rothman, 110 N.J. 204, 540 A.2d 504 (1988).

procedure, such as electroconvulsive therapy. However, it is conceivable that a malpractice suit might arise from an MHP who fails to warn patients about alternative treatment modalities and about the risks of a proposed psychotherapeutic treatment plan. Although a signed statement acknowledging the receipt of information and consenting to proposed treatment is not required, it is useful for documentation in court.

6.2

Right to Refuse Treatment

People who have the capacity to seek voluntary treatment, by definition, have the capacity to refuse such treatment. However, the right of involuntarily committed patients to refuse treatment has not always been recognized. The extent to which civilly committed mentally ill and developmentally disabled individuals have the right to refuse treatment is discussed in Chapters 5E.4 and 5E.7.

The right to refuse treatment has also been raised recently in cases involving terminally ill individuals who wish to forego treatment by life-sustaining medical technology. The New Jersey Supreme Court has supported the right of a patient to refuse medical treatment even at the risk of personal injury or death, subject to certain limitations.[1]

These rights and limitations are essentially incorporated into a new law known as the New Jersey Advance Directives for Health Care Act.[2] The law allows a person to execute an advance directive for health care at any time, which must be notarized or signed in the presence of two adult witnesses, who must attest that the declarant is of sound mind and free of duress and undue influence. The person may also revoke such a directive at any time, either orally or in writing.

The directive may state the person's treatment philosophy and specific wishes regarding the provision, withholding, or withdrawal of any form of health care, including life-sustaining treatment. A person may designate a health care representative, who may make decisions for the patient based on the advance directive when it is

---

1. *In re* Conroy, 98 N.J. 321, 486 A.2d 1209 (1985). *See also In re* Farrell, 108 N.J. 335, 529 A.2d 404 (1987).
2. N.J.S.A. 26: 2H-53 to 78 et al.

determined that the patient lacks capacity to make a particular health care decision.

The attending physician must determine, in writing, whether the patient lacks capacity to make such a decision. A determination must be based on an evaluation of the patient's ability to understand and appreciate the nature and consequences of the decision, including the benefit, risks, and alternatives to the proposed health care.

If the lack of capacity is not apparent, it must be confirmed by a second physician. If incapacity is due to a psychological impairment or developmental disability, and the physicians involved do not have expertise in that area, a physician with expertise, typically a psychiatrist or neurologist, must confirm the decision. If an incapacitated patient communicates a wish to continue life-sustaining treatment, such wish must be followed regardless of an advance directive.

Health care professionals, as well as private religiously affiliated health care institutions, do not have to treat a patient if an advance directive regarding treatment withdrawal goes against religious principles or sincerely held beliefs. In that case, arrangements must be made for the transfer of patient care to another health care professional or institution. Health care professionals are immune for liability for good faith actions performed in attempting to follow the law.

In case of a disagreement between the patient, health care representative, and attending physician concerning the patient's decision-making capacity or the appropriate interpretation and application of an advance directive, the parties may seek to resolve the disagreement by procedures developed by the hospital or institution, or a party may seek resolution in court.

Consistent with the terms of an advance directive, life-sustaining treatment may be withheld or withdrawn from a patient in any of the following circumstances:

1. The life-sustaining treatment is experimental and not a proven therapy, or is likely to be ineffective in prolonging life, or will merely prolong an imminent dying process;

2. the patient is permanently unconscious;

3. the patient is in a terminal condition; or

4. the patient has a serious irreversible illness or condition and the likely risks and burdens associated with the medical intervention outweigh the likely benefits, or imposition of the medical intervention on an unwilling patient would be inhumane.

6.3

Regulation of Aversive and Avoidance Conditioning

Despite their reported usefulness in treating certain disorders, behavioral therapies using aversive stimuli are carefully regulated in some states when they are intended for use with developmentally disabled or mentally ill individuals. In New Jersey, all services and programs regulated by the Division of Developmental Disabilities (see Chapter 5E.7), including developmental centers and facilities under contract, must work in conjunction with human rights committees.[1] Such committees have an advisory role to program administrators of reviewing, on a case-by-case basis, the use of procedures not prohibited by law or rule that may present an element of risk and/or restriction to an individual client's rights.[2] The committees are specifically authorized to review techniques utilizing aversive stimuli,[3] which are defined as[4]

> The presentation of stimuli or conditions to decrease the frequency, intensity, or duration of maladaptive behavior by inducing distress, discomfort or pain which may place the individual at some degree of risk of physical and/or psychological injury.

In reviewing aversive techniques, if the committee does not reach a consensus regarding a specific procedure, it may be approved if only one member disagrees with it.[5] However, if two or more members disagree with the technique, the committee cannot approve it, and the dissenting members must suggest alternative techniques.

---

1. N.J.A.C. 10:41-4.1 et seq.
2. N.J.A.C. 10:41-4.14.
3. N.J.A.C. 10:41-4.16.
4. N.J.A.C. 10:41-4.3.
5. N.J.A.C. 10:41-4.16.

In addition to the oversight of aversive techniques by the human rights committees, certain procedures on mentally ill or retarded individuals are independently regulated, such as shock treatment, physical restraint, isolation, and experimental research (see Chapters 5E.4 and 5E.7). Other behaviors are prohibited, such as corporal punishment. Any attempts to utilize such procedures and behaviors in the context of a behavior therapy program would need to conform to such statutory protections.

6.4

Quality Assurance for Hospital Care

Federal social service programs such as Medicare require that the governing body of every certified hospital establish a utilization review committee to review the professional practices within the hospital for the purposes of reducing morbidity and mortality and for the improvement of the care of patients in the hospital. The review does not need to identify the patient or doctor by name but may use a number system.

In addition to utilization review committees, hospitals are legally required to maintain a quality assurance program,[1] part of which must be for psychiatric services.[2] The ongoing quality assurance program of the psychiatric service must include incident review and monitoring of such areas as suicide, attempted suicide, elopement, assaults, slips and falls, patient abuse and neglect, use of seclusion, and use of restraints. The psychiatric staff must review use of restraints, discharge planning, and outcomes on at least an annual basis.

All members of utilization review and quality assurance committees are protected from liability to any person for any action taken or recommendation made without malice and in the reasonable belief that such action or recommendation was warranted upon the basis of facts disclosed.[3]

In New Jersey, all proceedings conducted and records and materials prepared in connection with utilization reviews are confidential and privileged, except for disclosure to a patient's attending

---

1. N.J.A.C. 8:43G-27.1 et seq.
2. N.J.A.C. 8:43G-26.14.
3. N.J.S.A. 2A:84A-22.10.

physician, the chief administrative officer of the hospital, the medical executive committee, government agencies in the performance of their duties, or any medical insurance company that authorizes the carrier to request and be given such information and data.[4]

These privileges and exceptions do not specifically apply to quality assurance committees. Members of such committees would therefore be governed by other statutory laws governing confidentiality and privilege (see Chapters 4.2 and 4.3), unless the courts interpret this law to include quality assurance committees in the future.

<hr/>

4. N.J.S.A. 2A:84A-22.8.

Malpractice Liability

A malpractice suit is a civil action in which the plaintiff alleges that he or she suffered damages as the consequence of an act or omission by a professional who did not exercise the level of ordinary and reasonable care possessed by the average member of that discipline. Although some states have codified laws of negligence and malpractice into their statutory laws, in New Jersey the appellate courts are the primary sources of the law.

Malpractice Law

Standard of Care

Although malpractice law has been developed primarily out of suits against physicians, any MHP may be subject to such claims. Although an MHP cannot guarantee a cure, when he or she does take a case, it[1]

> imposes upon him the duty to exercise in the treatment of his patient the degree of care, knowledge and skill ordinarily possessed and exercised in similar situations by the average member of the profession practicing in his field. Failure to have and to use such skill and care toward the patient as a result of which injury or damage results constitutes negligence.

The law recognizes that a good result may occur with poor treatment and that good treatment will not necessarily prevent a poor result.[2] Consequently, if the MHP has brought the requisite

---

1. Schueler v. Strelinger, 43 N.J. 330, 344, 204 A.2d 577, 584 (1964).
2. *Id.*

degree of care and skill to the patient, he or she is not liable simply because of failure to cure or for bad results that may follow. Nor is the MHP liable for an honest mistake in diagnosis or in judgment as to the course of treatment taken. An MHP is not liable for malpractice as long as he or she uses reasonable judgment and as long as that judgment does not represent a departure from the requirements of accepted professional practice or does not result in the failure to do something that accepted professional practice would obligate him or her to do.

If an MHP claims to be a specialist, then the standard of care is that not merely of the general practitioner, but the special degree of skill normally possessed by the average MHP who devotes special study and attention to the particular problem involved, with regard to the present state of scientific knowledge in the field.[3] For example, if a person states on a professional card that he or she is a forensic psychologist, then the standard of care would be that of the average forensic psychologist, rather than the average psychologist.

The standard of care recognized by the profession for the treatment of a patient's condition must ordinarily be proven by expert professional testimony.[4] However, where the asserted malpractice consists of conduct so obviously wanting in reasonable skill and prudence that it may be adjudged even by a lay person, expert testimony as to the standard offended is unnecessary.[5] Thus, a court would be likely to rule that expert testimony was unnecessary in a medical malpractice case where a surgeon left a sponge in a patient's body after an operation, or if an MHP made a faulty diagnosis using mental telepathy.

Proximate Cause

In addition to proving that an MHP failed to provide an acceptable standard of care to a patient, a plaintiff must also prove that such failure was a "proximate cause" of the harm suffered. Proximate cause has been traditionally defined as any cause that in a natural and continuous sequence, unbroken by an efficient intervening cause, produces the result complained of, without which the result would not have occurred.[6]

A second, more flexible proximate cause standard has recently been accepted in medical malpractice claims where negligence exacerbates a preexisting condition. It states that one who undertakes

---

3. Clark v. Wichman, 72 N.J. Super. 486, 179 A.2d 38 (App. Div. 1962).
4. Toy v. Rickert, 53 N.J. Super. 27, 146 A.2d 510 (App. Div. 1958).
5. Becker v. Eisenstodt, 60 N.J. Super. 240, 158 A.2d 706 (App. Div. 1960).
6. Fernandez v. Baruch, 96 N.J. Super. 125, 232 A.2d 661 (App. Div. 1967), *rev'd on other grounds*, 52 N.J. 127, 244 A.2d 109 (1968).

to render services to another is subject to liability for failure to exercise reasonable care if his or her failure increased the risk of harm and if such increased risk was a substantial factor in producing the condition suffered.[7]

In determining damages, where negligence has exacerbated a preexisting medical condition, the jury must apportion and award, on a percentage basis, the increased risk of harm proximately caused by a defendant, separately from the harm caused by the preexisting condition.[8]

Statute of Limitations

The statute of limitations is the period in which a client must file suit. For a malpractice claim, it must be filed within 2 years of the date of injury,[9] or within 2 years after the time when a patient's suspicions ripen into knowledge that his or her injuries may be attributable to the provider's faulty treatment.[10] Such knowledge refers to personal awareness, not documentation by an expert consultant.

Avoiding Malpractice

There are several considerations that may be of use in taking a preventive posture regarding malpractice litigation. First, the rules and regulations promulgated by the professional licensing boards (see Section 1) constitute a legally recognized standard of care. Second, ethical and practice standards provided by national and state MHP associations are an important source that frequently represent the highest codified standards of care. Finally, a knowledge of the literature on a particular method of assessment or treatment is important, especially because the plaintiff's experts may use that as the basis on which to judge rare or unusual techniques.[11]

Malpractice Review Committees

Some states require the submission of medical malpractice claims to an independent review committee. New Jersey formerly provided for a voluntary medical malpractice screening panel, which was abolished because of nonutilization.[12]

---

7. Evers v. Dollinger, 95 N.J. 399, 471 A.2d 405 (1984).
8. Scafidi v. Seiler, 119 N.J. 93, 574 A.2d 398 (1990).
9. N.J.S.A. 2A:14-2.
10. Brizak v. Needle, 239 N.J. Super. 415, 571 A.2d 975 (App. Div. 1990).
11. New Jersey v. Desoi, 42 N.J. 274, 200 A.2d 116 (1964).
12. R. 4:21.

6.6

Other Forms of Professional Liability

Generally, when clients sue MHPs, it is for malpractice (see Chapter 6.5), which covers suits alleging that a standard of care was violated in treating a patient. However, other legal causes of action may also be brought against a defendant. The right to bring suits on alternative legal grounds may be of importance in some situations because the period for filing a malpractice suit is limited to 2 years after a person realizes that he or she has been harmed as the result of such negligence (see Chapter 6.5). Other types of legal actions often have longer statutes of limitations. Although malpractice law has been interpreted flexibly enough in New Jersey to provide grounds for most suits against MHPs, alternative legal grounds against MHPs in other states, which could possibly be used in New Jersey, will be considered.

Intentional Torts

An intentional tort is a legal wrong involving action by the defendant that violated the legal rights of the plaintiff. In these cases, intent is defined as the desire to bring about physical results that the defendant knew or should have known were likely to occur. Moreover, the intent does not have to be hostile or a wish to do harm (e.g., a person who unlawfully restrains another commits false imprisonment even if "it is for the person's own good").

Criminal-Related Actions

An MHP who is liable under criminal law (see Chapter 6.7) will also be liable for the same behavior under civil law. Thus, an MHP who is liable for assault and battery under the criminal law will also be liable to the victim in a suit. The difference between a criminal and civil suit is that the state prosecutes the former and the victim brings the latter.

Defamation of Character

Defamation may be either oral or written. In the former case, it is referred to as slander, whereas in the latter it is considered a libel. In either form, the injury is to the reputation and good name of a person. This action generally requires that the defendant communicated information (or caused it to be communicated) to a third party that was of such a nature as to harm the plaintiff's reputation. There are two defenses to a defamation suit:[1] (a) the communication was true or (b) the defendant was privileged[2] (legally entitled) to communicate the information. Privilege may be absolute, such as in a judicial, legislative, or executive proceeding or publication. This means that a witness at a trial or legislative committee hearing may not be sued for defamation under any circumstances. A privilege is qualified where the defendant was acting in furtherance of a higher good as shown by the facts of that particular case.

Invasion of Privacy

This action involves communication of private information. It requires proof of a public disclosure that goes beyond an individual, or even a small group, of private facts that are not matters of public record or generally known and that would be offensive to a reasonable person of ordinary sensibilities. Note, however, that if a psychologist or psychiatrist was liable for invasion of privacy, that person usually would have violated ethical principles and laws concerning maintenance of confidences (see Chapters 4.2 and 4.3).

Malicious Prosecution, False Imprisonment, and Abuse of Process

A malicious prosecution suit alleges that the defendant brought civil or criminal proceedings without any reasonable basis. A false imprisonment charge may be brought if a person was physically detained without an authorizing legal order. In an abuse of process case, the plaintiff alleges that in the course of a legal, justified proceeding, the defendant engaged in some act not authorized by the process or sought some ulterior objective. For instance, an MHP who participated in detaining a person for involuntary commitment without legal authority to do so, or who brought commitment pro-

---

1. W. Prosser, The Law of Torts § 114 (4th ed. 1971).
2. Note difference from privileged communication concept (see Chapter 4.3).

ceedings for reasons not provided in the statute, would be subject to these suits. The commitment law (see Chapter 5E.4) provides a defense to these actions as they pertain to involuntary commitment.

Other Types of Civil Liability

An MHP may be liable on the basis of other types of suits that are based on his or her relationship with the client. The law will infer certain attributes into the relationship, such as the superior–subordinate positioning, or will require proof, such as a written contract. In any event, the MHP may be civilly liable for breaches of express or implied responsibilities arising out of the relationship with the client.

Breach of Fiduciary Duty

The law imposes a "fiduciary duty" on relationships where one party is in a superior position to and also enjoys the intimate trust of another with the understanding that the former will act primarily for the latter's benefit. The MHP–client relationship is very likely to be held a fiduciary relationship, although the law has not yet addressed this issue. If such an action were brought, any transactions between an MHP and client would be very closely examined to determine whether the practitioner took advantage of the client. For example, even though a stranger could legally drive a hard bargain with a client over a sale of an item, a similar deal between the MHP and client would be voided by a court.

Breach of Contract

Where an MHP contracts in writing to provide services, provide certain results, or provide any other tangible or intangible thing that has some value in exchange for something of value given by the client (i.e., payment), the MHP will be held liable for breach of contract if he or she fails to live up to the bargain. Unlike other actions (supra) in which the injured party asks for monetary compensation for injuries received as a result of the defendant's behavior, a breach-of-contract action generally results in payment by the defendant of a sum that places the plaintiff in the same position as if the contract had been performed. Computing what the amount of this determination should be involves complex legal issues (e.g., how does one calculate the pecuniary advantage of psychotherapy? Would the MHP merely be required to return any payments made?) that New Jersey law has not begun to address as they pertain to MHPs.

Criminal Liability

Some states have criminal statutes prohibiting MHPs from engaging in certain behaviors (e.g., sexual relations with a client). New Jersey does not have such a law, however; nor have the courts addressed the issue of whether any criminal laws specifically apply to MHPs. There are three criminal laws, though, that could be of relevance to an MHP.

Sexual Offenses

Before discussing specific offenses, it is necessary to review statutorily defined terms.[1] *Sexual penetration* means vaginal intercourse, cunnilingus, fellatio, or anal intercourse between persons, or insertion of the hand, finger, or object into the anus or vagina either by the actor or upon the actor's instruction. *Sexual contact* means an intentional touching by the victim or perpetrator of intimate parts. *Intimate parts* means sexual organs, genital area, anal area, inner thigh, groin, buttock, or breast of a person. *Mentally defective* means that condition in which a person suffers from a mental disease or defect that renders the person temporarily or permanently incapable of understanding the nature of the conduct. The New Jersey Supreme Court has held that a person is mentally defective if at the time of sexual activity the victim is unable to comprehend the distinctively sexual nature of the conduct or was incapable of understanding or exercising the right to refuse to engage in that type of conduct with another person.[2]

---

1. N.J.S.A. 2C:14-1.
2. State v. Olivio, 237 N.J. Super. 428, 568 A.2d (App. Div. 1989).

Mentally incapacitated means that condition in which a person is rendered temporarily incapable of understanding or controlling conduct because of the influence of a narcotic, anesthetic, intoxicant, or other substance administered to that person without prior knowledge or consent, or because of any other act upon the person that rendered the individual incapable of appraising or controlling the conduct.

A person is guilty of the most severe sexual crime, aggravated sexual assault, if there is an act of sexual penetration and the victim is less than 13 years old, or if the victim is between the ages of 13 and 16 and the perpetrator has supervisory power over the victim by virtue of professional or occupational status.[3] A person is guilty of sexual assault if there is an act of sexual penetration and the victim is one whom the perpetrator knew or should have known was physically helpless, mentally defective, or mentally incapacitated; or the victim is on probation or parole or detained in a hospital or other institution, and the perpetrator has supervisory or disciplinary power over the victim because of professional or occupational status. If there is sexual contact rather than sexual penetration, these crimes will be reduced to the crime of criminal sexual contact.[4]

Assault

A person is guilty of assault if he or she attempts to cause or purposely, knowingly, or recklessly causes bodily injury to another, or attempts by physical menace to put another in fear of imminent serious bodily injury.[5] An MHP might be charged with such a crime if at any time force is used to restrain a patient. However, force is not a crime if used in self-defense or to protect third persons against an assault. In addition, force by physicians and MHPs with special responsibility for the care, discipline, or safety of others is justified to the extent necessary to further that responsibility.[6]

Manslaughter

A person who purposefully aids or assists the commission of suicide or attempted suicide commits manslaughter.[7] However, an eval-

---

3. N.J.S.A. 2C:14-2.
4. N.J.S.A. 2C:14-3.
5. N.J.S.A. 2C:12-1.
6. N.J.S.A. 2C:3-8.
7. N.J.S.A. 2C:11-4.

uation of a person's competency to remove extraordinary life-sustaining devices is appropriate if performed under court guidelines (see Chapter 6.2).

6.8

Liability of Credentialing Boards

Certain branches of government, such as the legislature and judiciary, are immune from lawsuits. This originated from the maxim that "the King can do no wrong," but is now premised on the theory that it cannot be tortious (i.e., injurious) conduct for a government to govern. This absolute immunity does not extend to all aspects of government, however. The New Jersey Tort Claims Act has removed certain obstacles that in large part prevented suits against the state or its agents.[1]

However, the law specifically protects the decision-making powers of state licensing boards from negligence suits. This immunity is necessitated by the almost unlimited exposure to which public entities would otherwise be subjected if they were liable for the numerous occasions on which they issue, deny, suspend, or revoke licenses. In addition, most actions of this type by a public entity can be challenged through administrative or judicial review processes.

Existing Principles of Law

The law states,[2]

> A public entity is not liable for an injury caused by the issuance, denial, suspension or revocation of, or by the failure or refusal to issue, deny, suspend or revoke, any permit, license, certificate, approval, order, or similar authorization . . . .

---

1. N.J.S.A. 59:1-1.
2. N.J.S.A. 59:2-5.

Likewise, a public employee (e.g., a board member) cannot be held liable for an injury caused by his or her decisions regarding authorized licensing matters.[3]

However, immunity from liability is not absolute. An employee may be successfully sued if it is proven that the alleged conduct was outside the scope of his or her employment or constituted a crime, actual fraud, actual malice, or willful misconduct.[4] In addition, an employee or the board can be sued for negligence regarding routine tasks that do not contain decisional or discretionary elements,[5] except if the negligence occurs as part of the licensing process.[6] Thus, for example, a suit against a board arising from a car accident of the board secretary while on board business will succeed if the secretary were negligent.

3. N.J.S.A. 59:3-6.
4. N.J.S.A. 59:3-14.
5. N.J.S.A. 59:2-2 and 3-2.
6. Malloy v. State, 76 N.J. 515, 388 A.2d 622 (1978).

6.9

Antitrust Limitations
to Practice

Antitrust laws were enacted to prevent the formation of monopolies and prevent the abuses of economic power. In recent years, health care providers and their organizations increasingly have become defendants in antitrust litigation. Scrutinized activities include price fixing (an agreement among competitors to establish a common price or system for setting prices), division of markets (an agreement among competitors to allocate certain markets to certain participants), a group boycott (an agreement among competitors to patronize only certain businesses), and tying arrangements (where a party agrees to sell a certain product or service only on the condition that the buyer also purchases a different product). All of these fall under the general prohibition of "restraint of trade."

Most enforcement is through federal law in federal court. However, state law also applies. This chapter is limited to New Jersey antitrust law. It applies to any MHP or organization.

Prohibited Activities

The law states, "Every contract, combination in the form of trust or otherwise, or conspiracy in restraint of trade or commerce, in this State, shall be unlawful."[1]

Certain organizations and activities are exempt from the act, including legitimate trade and professional organizations, labor organizations, agricultural cooperatives, legitimate practices in industries regulated by the state, religious and charitable activities

---

1. N.J.S.A. 56:9-3.

of not-for-profit corporations, and state boards that recommend fee schedules or rates as guidelines.[2]

This law has had varied and complex applications in other jurisdictions against health professionals but has not been widely addressed in New Jersey. One business practice that has been considered, however, was the exclusive contract of a partnership of physicians to provide anesthesia services to a hospital.[3] The court ruled that the contract was a reasonable choice of the hospital and did not violate public policy or antitrust law, after weighing the competitive and anticompetitive effects of the practice under all relevant circumstances, using the "rule of reason," and considering the economics of the industry.

In the ruling, the court noted that courts normally do not interfere with a reasonable management decision concerning hospital staff privileges as long as the decision furthers the health-care mission of the hospital. The implications for MHPs are that such exclusive contracts, even to provide mental health care to hospitals, are likely to be upheld by the courts and not overturned as violations of the antitrust law. However, if the hospital staffing decisions arbitrarily discriminate against qualified applicants without serving a genuine public health objective, such practices may be overturned by the courts as being contrary to public policy, without applying antitrust law.[4]

---

2. N.J.S.A. 56:9-5.
3. Belmar v. Cipolla, 96 N.J. 199, 475 A.2d 533 (1984).
4. Desai v. St. Barnabas Medical Center, 103 N.J. 79, 510 A.2d 662 (1986).

Appendix

Table of Cases

Table of Statutes

Table of Rules of Court

Table of Administrative
Rules and Regulations

Table of Cases

References are to page numbers in this book

T

V

W

Table of Statutes

New Jersey Statutes Annotated

New Jersey Constitution

Table of Rules of Court

References are to page numbers in this book

Table of Administrative Rules and Regulations

References are to page numbers in this book

Index

W

WAIVING CONSTITUTIONAL RIGHTS
  Generally, 5D.2
WARD
  Conservatorship of adults, 5A.3
  Guardianship of adults, 5A.2
  Conservatorship of minors, 5A.12
  Guardianship of minors, 5A.11
WITNESS
  Competency to testify, 5C.4

Expert, generally, 5C.2
  Eyewitness identification, 5D.13
WORKERS' COMPENSATION
  Generally, 5B.2

Z

ZONING
  Community homes, 2.8

About the Author

James S. Wulach is a clinical psychologist, psychoanalyst, and attorney. He is Associate Professor of Psychology at John Jay College of Criminal Justice, City University of New York, where he is Graduate Coordinator of the Forensic Psychology Program. He is a member of the Council on Legislative Affairs of the New Jersey Psychological Association and the Board of Trustees of the New Jersey Academy of Psychologists. He is also a member of the Committee on Professional Practice and Standards of the American Psychological Association. He maintains a part-time practice of psychology in South Orange, New Jersey.

Dr. Wulach received his B.A. from Johns Hopkins University, J.D. from the University of Michigan Law School, and Ph.D. in Clinical Psychology from the City University of New York at City College. He received a Certificate in Psychoanalysis and Psychotherapy from the New York University Postdoctoral Program. He is the author of numerous articles on psychopathology and law. He resides in New Jersey with his wife, Sandra, a psychiatrist, and daughters, Laura and Suzanne.